IT'S ABOUT THYME!

An Herb Manual
and Cookbook of
Herb and Non-Herb Recipes

by *Marge Clark*

Cover Photography by Richard Clark
and Jim Barnett
Illustrations by Doan Helms
Cover Design by Bruce Sargent

IT'S ABOUT THYME!

by Marge Clark

If this book is not available locally,
it may be obtained from:

Marge Clark
R.1 - Box 69
West Lebanon, Indiana 47991

First Printing	5,000	September, 1988
Second Printing	5,000	September, 1989
Third Printing (Revised)	5,000	September, 1991
Fourth Printing	5,000	August, 1992
Fifth Printing	5,000	September, 1993

Library of Congress Catalog Card Number: 88-92078
ISBN: 0-9620692-0-5

Printed in the USA by

WIMMER
The Wimmer Companies, Inc.
Memphis • Dallas

It's About Thyme!

It's also about basil, rosemary and sage, and lots of other herbs as well. It's about planning an herb garden, planting that garden, harvesting and preserving the herbs from that garden. It's about herb garden designs, container gardening with soilless mix. It's about making your own potpourris. It tells you what herbs enhance which foods. It's about Christmas and how beautiful you can make it with herbs and spices.

But that isn't all! This book also has a special collection of new recipes, old recipes (such as many of Mother's) and recipes from far away places. Many of the recipes call for herbs — many don't. And I've also included menus to help you put these recipes to good use.

I want to thank my husband, Dick, for encouraging (no! practically making!) me write this book. I guess he got tired of hearing me *talk* about it, so he's the one who made me *do* something about it.

Special thanks to my son, Scott, and his Nancy for being clever enough to use that new-fangled computer of theirs! It baffles me . . . All typing on the revised edition was done by Nancy Clark.

Also, special thanks to four very talented people — To Doan Helms, my illustrator, for a remarkable job; to Bruce Sargent who designed the front and back covers; and to Jim Barnett, photographer, who can make anyone look good!; and to Dick for the front cover photo of our herb garden.

Well, enough — I think *It's About Thyme!* I started this book! This book is really a personal story. What you'll read here is what *I* have learned about herb gardening, cooking with herbs, etc. When I talk about herbs or cheese or olive oil, for example, it's what *I* have learned about these subjects through experience. It is my hope that this book will act as a guide for you.

Marge Clark
Oak Hill Farm

May 1, 1988

It's About Thyme! UPDATE . . .

After giving this much thought, I have decided to take about 100 of my favorite and best recipes from the book *Take A Little Thyme* by myself and my friend, Ann S. Harrison, and add those recipes, plus a few others, to this book. These additions are all truly special and will make *It's About Thyme!* even better! The following symbol

will denote recipes from *Take A Little Thyme.* Also look for *Thymely Footnotes* throughout the book.

Marge
Oak Hill Farm

May 1, 1991

Table of Contents

A Season of Herbs 6
A Potpourri of Ideas 44
Useful Addresses 64
Cooking Class Favorites 66
Some Old, Some New, Some Mother's,
Some Far Away 90

   1. Appetizers and Drinks 91
   2. Soups, Salads, Salad Dressings 107
   3. Fish and Seafood 129
   4. Chicken and Meat 139
   5. Fruits and Vegetables 163
   6. Breads and Coffee Cakes 179
   7. Cakes 207
   8. Pies 233
   9. Cookies 247
  10. Desserts 267
  11. Canning and Preserving 287

Menus 297
Index 305
Order Blanks 319

A SEASON OF HERBS

So many people say to me — "I'd love to raise a few herbs, but I don't have the time or I don't want to get too involved with a project. Is there a simple way to have a few herbs?" The answer, of course, is "yes"!

After my friend, Ann Harrison, and I wrote the cookbook, *Take a Little Thyme*, I have had literally hundreds of questions about planting herbs, how to cook with them, how to preserve them, etc. Let me stop here and say that I am not an expert — I enjoy what I've learned about herbs and I am always happy to share. I certainly know more about herbs than I did a few years ago! I guess that's the best place to start this story — a few years ago. . .

When our sons started moving away to begin their own lives and homes, I decided I needed to find a new outlet to keep myself busy — no more chauffeuring, not much laundry, not as many dirty dishes, etc. I had been reading and hearing a lot about herbs and I found myself getting more and more interested in that subject. I read as much as I could find (your local library is a good place to start) and I talked to as many people as I could find who knew anything about herbs.

Finally one day, I knew I wanted to start my own herb garden. Dick (my husband) and I spent many hours one winter sketching garden designs and planning which plants to use. We decided on a 20-foot by 20-foot plot. I decided to raise mainly culinary herbs (think of culinary herbs as the ones to cook with — there are groups of herbs used in medicine-making and another group used for dyeing purposes, but I am really mainly interested in culinary herbs).

I talked to my local garden supply man and he agreed to raise the plants for me from seeds in his greenhouse. (See Useful Addresses for some seed and plant sources that your local supply man may not sell.) I learned that herb seeds (in many cases) planted in the garden are very slow to germinate (some take several weeks), so I decided to use only plants. You can be harvesting herbs in less than a month if you start with plants. Be sure to get your seeds started in February or March — check germinating times on the package — so the plants are established enough to set out by May 10, or so. In mid-Indiana that is considered our frost-free date, so that's the date I aim for.

Spring finally arrived! Dick and I set out to build our herb garden. We chose a spot on the east side of our screened porch — an herb garden needs *at least* 6 or 8 hours of sun a day, so put your garden where it will get east, south, or west exposure to the sun. We removed the sod from the 20-foot by 20-foot plot. This turned out to be the hardest job of the entire project! We next laid down treated wooden beams for the boundary lines. Then we laid brick paths in sand in the shape of a cross. In the middle, we set a sun dial (available at nurseries or garden supply stores), and of course, we planted the herb Thyme around the sun dial! So, basically, we had a raised-bed garden with brick paths and a sun dial. Obviously, you can make your garden any shape that fits your space. Just keep in mind the growing habits of the plants — put short ones in front, tall ones in back, for example. See the article on 12 Culinary Herbs to help you with this.

Next, we tilled the soil in each quadrant (see Williamsburg Garden design — that's our garden), added several bags of top soil, mixed in some peat moss and the proper amount of fertilizer and tilled all that together so we had a nice medium to put the plants into. Before I leave this subject, I need to be a little more specific — if your soil is heavy clay or not very productive, add extra top soil and peat and perhaps even a few handfuls of gypsum to loosen the soil and enrich it. Dick brought in tractor scoops of 3 or 4 year-old dried cow manure (must be dried) and he tilled it in thoroughly. You can buy dried, sterilized manure at your garden supply store. After my garden was established, I set out my annual plants each Spring and hope that severe mid-western winters allow my perennials to come up.

Herbs like water and fertilizer just like most other plants. If you set your plants out in dry dirt, carefully water in the plants so they can get started. The first two or three weeks after I plant my garden, I make sure the soil stays moist. Do *not* overwater, however, because herbs require *good* drainage — don't ever let them stand in water. Sage, for example, will absolutely die if the roots stand in water.

Toward the end of June, I usually fertilize the herb garden, but with a *very light* dose of fertilizer. In late July, I give the garden another *very light* dose. Check your fertilizer package directions. Whatever rate is called for for your size plot, use ¼ that amount! Too much fertilizer will interfere with the volatile oils (the flavors) in the herbs.

📖 Williamsburg Garden

This is a sketch of our Williamsburg-type garden:

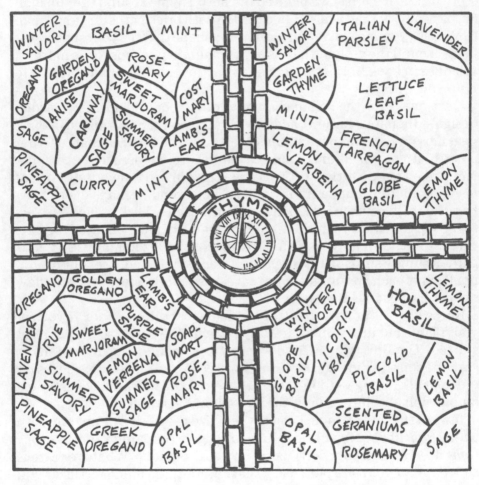

20 FT. BY 20 FT.

Don't think you have to start out with a 20-foot by 20-foot herb garden — you probably shouldn't! Study all garden designs that follow and choose one, or make up one, to suit your needs.

🏺 An Old Wagon Wheel Garden

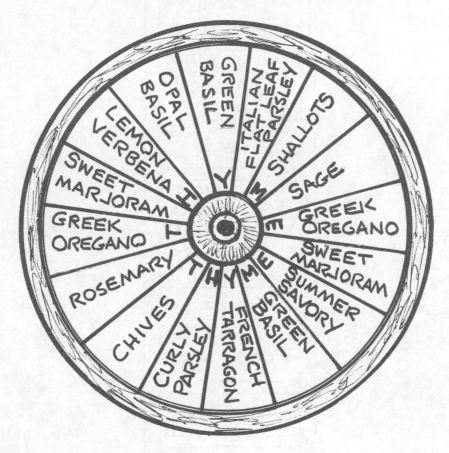

Lay down the wheel where you want your garden to be. Mark the area, then remove sod from that area. Till soil, add proper fertilizer and lay wheel onto tilled area. You're now ready to plant between the spokes.

An Old Ladder Herb Garden

Follow the same instructions for planting "An Old Wagon Wheel Garden."

A Kitchen Herb Garden

A kitchen herb garden should contain all or most of the herbs you would *normally* use in cooking. Nothing unusual or exotic, just the basics. The idea is to have the garden close enough to the back door (or kitchen door) that it's convenient to run out and snip what you need in a hurry.

You may want to add or subtract from this list, but this is my basic list of plants:

1 or 2 chive plants
3 to 6 (or more) sweet basil plants*
2 rosemary plants
1 lemon verbena plant
1 sage plant
3 Greek oregano plants
3 sweet marjoram plants
6 Italian parsley plants
3 French tarragon plants
3 thyme plants
You'll also need 2 or 3 dill plants and 1 or 2 mint plants.

Set out all the above plants, *except* dill and mint as near to the kitchen door as possible, just remembering to allow at least 6 to 8 hours of sun each day.

I recommend planting the dill and mint in spots in your garden or yard where they can come up each year and where they'll not interfere with other plants. Be careful because mint will take over wherever you plant it. I wish I had taken my own advice when I planted my herb garden a few years ago. I planted my mints in with my other herbs, and I am now in the process of digging them all out and replanting them where they won't interfere. Oh well, we learn from experience and mistakes.

If you let some of the dill heads go to seed and let them drop their seed, you'll have dill more or less in the same spot year after year. The size of the dill bed seems to grow also, so that is another reason why I recommend planting it away from the other plants.

*If you love *pesto*, better plant 8 or 10 sweet basil plants. Each recipe I will give you takes about 4 cups of leaves — besides, you can't have too much basil!

Suggested Placing of Plants in a Kitchen Herb Garden

This design uses 8 basil plants. There is room left in this garden for 1 or 2 other interesting plants you may find and want to use.

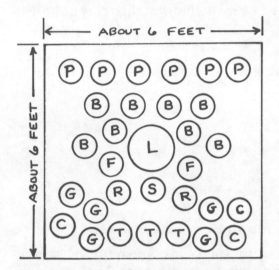

L = Lemon Verbena
P = Parsley (Italian, if possible)
B = Basil
F = French tarragon
S = Sage
R = Rosemary
C = Chives
G = Greek oregano
T = Thyme

THYME UPDATE ... Herbs and Flowers

Besides the garden designs I give you using only herbs, I also plant herbs in my flower garden and especially in flower containers. Many herbs work into the flower garden very beautifully. I love tall **Angelica**, for example, on the back fence of the flower garden where it reigns over the entire garden! **Southernwood** and other **artemisias** do well toward the back of the garden also. Every spring, spade around the artemisias to keep them more or less from spreading. **Purple Ruffles basil** plants set among medium tall **pink zinnias** are spectacular! As summer goes along, keep flower heads of the basil picked. Feel free to mix other herb plants in with your flowers — they help fill in bare spots and they add great beauty and fragrance to the garden. Just keep heights in mind as you plant.

Some of the most beautiful pots and containers on our patio are flower-herb combinations, such as: **pink geraniums**, **blue lobelia**, and **thyme** are beautiful in a large pot; **short yellow marigolds**, **Johnny Jump-Ups**, and **sweet marjoram** planted together; a barrel half of **3 or 4 pink geraniums** in the middle, **opal basil** plants around them, **Greek oregano** plants around them, and **thyme** plants around the rim to drape down over the side as summer progresses.

Another Small, Basic Garden

1 chive plant
2 French tarragon plants
4 basil plants
2 thyme plants
2 rosemary plants
4 sweet marjoram or Greek oregano plants
6 parsley plants
3 dill plants

These can all be planted in a 3 to 4 foot square or circle, such as:

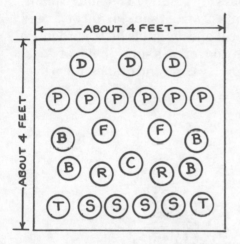

B = Basil
R = Rosemary
D = Dill
P = Parsley
T = Thyme
F = French Tarragon
S = Sweet Marjoram
C – Chives

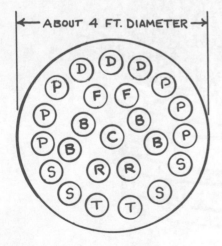

One of my favorite little gardens is:

🧂 A Barrel Half Garden

This is a perfect size garden for the beginner. It doesn't have all the herbs you might want, but it certainly has the important ones to give you the fresh taste of herbs to use in your summer cooking. First of all, drill 10 or 12 holes in the bottom of the barrel half — the holes should be about ½ inch in diameter. Set the barrel on bricks, flat side of bricks down. This is necessary for good drainage and for air circulation. Next, fill the barrel half with good-quality soil, or I prefer to use Soilless Mix (see article on Soilless Mix). Leave 3 or 4 inches of top space. Plant **1 chive** plant (it will come up every year), **2 parsley** plants, **1 rosemary** plant, **2 or 3 basil** plants, **2 or 3 thyme** plants, **2 sweet marjoram** or **Greek oregano** plants. This will be a beautiful and fragrant little garden, so be sure to place it outside your kitchen door or on a sunny patio or deck.

Plant the chive to one side — it gets pretty large and drapes down over the side of the barrel by late summer.

This is my last idea for an herb garden — the smallest one of all. I call it:

A Spaghetti Pot Herb Garden

I call this a spaghetti pot garden because it contains the herbs I snip for my fresh tomato sauces, spaghetti sauces, pasta dishes, etc. It consists of only 5 herbs, but by mid-summer, it's a beauty! I use at least a 12 inch pot. Fill it with soilless mix (put 6 or 8 small rocks or pieces of broken clay pots in the bottom for drainage) and plant **1 basil** plant in the middle of the pot. Around it, put **1 thyme** plant, **1 sweet marjoram** plant, **1 parsley** plant, and **1 Greek oregano** plant. Set the pot in a sunny spot and snip off the flavorful leaves as you need them for your summer sauces, herb butters, salad dressings, etc. The more you snip, the bushier the plants will get. Especially keep the basil trimmed or it will get very leggy. I always make several of these pots each Spring. I have brides ask me for one of these for a shower gift!

Container Gardening

Soilless mix is a *very* important part of container gardening, so I'll give you the recipe for it first. This is the mix Cornell University developed for pot and container gardening. I've changed the original somewhat to meet my needs.

5 cubic feet peat moss
4 cubic feet perlite
1 cubic foot vermiculite
about 1 gallon-size bucket of sand
1⅔ lbs. of limestone
1⅔ lbs. 5-10-10 fertilizer (or less, don't overdo!)
8 to 10 (or more) buckets warm water

You should be able to get all these ingredients at your nursery or garden supply store. Better take the pick-up truck if you have one because these are *big* bales to wrestle with — not heavy, just big.

You'll need a large flat surface to mix this on. I back out the car and mix on my garage floor! Carefully cut the tops off the bales (you need the bags later). Dump all the contents into a pile (it's a big one), add the warm water, a bucket at a time, and mix with a shovel until it's all moist and well-mixed. Scoop the mixture (you'll need someone to hold the bags) back into the big plastic bags the peat moss, perlite, etc., came in. Fold the tops down to keep the moisture in and store out of the way until you're ready to use it. This sounds like an awful job, but if you're filling several pots and containers, you can save quite a bit of money. A 5 cubic foot (bale) of ready-mixed soilless mix will cost from $20.00 up. The flowers and herbs you'll grow in this mixture is reward enough for all the work.

I use soilless mix in all my container and pot gardening. I also have all my houseplants planted in soilless mix. Many, if not all, of the plants you buy at the greenhouse or nursery are potted in this mixture, or a variation of this mixture. I mentioned above that you could buy large quantities of this mix, you can also buy small bags of it if you don't need to fill lots of containers.

So far, I've given you all the reasons why you *should* use soilless mix. I have to be fair and tell you there are a couple of cons also. The mix is of course very porous, so you must water more frequently than pots containing soil. Also, fertilizer leaches out more rapidly. But, the rewards for using this mix are great — the root system develops well and therefore you'll have tremendous bloom and foliage.

I apply a light dose of fertilizer every time I water my pots, barrel halves, and planter boxes. Before you say, "I can't do that!", let me tell you how I accomplish this. Go to your nursery or garden supply store and ask for a syphon system to water with — they'll know what you're talking about. It will cost in the $10.00 to $20.00 range. I won't attempt to tell you the mechanics of how it works, but basically, I set a 5 gallon bucket of fertilizer-water mix (5 gallons of water to 1 cup of Peter's 20-20-20 dry fertilizer — stir well to mix) next to the water spigot. A little hose meters and syphons the fertilizer into the watering hose, so that the correct amount of fertilizer is distributed. Remember that this dosage is for *light* fertilizing, so for once-a-week or once-a-month fertilizing, you would have to adjust the rate of fertilizer used. You can also buy 25 pound bags of the Peter's fertilizer from your garden supply store. It's much cheaper than in the small containers on the shelf. Another method of fertilizing, and the easiest, is to buy Stern's Miracle-Gro Garden and Flower feeder with fertilizer refills. Just attach to your garden hose and fertilizer as you water.

I do want to make clear that you should be fairly serious about your gardening before you invest too much money in huge piles of soilless mix, syphon systems and big bags of fertilizer! So analyze your needs, the size of your garden, how many pots you fill, etc., before investing too heavily. Besides the herbs I plant and fertilize this way, I water and fertilize all my flower pots and planters in the same manner. Remember, this discussion applies *only* to container gardening with soilless mix — *not* to your herbs or flowers planted in the ground.

🌿 Grow Your Own Gingerroot

Buy a piece of gingerroot at your supermarket. Plant it (shallow) in a pot of soilless mix. Set the pot in the sun and keep it watered. When the leaves begin to appear (it's slow!), continue to water until the leaves are 3 or 4 inches tall. When the weather permits, carefully remove the root (soil and all) from the pot and set it out in your garden. Plant it fairly shallow. This will allow the root to spread. After it is established, you can cut off a piece of the root with a sharp knife, wash it and refrigerate it for later use. The rest of the root will continue to grow. If you want to bring some inside for winter, chop off some of the root with leaves above it and re-pot. So, you can start with a small piece from the supermarket and grow it into quite a large ginger plant. It *won't* winter over in the ground in the Midwest.

Favorite Herbs

I have many favorite herbs — among my favorite **annual** herbs are: **basil, rosemary*, oregano*, sweet marjoram, summer savory,** and **parsley.** (*Actually, these are considered perennials, but not in mid-Indiana. Some oreganoes are hardy, but my Greek Oregano is often winter-killed. The winters are too harsh and often there is not enough snow cover for protection.) Another favorite annual herb (really a perennial!) is lemon verbena. I love it to dry for potpourri and to use in fresh herbal bouquets. The leaves are a lot like bay leaves — stiff, dry, shiny. Use them on baked fish fillets, or on baked chicken for a delightful lemony flavor, but discard leaf before serving, just as you would a bay leaf. Some of my favorite **perennial** herbs are **dill, chives, sage, mint, French tarragon,** and **thyme.** You will see in my garden that I have many other herbs besides these, but for the purposes of this book, I would like to talk mostly about 12 herbs. These are the 12 herbs I consider most necessary to the cook (the important word here is "I" — with experience, you will add to this list of 12).

On the following pages, we'll talk about these 12 herbs — what they look like, how tall they get, what they taste like, and other general characteristics.

Lemon Verbena

12 Culinary Herbs

Basil — Basil is a tender *annual*. There arc 40 or 50 varieties of Basil — new ones come along all the time (such as the All American winner Opal Basil, the new Purple Ruffles and Green Ruffles). The basil I refer to in all my recipes is *Sweet Green Basil* (sometimes called lettuce leaf basil), unless I state otherwise. Basil grows from 1 to 2 feet tall, or more. I put my plants about 8 to 10 inches apart. I've been told that Basil is the so-called royal herb — that it was once forbidden to anyone but royalty. Sure glad it isn't that way today since it is my favorite herb! The taste is described as slightly like a clove and with a very mild pepper flavor.

Rosemary — I treat Rosemary as an *annual*. It is native to the Mediterranean and I have seen it growing in France and Italy as shrubs in landscaping! For me, it grows to about 1 to 2 feet tall. Space plants about 1 foot apart. Rosemary has a distinctive pine flavor and aroma. The leaves even look like little pine needles. It is a beautiful plant to bring indoors for winter. Keep it well-watered and fertilize it occasionally. The leaves should be misted every 2 or 3 days inside a winter-dry house.

Oregano — Be very careful which oregano you plant. I prefer Greek Oregano. I snip off a leaf and taste it before I'll bring it home to plant. If it is sharp, tangy, peppery and wonderful tasting, it's Greek Oregano! If it has little or no taste, I consider it a weed. Oregano and Sweet Marjoram are related and similar. Oregano is a fairly hardy *perennial* but I treat it as an annual in Mid-Indiana. It has a stronger flavor than Sweet Marjoram. Oregano will grow 1 to 2 feet tall. Space the plants 8 to 10 inches apart.

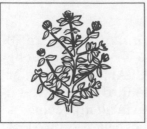

Sweet Marjoram — Sweet Marjoram is a tender *annual*. It will grow to about 1 foot tall, maybe a little taller under good conditions. I space marjoram plants no more than 8 inches apart. I love this little plant — it is mild and sweet and the leaves are a little smaller and a little paler green than Oregano leaves. It is very important to keep the blossoms snipped off this plant to keep the stems from getting leggy and woody. It also encourages side growth. The small white flowers are a tiny knot-like cluster of leaves. These little knots are what you want to keep clipped off.

Summer Savory — These plants will be 12 to 18 inches tall at peak growth. Plant them about 6 to 8 inches apart in your garden. Summer and Winter Savory are pepper-flavored. Summer Savory is milder in flavor than Winter Savory. It also has smaller, narrower leaves than Winter Savory. *Summer Savory* is a tender *annual*. *Winter Savory* is a hardy *perennial*.

Parsley — There are new varieties of Parsley popping up all the time. The plant will grow from about 8 to 18 inches tall. I put the plants 6 to 8 inches apart. I treat Parsley as an *annual*. I grow two varieties of curly Parsley (they're beautiful plants!), and I grow flat-leaf Italian Parsley for its flavor. Bring a nice Parsley plant inside in the winter. Give it lots more water and fertilizer than you'd ever guess it needed, and you should be able to snip Parsley all winter (keep the pot in a sunny window).

Dill — Dill will grow from 1½ to 3 feet tall. If you set out plants, put them 12 inches or more apart. You must set out smallish plants, because Dill has a tap root and so if the plant is very large, the tap root may be damaged in transplanting. Dill will re-seed itself, so it can be treated as a *perennial*. Dill is one herb I suggest you plant *away* from your herb garden. It is a beautiful plant, but the wind and birds scatter the seed and you'll find Dill growing everywhere you don't want it. The seeds and leaves of Dill have a sharp, slightly bitter taste — a little like Caraway seeds taste.

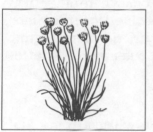

Chives — Chives is a hardy *perennial* that grows 1 to 2 feet tall. A well-established plant will get rather large, so space Chive plants at least 12 to 18 inches apart. Chives have round, hollow stems that taste like a mild onion. Snip these wonderful stems and cut into short lengths to dry or freeze for later use. If I have room in my refrigerator, I keep a bouquet of Chives in a glass jar filled ⅓ full with water. I can take out whatever I need, dry the stems and use. The flowers that appear on top are beautiful. They look like fresh clover blooms. These are pretty in fresh bouquets. I often dry the flower heads for potpourri, but I usually make a beautiful vinegar with them (see Herb Vinegar). One of my favorite Chives is *Garlic Chives*. Its stems are flat and the flowers are white and grow in tight clusters above the tips of the stems. The stems have a marvelous mild garlic flavor.

Sage — There are over 500 varieties of Sage. Sage will grow 1 to 2½ feet tall, depending on the variety. Place the plants at least 1 foot apart. Sage is a *perennial* plant. This is a gray-green herb and the leaves are long ovals and are rather coarse in texture. This is probably why Sage is usually ground or rubbed. The usual garden Sage has pretty lavender flowers on it. I try to dry all the Sage I need before allowing it to flower. I grow *Pineapple Sage* for its beauty and aroma. In the fall, it has beautiful trumpet-shaped red flowers on the plants —

the hummingbirds love these blooms! I also grow *Clary Sage* — I don't cook with it though. It's just a beautiful big plant. Sage has a strong flavor, so should be used sparingly. Of course it's indispensible at Thanksgiving time for the stuffing!

 **Mint** — There are many, many varieties of Mint. Among the widely known ones are Spearmint, Peppermint, Orange, Apple, Corsican, Pennyroyal. The Mints are hardy *perennials*. They will grow 1 to 2 feet tall. Don't worry about spacing them — plant only 1 of each variety you want and they will soon take over the area! This is another plant I would definitely suggest planting somewhere other than in the herb garden — along the back fence would be fine. I love the Mints, but they are difficult to contain. If you let several varieties of mints grow together, they will all tend to taste the same, so keep the varieties separated, if possible.

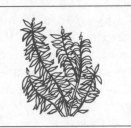 **French Tarragon** — Plants will get from 1 foot to nearly 3 feet tall. Space plants about 1 foot apart. French Tarragon is a *perennial,* but needs a little mulch if the temperature gets below -10°. It can *only* be grown from cuttings or root divisions. It does not set productive seeds, so you *cannot* grow French Tarragon from seeds. The leaves have no aroma, but they have a sharp licorice (anise) flavor. *Always* snip off a leaf and taste it before you buy it. If it doesn't taste like licorice, don't bring the plant home — it's the Russian variety and it's tasteless and of no value in cooking.

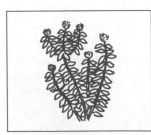 **Thyme** — There are over 100 varieties of Thyme. Sizes vary from creeping to up to 1 foot tall. I space these plants about 8 inches apart. Thyme is a *perennial*, and like French Tarragon, may need a mulch to get it through severe winters. As I've said before, the lack of snow seems to me to be the most damaging part of winter as far as plants are concerned (in my area). Thyme has a distinctive, slightly tangy

taste. One of my favorites is Lemon Thyme and it of course has a marvelous lemon flavor. Thyme grows on rather woody stems. It's a great herb for many uses. Besides cooking with it, I love it in herb and flower bouquets. It is probably the herb I use the most — it seems to enhance anything you add it to.

If you keep the above herb facts in mind, they should help you plan and plant your herb garden.

Finally, we come to the fun part — when to harvest your herbs, some ways to preserve them, and some great recipes I hope you will enjoy.

🏛 When to Harvest Herbs

If you set out your herb plants in early May (I hope to plant mine by May 10, if possible), you'll be able to harvest herbs by mid to late June. July and August are the peak months to harvest herbs in my area. The plants should be nice and leafy and well-branched. After your plants are in the ground, you may need to snip the centers out to encourage side growth. (These little snips are always the first herbs of the season and I can hardly wait to get them to the kitchen!).

I like to harvest herbs before they bloom. I find that if they do bloom, the plants tend to get leggy and woody-stemmed and they stop putting on new leaves. So, I think snipping off the blooms is a very important step in your herb gardening. I particularly won't let my basil plants flower — they really get leggy and stemmy if you do.

When you do harvest your herbs, cut the stems when the morning dew has dried away, and before the sun is too hot. Hot sun may harm the volatile oils (the tastes) of the herbs.

After you have cut your herbs, be sure to feed and water your plants to encourage new growth. They will almost always come back for a second growth in the same season, particularly the perennial herbs. Remember that annual herbs are like our annual garden and flower plants — they'll do their thing for so long, then because they are annuals, they will die. But, as I said before, they can often be encouraged into new growth. Don't *ever* cut the stems to the ground or remove the whole plant. You must leave several leaves to encourage the plant to grow again.

How to Preserve Herbs

There are several ways to dry and preserve herbs. If I'm drying herbs for culinary (cooking) use, I·bring them into the kitchen and give them a quick swish in a sinkful of tepid water — *not* hot. I line my counter with old towels and lay the herbs on them so they'll dry thoroughly. (If the herbs I'm drying are for potpourris or for other decorative purposes, I don't give them this bath).

The trick with drying fresh herbs is to dry them as quickly as possible so they'll retain their color and flavor. So with that in mind, I'll list some ways to do just that:

(1) Cut several stems, tie in a bunch and *hang to dry suspended in a brown paper bag*. Punch a few holes in the bag for air circulation. If you came to my house you would see several bunches of herbs hanging from the kitchen beams — but I have no intention of cooking with those dried bunches. If your house is like my house, things get dusty! Besides, these herbs will soon lose their flavor and color — but they do look and smell wonderful for awhile! So, back to the brown bag drying — leave them alone for 10 days to 2 weeks, then carefully check the bag. There should be several nice dry leaves resting on the bottom of the bag. Strip the rest of the leaves off the stems and store them in air-tight bottles or jars away from heat and light. By the way, I store as many dry whole-leaf herbs as possible — once you crush or grind them, they lose their flavor more rapidly.

(2) Another natural method of drying is to *lay leaves of certain herbs (particularly thicker-leaved herbs such as basil, sage, etc.) on old window screens*. Put these screens in an unused dark room, but one where air circulates freely. I use one (or two!) of the boys' bedrooms upstairs. Pull the blinds or close the draperies, but leave the door open. After three or four days of drying like this, I'll cover the partially dried leaves with a loose layer of paper towels. They'll go ahead and finish drying and I find the color is much better. There is no way to say how long they need to dry. Every few days, test a leaf — when it's crispy dry, it's ready to package as in number (1) above.

(3) I have had pretty good luck *drying herbs in a warm oven*. Put a layer of fresh-cut, clean herbs on a cookie sheet. Set your oven to slightly above WARM and dry herbs for 10 to 30 minutes, or more or less, depending on leaf size, leaf thickness, etc. Leave the oven door ajar. You must be aware of two important factors if you choose this method of drying: 1. Do not put too many herbs to be dried on the cookie sheet — they must be in a single layer; and 2. If you are impatient and use too high heat, you will destroy all the aroma and flavor in the leaves. Heat will

destroy the volatile oils. Otherwise, I find this a fairly satisfactory method of preserving herbs. When the leaves are dry, again follow directions to store as in number (1) above.

(4) I find a good way to *dry many herbs is in my microwave oven.* Place a single layer of herbs on a microwave plate. Cover with microwave-safe paper and microwave on HIGH for about 1 minute. Test to see if leaves are crisp. If not, microwave another 30 to 60 seconds. This method retains the color and flavor, *but* don't overdo, or you'll destroy all the flavor. You'll learn with experience which herbs dry best with this method.

(5) You may *freeze chopped fresh herbs* in air-tight containers. Do *not* blanch the leaves first. If you rinse them, be sure leaves are thoroughly dry before freezing them. Package in small quantities, because once these are thawed, they have to be used immediately. The thawed herbs will be too limp to use as a garnish, but they are fine to chop with your scissors to add to your cooking.

Here is another way to freeze herbs. Place chopped fresh herbs in sections of ice cube trays. Fill with water and freeze. Pop out the cubes and freeze them in plastic bags. Use individual cubes at a later day for soups or stews.

There are other methods of preserving your herb harvest. You can *layer herbs in salt* — then you have an herb-flavored salt to use as well as the preserved leaves.

A good way to preserve *basil is in olive oil.* Remove the leaves needed, rinse oil off leaves, pat dry with paper towels and chop. Then, of course, you also have a lovely basil-flavored olive oil to use.

So, you can see there are many methods of preserving your harvest. Experiment and see what works best for you. (Two or three farm women at the Farm Progress Show told me they used their food dehydrator to dry herbs and it worked very well. If you have one, it would be worth a try.)

I should mention one other thing here. If you have dill, fennel, anise, caraway, etc., and would like to dry seeds from these plants, cut the stems at the end of summer, but before the seeds drop (or before the birds get them!). Carefully cut the stems (don't handle them roughly or they'll shatter) and use the brown paper bag method for drying. When the seeds are dried, shake the bag and all the seeds will fall into the bottom of the bag. Store the dried seeds in air-tight containers.

When we talk about preserving herbs, we also need to talk about preserving herbs *and* flowers for potpourri. The method for drying the flower petals is basically the same as for drying herbs. I dry almost all my flowers for potpourri on old window screens in a dark room, or I spread out an old sheet on the floor and scatter the petals on the sheet in one layer. Every 2 or 3 days, stir the petals around gently to dry all sides evenly. Always remember — herb and flower leaves and petals are dry when they feel crispy-dry, but are still aromatic. After a batch is dried, I label brown paper bags with that flower or herb and store the closed bags in a dark closet until I have enough things dried for a batch of potpourri. Following is a very basic Flower and Herb Potpourri recipe.

🏛 Basic Flower and Herb Potpourri

Sometimes in a Fall Cooking Class, after drying flowers and herbs throughout the summer, I'll make this basic potpourri for the class. They love to see it go together.

1	to 2 quarts dried flower petals*
1	to 2 cups dried herb leaves (a mixture is best)**
¼	to ½ cup fixative (such as cut orris root, *not* powdered)
1	to 2 tablespoons spices (such as pieces of cinnamon bark, whole cloves, whole allspice, and a whole nutmeg, shaved into pieces)
1	to 2 tablespoons crushed herb seeds (such as anise, coriander, caraway seeds)
1	to 2 tablespoons dried citrus peels (orange and/or lemon)
20	drops rose oil
5	to 8 drops patchouli oil
8	to 10 drops orange oil
5	to 8 drops verbena *or* honeysuckle oil

Mix the flowers, herbs, spices, herb seeds and citrus peels together in a large glass jar with a screw-on lid. Drop the oils onto the fixative (cut orris root). Gently mix this into the contents in the glass jar (or mix all together in a huge bowl, then put in the container). Let potpourri age in a dark room (lid on) for 5 or 6 weeks for full blending of scents. Stir gently once in awhile. Always give potpourri as a gift in a covered container.

*Such as *rose, blue salvia, peony petals (not* white or pale pink — they want to turn yellowish or brown), *statice, delphinium, stock, lavender,* etc. I always say to dry what's pretty — if it doesn't dry really beautiful, throw it away. Your potpourri will only look as good as the petals you put in it.

**Such as *lemon verbena leaves* (the main reason I grow lemon verbena is for the beautiful green leaves for potpourri — you'll learn that many green leaves *won't* dry green. If they aren't green when dried, throw them away), *opal basil leaves* (beautiful!), *bay leaves, rosemary, sweet marjoram, scented geranium leaves, costmary leaves, thyme, flower heads of chives, some artemisias, lavender, lamb's ear,* etc.

A Word on Orris Root

Orris root is a common fixative used in potpourri. It is the dried root (or corm) of the German iris plant. This dried root is then powdered or cut into small pieces. There are many fixatives, but I find orris root most readily available. I used to use the powdered orris root until I got smarter! Now I use only the cut orris root for my potpourri. The powdered orris root leaves an unsightly powdery residue on the beautiful petals and leaves. After you have worked hard all summer drying the petals, you don't want to ruin them with the wrong fixative. For this same reason, don't use ground spices such as ground cinnamon, ground cloves, etc. Now I put my essential oil drops on the cut orris root and then mix the root into the other potpourri ingredients. I have been much more pleased with the quality and color of my potpourris. If you can't get orris root locally, Nichol's Nursery (see Useful Addresses, page 64) has top quality potpourri supplies. But do try your local nurseryman or garden supply man first. If he doesn't have what you want, he'll probably be very happy to get it for you. Other very good fixatives are: oak moss, frankincense tears, sandalwood chips, deer tongue, gum benzoin, vetiver root, etc.

How to Dry Orange Peel

To dry orange or lemon peel for your potpourri, remove the peel with a sharp knife and try not to get into the white part of the rind. Place in a single layer on a paper plate. Cover with paper towel and let set at room temperature for 2 or 3 days, or until peel is dry. To dry in your microwave, arrange pieces of peel, not touching, on a paper plate. Microwave on high for 2 or 3 minutes, turning plate ½ turn after 1 minute, until peel curls up and is dried. This is a quick way to prepare peels for potpourri, spiced tea mixes, etc.

*A **Thymely Footnote** . . . I have found that the leaves from **hot house roses** dry a beautiful green. I add these to my potpourri mixture when I have a short supply of dried green herb leaves.*

 Herb Bath Sachet

If you're clever with a sewing machine, make pretty bags from calicos, muslins, prints, etc. Fill a bag with dried herbs and sew it shut. Add a ribbon or string long enough to tie or hang onto the tub faucet. Let your warm bath water run over the sachet to perfume it. A jar of these would make a lovely and unique gift. Some of the herbs I use are: *dried mint leaves, dried rosemary, dried lemon verbena, dried lavender, dried scented geranium leaves.* Let the bag dry and use it once or twice more — after that, most of the scent will be gone. Store the dry bag or bags in a large air-tight jar to retain the fragrance.

Well, we have spent considerable time on planning the garden, preparing the garden, planting the garden, when to harvest, and how to harvest the garden. Now, I would like to tell you some wonderful ways to use your herbs, so I have prepared a list of foods to go with the 12 herbs I have emphasized. Following is a **Culinary Chart** for those herbs. Following that are some great herb recipes — how to make herb vinegars, herb seasonings and herb butters.

Culinary Chart

Basil — herb vinegars, herb butters, tomatoes, tomato dishes, summer squash, salads, seafood, pesto, soups, cheese balls, dips, bread crumbs for fish or chicken, marinades, bouquet garnis, mayonnaise

Rosemary — herb vinegars, lamb, chicken, marinades, herb mustard, herb butters, bouquet garnis

Oregano — fish, shellfish, lamb, poultry, tomato sauces, herb butters, meat marinades, eggs, mushrooms, pizza, zucchini, green beans, cheeses, dips, soups, vinegars, beef, pork, bouquet garnis

Sweet Marjoram — interchangeable with oregano. The good Greek oregano is a little more powerful in flavor than marjoram.

Summer Savory — most any green vegetable, especially green beans, herb butters, beef, pork, eggs, dips, vinegars

Parsley — meats, salads, all vegetables, stews, quiches, cheese dips, tomato sauces, soups, herb butters, stews, bouquet garnis, eggs, fish, shellfish

Dill — salmon, cucumbers, sour cream, herb butters, shrimp, salads, potato salad, green beans, cabbage, cauliflower, herb vinegars, bread

Chives — potato salad, vegetables, salads, herb butter, breads, fish, seafood, chicken, soups, cheese dips, egg dishes, sour cream, herb vinegar (use the flower heads)

Sage — pork, poultry, stuffing, pork marinades, egg dishes, breads, vinegars, herb butter

Mint — peas, tea, apple jelly, lemonade, iced tea, punches, dried leaves for potpourri, lamb, mint jelly, marinades

French Tarragon — chicken, salads, fish, herb vinegars, herb butters, mayonnaise, salad dressings, green beans, marinades, bouquet garnis

Thyme — herb vinegars, carrots, bouquet garnis, salads, salad dressings, meat marinades, soups, stews, sauces, pork, beef, lamb, poultry, any green vegetable, herb butters, egg dishes, fish, seafood

🍶 Some Special Herb Recipes

Mixed Herb Vinegar

❧ This is my favorite of all the vinegars I make.

Pick herbs late in the morning (when dew is dried away). Wash gently, but thoroughly. Lay out on towels and blot with another towel. Pack herbs in a 1 gallon glass jar which has been sterilized. Heat white distilled vinegar to *nearly* boiling point. Pour over herbs. Cover with a glass lid or cover with waxed paper or plastic wrap, then with a regular jar lid. (Don't use metal lid directly on jar because of a reaction with the vinegar.) Let steep 3 weeks. Taste. If strong enough, strain out herbs. (Throw herbs away.) Run vinegar through a coffee filter into a clean, sterilized jar or a pretty bottle. Cork, label, enjoy! The herbs I use are: **2 handfuls green basil leaves, 1 handful of thyme, 1 handful of sweet marjoram, 1 handful Greek or true oregano, 3 or 4 peeled cloves of garlic, 10 whole peppercorns** and **1 dried hot cayenne pepper** (or ½ to 1 teaspoon dried hot pepper flakes).

Herb Vinegars

❧ Some herbs to use for flavoring vinegars are:

Green Sweet Basil — use the whole leaves and stems if not too woody.
Opal Basil *or* **Purple Ruffles Basil** — use the whole leaves and stems. This makes an incredibly beautiful, bright pink vinegar. One of my favorites.
Tarragon (French) — use the leaves and tender stems.
Dill-Garlic — For one gallon of vinegar, use leaves and seeds of dill and 4 or 5 whole bulbs of garlic which have been peeled and separated into cloves.
Chive Blossoms — use the pink-lavender colored blossoms only. The vinegar will become a beautiful pale mauve color with a very oniony flavor.
Thyme — use the leaves and tender new stems.
Mint — use the leaves and tender stems.
Dill — use leaves and seeds

To make these vinegars, follow the directions for my Mixed Herb Vinegar. (I use white distilled vinegar for all these herb vinegars.)

No-Salt Herb Blend I

5 teaspoons onion powder
2½ teaspoons garlic powder
2½ teaspoons Hungarian sweet paprika
2½ teaspoons dry mustard
1¼ teaspoons thyme
½ teaspoon ground white pepper
¼ teaspoon celery seed

Combine all ingredients and mix well. Spoon into a shaker. Makes about ⅓ cup. If you want to double or triple recipe, store extra blend in a covered glass jar to keep fresh.

No-Salt Herb Blend II

This will make about 1 cup.
4 tablespoons dried, crumbled oregano leaves
4 tablespoons onion powder
4 teaspoons dried, crumbled marjoram leaves
4 teaspoons dried, crumbled basil leaves
4 teaspoons dried, crumbled savory leaves
4 teaspoons garlic powder
2 teaspoons dried, crumbled thyme leaves
2 teaspoons dried, crumbled rosemary leaves
1 teaspoon dried, crumbled sage leaves
1 teaspoon ground black pepper

Combine all ingredients and put some in a shaker. Store any unused portion in a covered glass jar. Sprinkle on fish, chicken, vegetables.

A Thymely Footnote . . . To make sure that little worms which become little moths don't ruin your dried potpourri materials, place zip-loc bags of dried potpourri materials in your freezer for 2 or 3 days. This will eliminate the insect larvae completely.

Gourmet Seasoned Salt

This is a marvelous seasoning you'll reach for every day. It's really good.

       1 **cup salt**
       2 **teaspoons dry mustard**
    1½ **teaspoons dried oregano leaves**
       1 **teaspoon dried marjoram leaves**
       1 **teaspoon dried thyme**
       1 **teaspoon garlic powder**
     ½ **to 1 teaspoon curry powder (optional)**
     ½ **teaspoon onion powder**
     ½ **teaspoon celery seeds**
     ¼ **teaspoon dried dill weed**

Combine all and mix well. Store in an airtight container. Makes about 1¼ cups. (I usually mix this in my blender or food processor because I like this mixture rather fine.)

Bouquet Garnis

No herb chapter would be complete without a recipe for bouquet garnis! Here are two favorite recipes.

Garni No. 1:
1 **bay leaf**
1 **tablespoon dried tarragon**
1 **tablespoon dried parsley**
1 **teaspoon dried rosemary**
1 **teaspoon dried thyme**
5 **or 6 peppercorns**

Garni No. 2:
1 **peeled garlic clove**
1 **tablespoon dried parsley**
1 **teaspoon dried basil**
1 **teaspoon dried rosemary**
1 **teaspoon dried oregano**
2 **bay leaves**
6 **whole peppercorns**

Put herbs in the middle of a coffee filter. Gather up into a bag and tie with white kitchen string. I make an assembly line of ingredients and fix several of these at a time. Store garnis in an airtight glass jar.

Use bouquet garnis to flavor your soup or stew pot.

Fine Herbes

* *Make your own classic French mixture of herbs. The French call the mixture "Fine Herbes," and they use it in much of their cooking.*

Mix equal parts of:
Parsley
Chervil*
Chives
French Tarragon

*Chervil is a very nice herb. It reminds me of parsley in both looks and taste. It is the monosodium glutamate (MSG) of the herb world because it enhances other herb flavors. That is why it is almost *always* used in combination with other herbs. Chervil has a slight anise (licorice) flavor.

Herb Butter I

* *This butter is especially good on broiled fish.*

⅓ **cup minced fresh parsley**
2 **green onions, minced**
½ **cup snipped fresh dill, OR 2 teaspoons dried**
2 **tablespoons chopped fresh tarragon, OR 2 teaspoons dried**
1 **tablespoon chopped fresh chervil, OR 1 teaspoon dried OR 1 tablespoon chopped fresh celery leaves**
2 **sticks unsalted butter, softened**
2 **tablespoons fresh lemon juice**
   salt and pepper to taste

Combine first 6 ingredients in a blender or food processor. Add the lemon juice and salt and pepper and blend until mixture is combined well. Store in a pretty crock, covered, in the refrigerator until ready to use. Makes about 1 cup of wonderful butter.

Herb Butter II

🌿 *This herb butter is especially good on baked or broiled chicken.*

1 cup butter, softened
3 garlic cloves, chopped fine
2 tablespoons chopped fresh rosemary, or 1½ teaspoons dried
1 tablespoon chopped fresh Italian parsley (or regular parsley will do) or 1 teaspoon dried
2 teaspoons finely grated lemon peel
salt and pepper to taste

Combine all ingredients in mixing bowl or food processor. Makes 1 cup. Besides using herb butters on meat and fish, try some on a baked potato, on a chicken or turkey sandwich, on thick slices of French bread to toast in the oven. Spread some on a grilled or broiled hamburger. You'll think of all kinds of delicious ways to use these butters.

Herb Butter III

Mix thoroughly:
½ cup butter, softened
¼ cup grated Parmesan cheese
1 tablespoon chopped fresh parsley, or 1 teaspoon dried
1 tablespoon chopped fresh oregano, or 1 teaspoon dried
¼ teaspoon garlic powder
1 tablespoon lemon juice

Spread on thick slices of French or Italian bread. Toast under broiler. Watch closely. Delicious!

A Thymely Footnote . . . Watercress is a peppery-tasting perennial. Requires a lot of water for good growth. Toss a few leaves into a green salad and of course watercress sandwiches on the tea table are almost a necessity!

Fine Herbes Butter

&. *This too is a basic herb recipe. If you are served an herb butter in a French restaurant or café, it most likely is a variation of this one:*

Combine:
- 1 **cup butter, softened**
- 2 **tablespoons dried parsley flakes**
- 2 **tablespoons chopped fresh chives**
- 1 **teaspoon dried tarragon**
- 1 **teaspoon dried chervil**
- ½ **teaspoon salt**
  dash of freshly grated pepper

Blend well. Put on slices of French bread to toast under the broiler; put on a grilled steak; dab on chicken to be broiled or baked.

Parsley Butter

&. *If you don't raise any herbs, and would like to use an herb butter, Parsley Butter is for you. Parsley is available in most all groceries most all year.*

- 1 **cup unsalted butter, softened**
- 1 **cup chopped fresh parsley leaves**
  freshly grated black pepper, to taste
- 1 **tablespoon fresh lemon juice**
- 1 **or 2 cloves garlic, minced**

Combine all thoroughly. Cover tightly and refrigerate up to 2 weeks. Good on any meat, fish, chicken, bread or vegetable. People ask if they can freeze herb butters — yes, if you wrap the butter *very* well and use within a few weeks. Let thaw in refrigerator, if possible, before using.

A Thymely Footnote . . . Bay leaf *(bay laurel) is a sweet aromatic evergreen. California bay is 3 times stronger in flavor than its Mediterranean cousin.*

The Best Fresh Herb Butter I Know Of!

❧ Keep this butter in the refrigerator and bring to room temperature to use. The title tells you my opinion of it!

- 2   **sticks unsalted butter, room temperature**
- 1   **tablespoon chopped fresh green basil**
- 1   **tablespoon chopped fresh marjoram**
- 1   **tablespoon chopped fresh chives**
- 1   **teaspoon chopped fresh rosemary**
- 1   **teaspoon fresh lemon juice**

Use your kitchen scissors and chop the herbs fairly fine. Blend all herbs and the lemon juice into the butter with a wooden spoon. Don't use your electric mixer, food processor or blender unless you like your butter to be green. Make this butter a day or two before using it so flavors will blend.

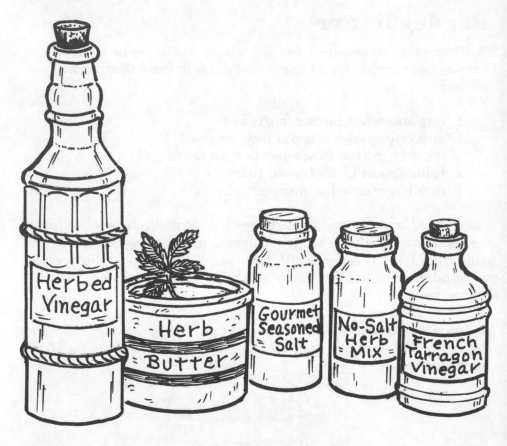

My herb garden wouldn't be complete without members of the Allium family. Here is a little information on them:

The Allium Family

This family includes onions, leeks, shallots, garlic, chives. The Allium family is a member of the Lily family.

There are many varieties of onions in the world, among them five sweet ones that I'm familiar with — they are *so* good they deserve a few words.

The one we probably hear about most is the Vidalia Sweet, from the Vidalia, Georgia area; another is the Walla Walla Sweet, from Walla Walla, Washington; and the Florida Sweet which is raised in the Florida interior. Also, the Texas Sweet and the Maui Sweet from Hawaii. These sweet onions cost a little more, but any time you see them in your grocery or market, treat yourself to some. The season for these sweets is fairly short.

Many cooks are discovering leeks and how good they are. They look like huge green onions, but they're very mild in taste. They are wonderful braised or creamed.

Shallots are somewhat of a cross between garlic and onions. They are indispensable in French cooking.

Onion sets or plants are available at any garden supply or nursery in the spring. Leeks are easiest to raise from tiny plants. You can sow seeds, but the seedlings are so slow to emerge. I find the plants more satisfactory.

Buy shallots and garlic bulbs from your garden supply and grow your own. Separate the bulbs into cloves and plant the cloves. Plant these just as you do your onion sets.

Be sure to harvest all onion-family plants when the tops have died down in late summer or early fall and when the tops have fallen over. Be sure to dig or pull them before the fall rains begin. The mature bulbs will rot very quickly in cool, wet soil. Lay the harvested bulbs on several layers of newspaper in a dry, warm place until the outer skins are crispy dry.

Plant your chives where they can come up every year. It is one of the first plants to emerge in the spring at my house. I always know nice weather isn't far away when I see the chives coming through the ground. After you have cut the chives several times, let them flower and either dry the pink blooms for potpourri or make chive vinegar (recipe appears on page 30). After you cut off the blooms, cut rest of the chives to within 2 or 3 inches of the ground. Use your scissors and cut the stems into tiny pieces. Either dry these or put into small packages and freeze them. I particularly like to freeze them. With rain and sunshine, your chive plants will come back and produce another crop.

If you're interested, the garlic that is purplish in color is Mexican garlic. The white is U.S. or European garlic.

A final word on garlic — it's easy to peel garlic. Drop the cloves in hot water briefly. Remove from the water and the skin will pop off easily. Another easy way to remove the skins is to hit the clove sharply with the flat edge of a large knife. The skins slip right off.

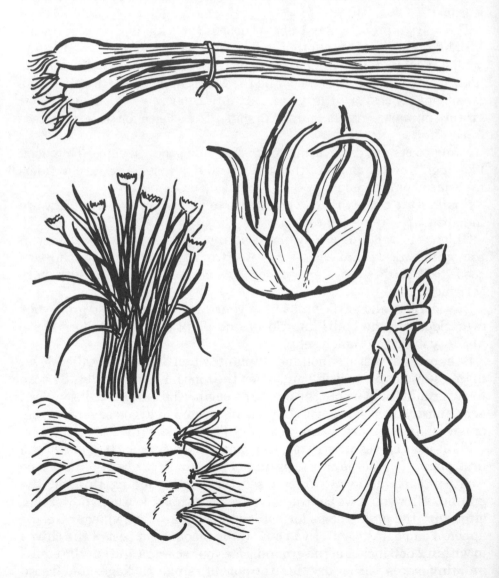

Christmas with Herbs and Spices

I have put together some recipes and ideas for you to use in your Christmas decorating. These are all beautiful and relatively easy to make. Do try one or all of these. Your house will smell like Christmas!

Christmas Potpourri

🍃 *This recipe is also from* Take a Little Thyme. *I have discovered something important about this recipe (that differs from other pot-pourris). Because salt was used as the fixative (orris root is the usual fixative in floral potpourris) in this recipe, you must never cover your container. If covered, moisture collects inside the jar and causes the greens to turn blackish. So, enjoy this potpourri uncovered! I made this discovery at the Farm Progress Show in Iowa. Since I was one of the speakers for the Women's Program, I had of course taken lots of my herb vinegars, potpourris, etc. It was typical late September weather — hot in the daytime and quite chilly at night. By the third day, I noticed my beautiful Christmas Potpourri was turning black — that's when I discovered the contents were almost wet. With the temperature changes, moisture had condensed on the inside of the jar. Needless to say, I was horrified! As I said in my speech that day, "hardly a day goes by that I don't learn something new about the world of herbs and spices." If you begin to lose the fragrance (and you will with it uncov-ered all the time), just add another vial of cinnamon oil, stir it in good, and you're back in business. Now for the recipe:*

To make about 1 gallon —

Collect small pieces of evergreen and lay on an old clean window screen to dry (will take a week or two, depending on humidity, heat, etc.). Some of the best greenery to cut are spruce, juniper (especially blueberry juniper), cedar, pfitzers, and arborvitae. Don't cut yews — they dry brown. Mix about **1 gallon of the dried evergreen sprigs, 1 quart small pine cones** (hemlock are perfect), **1 cup, or less, dried orange peel, ½ cup, or less, whole cloves, 1 cup , or less, broken cinnamon sticks, ½ cup, or less, whole allspice, about 1 cup fixative*,** such as **large cut cellulose, reindeer moss, or oak moss and 10 to 20 drops of cinnamon oil** (get this from your drug store). I usually add **a big handful of dried flowers** (stick with one color). (The dark red dried peony petals are beautiful to use here, but use whatever you have.)

*Place the fixative (cellulose or moss) in a quart glass jar. Add the cinnamon oil to the jar and shake jar well. Put on lid and let oil soak into the fixative for a day or so before adding to the potpourri. Thanks to Linda Cloutier of The Potpourri Patch, Auburn, Maine, for this suggestion.

THYME UPDATE . . . Note that I don't use salt as a fixative now — no more condensation problems!

Pomander Balls #1

These pomanders are not treated with spices and orris root (see #2), because I fix these for the beautiful orange color to show through. They are rather short-lived (they'll start to decay after a few days), so fix these just a day or two before you want to use them. For one pomander, you'll need **1 navel orange and 2 or 3 tablespoons of whole cloves.** Use only navel oranges because the skin is easier to penetrate. Arrange the cloves in rows, circles, or any decorative way you choose (see illustration for ideas). Pile these oranges in a beautiful footed bowl. Tuck sprigs of fresh greenery among and between the oranges. A simple and beautiful centerpiece or decoration.

Pomander Balls #2

These pomanders are completely covered with whole cloves, then rolled in a mixture of ground spices and ground orris root so that the orange is preserved. These are the kind you tie a ribbon around and hang in your closet or put in linen drawers. A bowl of these is also pretty, but no orange color shows through. For decorative purposes, I like Pomander #1 better. For long lasting, aromatic purposes, I'd choose Pomander #2.

Cover a **navel orange** completely with **whole cloves** (this takes awhile and also produces sore thumbs!). Combine **2 or 3 tablespoons ground cinnamon, 1 to 2 tablespoons ground cloves, 1 to 2 tablespoons ground allspice,** and **2 to 3 tablespoons ground orris root.** Mix well and roll the clove-studded orange in this mixture. Gently shake off excess, then lay orange on newspapers or paper towels to cure and dry. They need to dry a couple of weeks before hanging in your closet. These make nice little gifts.

Keep any spice-orris root mixture that is left over in a closed airtight container. Be sure to mark it well and do *not* use for cooking purposes.

Mini Potpourri Wreaths and Mini Spice Wreaths

❧ I often make these in a Holiday Cooking or Gift class — everyone wants to rush home and make some!

For 1 wreath, you'll need:
- ¾ **to 1 cup potpourri or 1 cup Holiday Spices (recipe follows)**
- 1 **tablespoon white glue (such as Elmer's)**
- 1 **tablespoon water**

Grease a 2½" to 3" ring mold — I use a doughnut cutter — with soft oleo or salad oil. Use a cottage cheese carton (or some other disposable container) and mix the water and white glue together to make a thin paste. Add the potpourri and stir well to coat the leaves and petals with the thin glue mixture. Pack this mixture into your prepared mold and tamp it down with your fingertips — don't worry about the glue, it will dry clear. Let the mold set for a couple of minutes, then turn upside down on a paper plate. Three to six hours later, run a knife around the inside and outside edge of the mold and gently remove the wreath from the mold. Let dry for several days, turning occasionally to dry evenly on both sides. Tie wreath on the tree with a pretty ribbon. These are delightful to hang on your Christmas tree or on a small kitchen tree.

Holiday Spices for Mini Spice Wreaths

Combine **whole cloves**, **broken cinnamon stick pieces** (I put mine in a plastic bag and hit with a hammer or rolling pin), **whole allspice**, **whole nutmeg** (also broken up), **dried orange or lemon peel**. I have also added **finely chopped whole vanilla beans**, plus **other aromatic whole spices** from the spice shelves. Follow the procedure to make Mini Potpourri Wreaths.

A Thymely Footnote . . . Costmary (Bible leaf) is a perennial with rather bitter leaves, so it isn't usually used in cooking. The Puritans used a leaf of costmary as a Bible marker, hence, the name Bible leaf evolved.

Dried Cinnamon Apple Rings

These are fragrant decorations to add to your Christmas tree.

Cut firm-skinned apples (such as Red Delicious) into ½ inch slices. Carefully remove the core from each slice. Roll **apple ring** in a mixture of **ground cinnamon** and **ground orris root** (2 parts cinnamon to 1 part orris root). Cover the apple surface completely. Put rings on a cookie sheet and place in a WARM oven for 2 to 3 hours. Turn apple rings 2 or 3 times. This will dry most of the moisture out. Remove apple rings from cookie sheet and put on paper towels to dry another week or more, turning occasionally.

Tie these dried apple rings on your tree with a pretty ribbon.

The Smell of Christmas

Use an old pan with a loose-fitting lid. Combine in the pan:

2   to 3 tablespoons whole cloves
4   or 5 cinnamon sticks
1   to 2 tablespoons whole allspice
1   whole nutmeg, chopped coarsely
    piece of a vanilla bean, if available
    peel from 1 or 2 oranges, not dried

Cover the above with water. Put the pan in the oven (200° to 250°) and enjoy the wonderful spicy aroma. I usually have this mixture, or one like it, in the oven from Thanksgiving to Christmas. Keep adding water to the pan. After several days of brewing, it's best to throw away the spices, clean up the pan, and start over. The pan turns black, but don't worry — an SOS pad takes it right out!

Fruit and Spice Christmas Scent

3 sticks cinnamon
3 bay leaves
¼ cup whole cloves
1 lemon, cut in half
1 orange, cut in half
4 to 6 cups water

Combine all ingredients in a saucepan. Bring to a boil. Reduce heat and simmer on the back of the stove or put in a slow oven (200° or so) so the aroma will go all through the house. Check occasionally and don't let the pan boil dry. You can re-use this mixture 2 or 3 times — just add more water each time and refrigerate when not using it.

Fresh Christmas Greens

Put fresh-cut greens in a bucket of cool water and leave overnight in a cool place, like the garage. The stems need to absorb as much water as possible. This is called **conditioning.**

If you have holly, condition as above, then dry the stem ends. Lastly, dip the ends in melted candle wax or paraffin. Cool. This seals in the resin and the holly can be arranged then as you wish. (Do not arrange in water though.)

To keep ivy and boxwood fresh for a week or 10 days, condition stems in water overnight. Dry the stems and dip the entire cutting (leaves *and* stems) in clear liquid floor wax. Lay out on old newspapers to dry. Again, do not use any water in the arrangements.

A POTPOURRI OF IDEAS

A potpourri is a mixture of lots of good things. That's what I call this section — A Potpourri. There is a little bit of everything here, from making Pesto to making Pasta; from Herbed Olive Oil to Herbed Flour; from how to roast peppers to what vanilla beans to buy. Plus lots more — I'll tell you a little about spices, olive oil, and cheese, and how to make your own herb wreath. As you will see, none of these things go together, and yet they *all* go together.

Cheese Market Day in Alkmaar, Holland

Cooking with Fresh Herbs

If you're adding fresh herbs to sauces, sauté dishes, etc., add them toward the end of cooking time. The heat will destroy the volatile oils and the green color if allowed to cook too long. Usually the last three to five minutes of cooking time is about right — the flavor will go into the food, but will not be destroyed by over-cooking.

I have found the best way to chop fresh herbs is with a pair of sharp kitchen scissors. The electric choppers, food processors, etc., chop the delicate leaves so fine that much of the flavor is destroyed.

A good basic rule to follow:

1 tablespoon fresh herbs = 1 teaspoon dried herbs

Whether you use fresh or dried herbs, the herb should never overpower a dish. You just want the delicate and distinctive herb flavor to come through.

Herbed Olive Oil

A cooking class favorite —

- 6 **fresh rosemary sprigs, OR 1 teaspoon dried**
- 6 **whole black peppercorns**
- 3 **garlic cloves, coarsely chopped**
- 1 **Spice Island bay leaf, OR 3 others**
- 2 **fresh thyme sprigs, OR ½ teaspoon dried**
- 2 **fresh oregano sprigs, OR ½ teaspoon dried**
  Good quality olive oil

Put herbs and other seasonings in a clean quart glass jar or bottle. Add olive oil (use *only* a good grade virgin or extra-virgin oil) to nearly fill the bottle. Cork or put tight lid on. Store in a cool, dark place for a week to 10 days before using. Use in vinegar and oil salad dressings and in marinades. Sauté hamburgers or chicken breasts in it. This is wonderful to keep or to give! Makes 1 quart.

Keep refrigerated when not using. Olive oil will congeal when it's cold, so set the bottle out of the refrigerator for a little while before you want to use the oil.

Olive Oil — the Good and the Bad!

When my recipes call for "good olive oil," I mean an oil that is light to medium green in color, clear, and fragrant with no musty smell. This would be an oil labled as "extra virgin" or "first pressed" or "cold pressed."

The "bad" olive oil (my opinion) is the yellowish oil with not much flavor or aroma. It seems to often smell musty. Unfortunately, most olive oils in the grocery is this latter kind. You may have to go to a specialty food store or order your oil from a store like Williams-Sonoma (see Useful Addresses) to get a "good" one. I do, however, see signs of better grades of olive oil in our groceries. Speak to your grocer — he is almost always anxious to put things in his store that you, his customer, want. I'll name a few brands later that I particularly like.

There are many grades of olive oil, many colors, tastes, and aromas. Most olive oils come from Italy, Spain, Greece, Portugal, France and California. Considering all the climate, soil and processing conditions in all these places, it's no wonder that the oils are so different.

"Extra virgin" olive oil may *not* contain more than 1% of oleic acid. "Virgin" oil may have more acidity than that — up to 4%. "Extra virgin" oil is almost always from the first pressing of very high quality olives and the label will also almost always say "cold pressed," which means no heat was used in the processing.

When I buy an oil, I look for one that smells very "fruity," as they say. That means that it smells very much like green olives.

So, a lot of our grocery store oils are marked "virgin" or "pure." This means the oils have more acidity, they are from poorer quality olives, and they are often made from second and third pressings of the olive pulp. They are often processed with heat (therefore, not cold pressed) and also have chemicals added, whereas the extra virgin oils do not.

It's true that a good extra virgin oil is expensive, so I usually buy 2 or 3 grades. The best grade I save for salad dressings, for drizzling on fresh tomatoes or other salads, for my Herbed Olive Oil, for marinating cheese, etc. I use a less expensive oil for sautéeing and for general cooking.

Always store your olive oil, expensive or not, in a cool, dark place. But do not refrigerate it, or it will congeal. When I make salad dressings with olive oil and refrigerate the dressing, it will congeal. Just set it out at room temperature for awhile until you can shake it and make it liquid again. Olive oil doesn't have as long a shelf life as other vegetable oils. Six months to a year is probably maximum, so try to use it when it's fresh.

My husband is a farmer, so I won't abandon the wonderful American soybean and corn oils that we use nearly every day. I use my fruity, aromatic olive oil when I want to add that extra flavor to my dishes.

I'm not an expert on olive oils — I haven't tried dozens of brands to compare. But I have tried several, so I can talk about them. One of the best, and least expensive extra virgin oil is from Zabar's. Zabar's is a most wonderful food store in New York City. I know there are lots more, but Zabar's is the one I'm familiar with. When I was in New York City, I made a trip to Zabar's just to buy olive oil! The label says the oil came from Italy, so I assume they buy it in large quantities and bottle it with their own labels. At any rate, it is one of the best ones I've tried for the money. This is a food shopper's paradise! If you're a cook (or even if you're not) and if you ever go to New York, plan to spend an hour or two at Zabar's — quite an experience.

There are some great olive oils from California that are relatively inexpensive. One is from The Market Square Food Company. The oil is called "An American Delicacy" — "California Olive Oil." I brought home a 3 liter bottle of wonderful oil from the Napa Valley Olive Oil Manufactory in St. Helena, California. It was very green, very fruity and aromatic, and tasted great. It was also inexpensive.

I have tried the Old Monk brand from France but was disappointed. It is gold in color, very mild, and not much olive taste.

I carried some marvelous oil home on my lap from Mallorca, Spain. I bought it in a little busy market in a small town on the coast road. I can't even tell you the name of the oil — I'm sure it was pressed at a small farm operation that perhaps only sold to neighbors and at the local market. (The olives from that same market were unbelievable! The best green olives I ever tasted).

From Italy, I have tried the expensive Antinori. It is very good, but also very expensive. Antinori is a famous name in the olive oil and wine industries in Italy, so I suspect part of the cost is in the name. Also from Italy comes the oil most often found in our grocery stores — Bertolli. It is fairly inexpensive, golden in color and pretty bland. Not much olive taste or smell.

In my opinion, the best all-around oil from Italy and one that seems to be very available in the U.S. is the Colavita brand. It is inexpensive, golden-green in color, very smooth, and fairly aromatic. Ask your grocer to carry this brand in his store. Your friends will thank you for it.

I don't know much about the oils from Greece. I do know there are many great ones. One of the really great ones, and the only one I'm familiar with, is the Peloponnese brand. It is not green, it's gold, but very smooth, olive tasting, and very fragrant. It's also expensive.

I have rambled on longer than I intended on "olive oil," but I do think it's become an important cooking tool, and it's always fun to learn all we can about a subject. So, there you have it — the little I know about Olive Oil!

Hot Stir Fry Oil

❧ *This is a wonderful flavored oil to use in your wok or stir-fry pan.*

2   **cups vegetable oil**
2   **tablespoons fresh gingerroot, chopped**
2   **tablespoons dried red pepper flakes**
2   **or 3 large cloves garlic, chopped**

Combine ingredients in a saucepan and heat several minutes, but do not let oil get too hot. Cool. Put into a covered pint jar and refrigerate. Let jar set in refrigerator for several days before using. When you want to use some oil, strain the amount needed and put the rest back in the refrigerator.

Pesto I

❧ *This pesto is a little different from the one in* Take a Little Thyme. *This one has butter added for a little more flavor. Besides the pasta dishes we use pesto for, try some on broiled or baked chicken breasts — a marvelous flavor.*

4   **cups coarsely chopped fresh green basil leaves**
1   **cup pine nuts (available at specialty food stores)**
½   **cup extra virgin olive oil (or best available)**
1   **cup grated Parmesan cheese (fresh is best)**
¼   **cup unsalted butter, softened**
2   **cloves garlic, crushed**

In blender or food processor, puree the basil with pine nuts, oil, Parmesan cheese, butter, garlic and a little salt. Put pesto in a glass jar. Pour a thin layer of olive oil on top — this helps keep pesto fresh. Screw on lid and keep refrigerated for a week or two. If you wrap it really well, you can freeze pesto. Makes 1½ to 2 cups.

Pesto is truly a terrific Italian concoction. If I freeze pesto, I usually add the grated Parmesan cheese to it just before using — in other words, after it's thawed. It will taste fresher.

Pesto II

❧ I'm putting this pesto recipe in the book for those who can't find pine nuts. This recipe calls for walnuts, which are almost as good, just not quite as authentic. There is no butter in this one either.

4   cups fresh basil leaves (wash and dry thoroughly)
2   garlic cloves, coarsely chopped
½   cup toasted walnuts
½   teaspoon salt
    freshly ground pepper
3   tablespoons freshly grated Parmesan cheese*
½   cup extra virgin olive oil
2   tablespoons extra virgin olive oil

Use your food processor. Add all ingredients, except the olive oil. Process about 10 seconds. With the motor running, slowly pour in the ½ cup olive oil and process another 10 seconds, or until all the oil is absorbed. Stop motor, scrape sides, then process 5 to 10 seconds longer. Put pesto in a glass jar with a lid. Cover pesto with the other 2 tablespoons of oil. Cover tightly and store in the refrigerator for up to one week. Makes about 1 cup.

*If you don't have freshly grated Parmesan cheese, don't let that keep you from making this pesto. Use the regular Parmesan you buy in a can or glass jar. You know by now that if it's at *all* possible, I use the fresh product!

Herbed Flour

❧ I like to keep a batch of this herbed flour mixed up to use for frying chicken, fish, pork chops, etc. It's also nice to use the next time you make plain biscuits or rolls.

Combine: **4 cups all-purpose flour** and **3 to 4 tablespoons dried herbs** (I like equal parts of parsley, oregano, thyme, basil and dill). This flour must be stored in an airtight jar or can.

About Pasta

It seems that everyone is interested in pasta these days. I've only been making my own two or three years, but I have discovered that it is not difficult to make (see Pasta recipe in Cooking Class Favorites), and usually it is better than the store-bought variety. *However,* I have to tell you that some of the *fresh pastas* from the refrigerator section of your grocery are very good (and also a little on the expensive side), and if you can find them, *Prince's Presidents' Silver Award pastas* (the dried, boxed varieties on your grocery shelf), are exceptionally good.

A few things I have learned about pastas are:

1. If you're making your own dough, use unbleached white flour. It seems to make the best-textured dough.

2. You can make the dough and freeze it with good results. Lay pasta, separated as much as possible, on a large baking or cookie sheet. Put in the freezer. In an hour or two (or when dough is frozen), remove from the freezer and wrap very well in plastic wrap or put in plastic freezer bags. Put back into the freezer until you need it.

3. Fresh, undried pasta will cook in 45 seconds to 2 or 3 minutes in boiling, salted water. Dried pasta will take 7 to 10 minutes, depending on thickness, etc., of the dough.

4. Delicate pasta (angel hair, spaghettini, linguini, etc.) require a delicate, light sauce. The heavy, robust pastas (macaroni, lasagne, etc.) usually require a heavier sauce, such as meat, seafoods, cheeses, etc.

5. If you add a tablespoon of butter, olive oil, or vegetable oil to the boiling water, it will help do two things — it will help keep the pot from boiling over and it will help keep the strands of dough from sticking to each other.

6. The simplest pasta recipe I know (and one I use more than any other in the summertime) is: To feed 4 people, cook a **pound of pasta** (usually I use fettucine or linguini) until al dente*; drain; put pasta back into the cooking pot; add ¼ **cup butter** and **2 to 4 tablespoons chopped fresh herbs****. Toss until butter is melted and herbs are mixed in well. Add ¾ **to 1 cup heavy cream, salt** and **freshly ground pepper** to taste and about ½ **cup grated Parmesan cheese.** Toss again until pasta is well-coated. Distribute among four warmed plates and grate more **cheese** over the top. Serve. Delicious by itself or as a wonderful side dish.

*Al dente — an Italian word meaning "to the tooth." What it really means is "don't overcook!"

Fresh Herbs — my favorites for this recipe are one or a combination of the following: **basil, Greek oregano, sweet marjoram, thyme,

parsley, chives, or **garlic chives** (wonderful!). Experiment. You may want to use more than the 2 to 4 tablespoons of fresh herbs.

7. My second favorite pasta recipe is also a simple one: Make your favorite **Pesto** (see recipes in this chapter). For 4 people, cook about a **pound of pasta** in boiling, salted water. Drain. Return pasta to the pot. Use about **1 cup of your Pesto** and toss until the pesto has melted and coated all the pasta. (This isn't as confusing as it sounds, really! Just don't get the *pasta* and the *pesto* mixed up!). Add about **2 cups of broiled or sautéed chicken breast pieces or strips.** Add **salt and pepper** to taste. Toss again. Serve on warmed plates. Pass more grated **Parmesan cheese.**

I guarantee, if you like to cook and if you like to putter around in your kitchen, you will at some time be tempted to try one of these 2 recipes. At that point, you're hooked!

Roasted Peppers

❧ *So many recipes today call for roasted peppers. They're easy to do.*

Arrange peppers (as many as you want to roast) on a large baking sheet with sides. Broil close to the broiling element (or source of heat). Turn occasionally. Broil until peppers are totally blackened all over. This will take several minutes. (The first time I did this, I just knew I had ruined them — but not so!) Put blackened peppers in a large brown paper bag. Close the top and let them stand for 10 minutes — this loosens the skins. Hold each pepper under cold running water and carefully peel the blackened skin off. Drain peeled peppers on paper towels. Cut each pepper into fourths and gently remove the stem, seeds and ribs. They are now ready to use whenever roasted peppers are called for.

If you want to preserve the roasted peppers, put the pepper quarters in a clean glass quart jar. Add to the jar **2 sprigs of fresh rosemary, or ½ teaspoon dried, 2 bay leaves,** and **2 cloves garlic,** coarsely chopped. Fill jar with olive oil to the top. Put lid on and refrigerate.

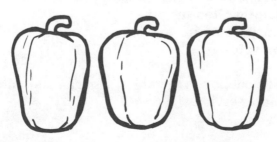

Clouté

To add wonderful flavor to your white sauce, fasten a couple of bay leaves to a peeled white onion with whole cloves. Add this onion to the milk you're scalding for a white sauce. Remove onion and add hot milk to butter-flour mixture (called a roux) and stir to make a smooth white sauce. This studded onion is called a Clouté by the French.

Lemon-Dill Sauce

ᔌ *This sauce is so good on grilled, broiled, or baked meats or chicken.*

To make 1 cup of sauce:
- 6 tablespoons mayonnaise
- 4 tablespoons Dijon mustard
- 4 tablespoons fresh lemon juice
- 4 teaspoons chopped fresh dill, OR 1 teaspoon dried
- 1 teaspoon grated lemon rind

Mix ingredients together. Brush on meat or chicken a minute or two before removing from the source of heat. Pass the sauce at the table. Any left-over can be refrigerated and used within a week.

Salsa

ᔌ *This isn't an herb dish, but it's a wonderful condiment, loaded with flavor. Serve with plain tortilla chips.*

- 4 ripe tomatoes, chopped fine
- 2 medium onions, chopped medium fine
- 2 4 ounce cans green chilies, chopped
- 1 tablespoon white vinegar
- ½ teaspoon garlic salt
- ¼ teaspoon salt

Combine chopped vegetables, vinegar, and salts. Refrigerate 2 or 3 hours before serving.

Herbes de Provence Toasts

❧ These toasts are delicious to serve with meat patés or with cheeses.

7   to 8 teaspoons Herbes de Provence*
½   teaspoon salt
16 slices of narrow French bread, sliced diagonally about ½ inch thick
½   cup extra virgin olive oil

Crush herbs and salt together to make a fairly fine mixture. Use your blender or food processor to do this. Brush both sides of the bread with olive oil. Arrange slices in a single layer on a baking sheet, or sheets, and sprinkle about ¼ teaspoon herb mixture on top side of each slice. Bake in a 400° oven for about 5 minutes or until golden brown. Turn slices over, sprinkle other side with about ¼ teaspoon herbs per slice. Bake again for about 5 minutes, but watch closely — do not burn. These are best served slightly warm. Store any leftover herb mixture in an airtight container.

*Read about Herbes de Provence in this Chapter.

 Spices

Spices and herbs are used so often together that it's hardly fair to talk about one and not the other. Spices are usually harvested from the root, bark, seed, fruit or berries of perennial tropical plants or trees. Herbs are usually the leafy parts of annual and perennial shrubs or plants.

Whole spices such as allspice, whole cloves, etc., will stay fresh longer than ground spices. A good rule for spices, as well as herbs, is if you can't smell it, you probably can't taste it. Store all herbs and spices in air-tight containers.

Some of the more common spices are **cinnamon, cloves, allspice, nutmeg, ginger, paprika** and the **peppercorns.** I find this subject interesting, so I've done a little research on these common spices.

Cinnamon is rolled, dried bark of the Cassia tree or cinnamon tree. Cinnamon bark comes from Sri Lanka (we used to call it Ceylon) and India. Cinnamon bark is mild in flavor compared to bark from the Cassia tree (native to China). I was fortunate to see cinnamon trees in Sri Lanka and we watched the workers shave the bark off in long strips. They are then rolled and dried and finally cut into the desired lengths.

Cloves are the unopened buds of a tree native to Indonesia. Trees now grow also in parts of Africa, South America and in the West Indies. These buds are harvested and dried. Broken ones get ground.

Allspice actually has the flavor of many spices, hence the name, but it's really a spice of it's own in the form of a berry. Trees that bear allspice are native to the West Indies. They also grow in other hot, tropical countries.

Nutmeg is really two spices in one. It is native to Indonesia, but I picked one off a tree in the West Indies and was surprised to see fruit about the size of a pecan, covered with a red web-like substance. That substance is **mace.** So the mace is separated and each spice is dried separately. By the way, if you ever visit the island called Grenada in the Caribbean, this is the island known as the Spice Island. It is well worth the trip ashore to visit these spice tree farms and see for yourself where your spices come from.

Ginger is the root of a plant native to parts of Asia. It now grows in many islands of the West Indies. The root is dug and dried. It is then ground, left in whole pieces or crystallized. See how to grow your own gingerroot in this chapter.

Paprika comes in many forms. Paprika is ground, dried pods of peppers called Capsicum annuum. These peppers can be mild in flavor or very hot. My favorite paprika is the Sweet Hungarian Paprika, native to Hungary. A shop keeper in Budapest told me to keep my Hungarian paprika in the refrigerator so it would stay fresh and keep it's pretty color.

Peppercorns are the dried berries of a vine. It is not related to our garden variety red and green peppers. This vine is native to Indonesia, but it also grows in many hot, tropical areas of the world. The workers harvest black, white and green peppercorns from the same plant. **Black peppercorns** are immature berries that are picked and dried. For **white pepper,** the dark brown skin is rubbed off the black peppercorns and the lighter colored middle is left. **Green peppercorns** are just that. They are unripe berries and picked when they're still green. These are often canned in water or brine, rather than dried, but they are available dried also.

Most black peppercorns come from an area in India, called the Malabar Coast. This coast produces two peppercorns. The ones from the southern end of the coast are called "Malabar" peppercorns. The ones from the northern end of the coast are called "Tellicherry" peppercorns. The Tellicherry peppercorns are generally regarded as the better of the two. They are larger and milder and of course more expensive. I buy Tellicherry peppercorns from White Flower Farm in Connecticut. They import nice ones. See Useful Addresses for their address — you can order by mail.

Some of the above information came from my encyclopedia. This is a fascinating subject! Perhaps you will enjoy reading more about these and other spices — check your library.

Pumpkin Pie Spices

ക *Make your own!*

For one pie, combine:
  - ¾ **teaspoon ground cinnamon**
  - ¼ **teaspoon ground nutmeg**
  - ⅛ **teaspoon ground ginger**
  - ⅛ **teaspoon ground cloves**

Mix well and use to season one pumpkin pie.

Cajun Seasonings

✿ Cajun-style cooking is very popular. If you ever go to New Orleans and have an extra day, be sure to drive through the Cajun country. The area begins about 50 miles west of New Orleans and goes to Lafayette, Louisiana. New Iberia is probably the heart of Cajun country — this is where Tabasco Sauce is made. There is also a wonderful restaurant there called Patout's. We went there for dinner one night. It was so good, we stayed overnight in town and went back for lunch!

3   teaspoons salt
2   teaspoons pepper
2   teaspoons onion powder
2   teaspoons cayenne powder
2   teaspoons Hungarian sweet paprika
2   teaspoons dried thyme

Blend all together in blender. Use to season meat, fish, or chicken. Store any leftover mix in an air-tight jar. Makes 4 tablespoons.

Louisiana Seasonings

✿ Use this seasoning in Creole or Cajun dishes.

1   tablespoon dried basil
1   tablespoon dried oregano
1½   tablespoons paprika
1½   teaspoons dried thyme
½   teaspoon ground red pepper
¼   teaspoon ground black pepper
1   teaspoon garlic powder
½   teaspoon mace
1   bay leaf

Combine all ingredients in a blender. Blend well, until bay leaf is ground into powder. Store in an air-tight container. Makes about ¼ cup.

This is a seasoning you might want to try for blackening fish, chicken, etc. Dip the fish, chicken, or meat in melted butter, then coat all surfaces with the above seasonings. Fry in a **very** hot black iron skillet. Drizzle a little melted butter over the top, turn and blacken that side. Fry quickly and be prepared for the smoke alarm to go off!

A Blend of Fine Spices

Combine:

1 teaspoon ground white or black pepper
1 teaspoon ground red pepper
1 teaspoon ground mace
1 teaspoon ground sage
1 teaspoon ground marjoram
1 teaspoon ground rosemary
1 teaspoon ground French tarragon
1 teaspoon ground cinnamon
1 teaspoon ground nutmeg

Blend thoroughly and store in an air-tight container. Note that this is a mixture of herbs and spices. A good blend of **Fine Spices** is expensive to buy, so you'll enjoy making your own. Use to season meats, vegetables, stews, sauces, etc.

Herbed Olives

❧ I concocted this recipe for a cooking demonstration stressing the use of fresh herbs. These olives are great on the relish or antipasto tray.

For 1 quart of herbed olives:

2 7 ounce jars whole green olives (pit still in), drained and save juice
3 or 4 cloves garlic, chopped
½ to 1 teaspoon hot red pepper flakes
2 or 3 sprigs fresh rosemary, or 1 teaspoon dried
2 or 3 sprigs fresh thyme, or 1 teaspoon dried
2 or 3 sprigs fresh sweet marjoram, or 1 teaspoon dried
8 to 10 whole peppercorns

Use a clean glass quart jar. Put drained olives, and rest of ingredients in the jar. Fill the jar with the saved juice. Put lid on and refrigerate for at least a week to develop flavors.

🏺 Herbes de Provence

The Provence (an area in southern France) is famous for herbs, olive oils, and many wonderful foods. Herbes de Provence is a mixture of the herbs that grow in that area. If you visit the Provence, you'll see *fields* of lavender and thyme growing to be harvested for this mixture. It is an incredible sight! Herbes de Provence is a blend of very aromatic herbs. They are: **thyme, basil, savory, fennel** and **rosemary**. **Lavender** is usually included. These herbs are dried, then mixed and sold in covered earthenware jars or pots. If you go, bring a big pot home with you! If you can't go, order some from Williams-Sonoma (see Useful Addresses on page 64) or specialty food stores in your area.

🏺 Herb Bouquets

Some herbs can be cut and added to floral bouquets for extra color and wonderful aroma. I've listed a few good ones to cut that won't wilt down and will also last a long time in water. These herbs are — **mints, scented geraniums, sage, rosemary, lemon verbena, opal basil, green basil** and **thyme**. There are others, of course, especially non-culinary ones, such as **lavender, santolina,** and **yarrow**. Gather the herbs (just like your flowers) from the garden before the heat of the day. As soon as you cut the stems, they should be plunged into water (I carry a pail with me to the garden). Let the stems take up as much water as they can, then add them to your favorite bouquets.

One of my favorite summer arrangements is **pink zinnias, opal basil** and **scented geraniums** in an antique country basket. Keep the water level up and this arrangement should be beautiful for several days. Sometimes I'll make a big arrangement of just fresh herbs for the supper table — pure heaven!

Another good combination is **blue salvia, rosemary** and **green basil**. Another is **yellow marigolds, thyme** and **sage**. Experiment — you'll love putting these beautiful and fragrant bouquets together.

*A Thymely Footnote . . . I like to grow **nasturtiums, violas, borage** and **lemon gem marigolds** for edible flowers. They are beautiful tossed in a green salad. Most are peppery-tasting.*

About Vanilla Beans

Did you know the vanilla bean is the long seed pod of a certain orchid? I was fascinated to learn that! The pod is picked and dried a certain way and then used to make vanilla extract. You can make your own extract by soaking and preserving beans in an alcohol solution. Split **4 or 5 beans** and add them to **2 cups of brandy, bourbon or vodka**. Cover tightly and let stand for 2 weeks or more. The extract will keep indefinitely.

There are many varieties of vanilla beans. The most common, and the ones we usually buy because they're most available, are the Madagascar beans. But the very best, and the most expensive, are the Tahitian vanilla beans. They're also a little difficult to find. You can order them from: Tahitian Imports, Box 67A54, Century City Station, Los Angeles, CA 90067.

Herb Wreath

Use a straw wreath for a base — 8", 10" or 12" are the usual sizes. Gather dry herbs (no dew or rain on them) before the heat of the day. Gather herbs into small bundles. You may use one variety of herb, such as thyme, or you may use several varieties. Lay a little bundle of herbs on the wreath and secure with a craft pin (get from your florist or from a craft shop). Or, buy thin florist's wire and wrap the stems going around and around the wreath. Lay another bundle on the wreath so that the herb tops cover the craft pin or the wire. Continue around the wreath until the top is entirely covered. If you don't like the straw wreath showing around the edges, fill those areas in with other herbs, such as artemisia. It takes quite a lot of herbs to cover a wreath entirely (helps explain why a full, beautiful one is expensive!). You can add a few flowers or everlastings as you wish. I always use *fresh* herbs in my wreaths and hang them to let them dry naturally. If you use dried bunches of herbs, you end up with a table full of ground herbs.

*A **Thymely** Footnote . . . If you grow **mint**, you know how invasive it can become. To keep it from spreading throughout the garden, sink a large clay tile or an old plastic bucket (without the bottom) into the ground. Plant your mint in the tile or bucket for a nice round mound. By the way, all mint stems are square.*

A Few More Herb Ideas...

1. If you serve **lemon wedges** with fish dishes, chop some **fresh dill** and dip the cut edge of the lemon in the dill. Pretty and delicious.

2. Freeze whole rinsed **mint leaves in ice cubes** for summertime drinks. Wonderful in lemonade and iced tea.

3. For a delicious **Herbed Honey,** add 2 or 3 sprigs of fresh **rosemary** or **thyme** to a jar of honey. Cover and let set for 2 or 3 weeks before using.

4. For an **Herb Basting Brush** — tie a few sprigs of **rosemary** or **thyme** together and use as a little basting brush when you're barbecuing either inside or out. The herb flavor will go into the sauce.

5. For **Herb Favors** — for a beautiful summer table setting, tie little bunches of fresh herbs together into a bouquet. Tie with a narrow ribbon to match your table decor. Lay one of the little bouquets on each napkin or at the top of each plate. I have never had one of these little bouquets left after a meal! They mysteriously disappear into a pocket or purse to be taken home. Make these up ahead of time, put into an *unclosed* plastic bag, sprinkle with a little water, then refrigerate until you're ready to put them out on the table. Some herbs I use for these little bouquets are: **thyme sprigs, opal basil sprigs, mint, French tarragon, oregano, marjoram,** and **summer savory.** Stay away from the larger leaf herbs, such as scented geraniums or green basil. Keep the bouquets small and delicate.

6. For a wonderful luncheon dish, add **a tablespoon of finely chopped fresh herbs** (parsley, oregano, basil, thyme, etc.) to **crepe batter.** Make crepes, fill with **chopped cooked chicken, seafood,** or **cheese.** Roll up crepes and lay in a greased baking dish. Cover with an **herbed cheese white sauce** (use same herbs as in crepe batter). Bake, enjoy!

 Cheese

I really got interested in cheese after I saw it made and being aged in the Roquefort caves in southern France. I still don't know very much about cheese, but what I have learned is fascinating.

Roquefort is one of the blue cheeses. The story goes that a shepherd boy left his lunch in a cave one day, forgot about it, and when he returned to the same cave several weeks later, his white cheese was now mottled with blue veins and was creamy and delicious. Those caves are in Mount Combalou in southern France. There is a blue mold called penicillium roqueforti that apparently grows only in these caves on this mountain. The caves are always 45° and are almost 100% in humidity. Roquefort (the name) is protected by international trade agreements and *all* Roquefort is made by only 9 producers. These 9 all own or control certain areas of these caves. Roquefort is rather unique in that it is the only well-known blue cheese made only from sheep's milk. The cheese wheels are made throughout the area, but they are all shipped to Mount Combalou to ripen and take on the blue veins. The wheels ripen for 3 to 6 months. Real Roquefort cheese bears an emblem of a red sheep in an oval. *Only* Roquefort can have this emblem. Most of this cheese is consumed in France. Only about 10% of it is exported to the rest of the world — no wonder it's so expensive. If you're ever in southern France, do visit these caves — it's fascinating. I got the above information from an English (thank goodness!) hand-out they gave us as we made our way through the caves.

Another excellent cheese is **Stilton** — also a blue cheese. It comes from, not Stilton, but from Leicestershire, England. We didn't see this cheese made, but I learned a little about it when we were in that area. The law states that all the cow's milk for Stilton Cheese must come from Leicestershire, Nottinghamshire and Derbyshire. Only seven dairies produce Stilton. Stilton is creamy color on the inside, whereas, Roquefort is snow white, and to be ripe, it must be semi-firm and buttery textured. It also is exposed to certain penicillium molds to produce the distinctive blue veins. A good Stilton ages 4 to 6 months.

Gorgonzola is the famous blue cheese of Italy. It is made in Gorgonzola, a little town near Milan. It is made from cow's milk. The cheese is also exposed to certain penicillium that makes the blue veins. Gorgonzola needs to age 2 or 3 months — the younger the cheese, the milder. Of these three famous blue cheeses, I like a young Gorgonzola the best — it is soft, creamy and not so salty or sharp. One that is more aged, is, however, a different story. It is strong and crumbly and I don't like it much.

There are several good blue cheeses from the U.S. A really good one is called **Maytag Blue,** made in Newton, Iowa, just east of Des Moines. It is aged for about 6 months and it's very white and very tangy. They produce several hundred pounds a day. You can order this cheese from the company (by mail). I was told that the Maytag family and Iowa State University are responsible for making this great cheese.

Another good blue cheese from the U.S. is called **Treasure Cave,** and it's made in caves in Faribault, Minnesota. I see it in many of our grocery stores.

One of the best of all blues is called **Saga Blue** and it's made in Denmark. A good Saga is buttery smooth and delicious.

If you're ever in Holland, check your guide books and try to arrive in some small town on cheese market day. You will never again see so much cheese in one place in your life!

The French say you must serve their **Roquefort with Sauternes wines;** the English say you must serve their **Stilton with Port wine;** and the Italians say you must serve their **Gorgonzola with Barolo wine.**

It is often difficult to find really fine cheese. Our groceries are stocking more and more in their stores, but you'll need to locate a good cheese shop to find a lot of the really good cheeses.

Here are the names of a few favorite cheeses and their origin (besides the ones mentioned above):

Edam - Holland
Gouda - Holland
Munster - Alsace region of France
Monterey Jack - California
Parmigiano-Reggiano - Italy
Romano - Italy
Provolone - Italy
Pont L'Eveque - Normandy, France
Reblochon - Switzerland
Monterey (herbed cheese) - Massachusetts
Cantal - France
Belle Etoile (triple cream cheese) - France
Cream Havarti (or Dill) - Denmark
Oka - Canada (one of the best Cheddars)
Cotswold (also a Cheddar) - England
White Cheddar - Vermont (Cabot brand is excellent)
Gloucester - England - a famous Cheddar
Huntsman - England (a layered cheese of Gloucester and Stilton)
Camembert - Normandy, France (*real* Camembert is made from un-

pasteurized milk and therefore, it cannot be exported to the U.S. A cheese shopkeeper in Normandy told me this.) By the way, cheese in France is called fromage. A cheese shop is called a fromagerie.

There are literally hundreds and hundreds of cheeses throughout the world. So the ones I've mentioned here are barely a sampling.

Here are a few other things I've found out about cheese:

1. Use only low heat to melt cheese. The protein in cheese becomes stringy if the heat is too high.

2. The longer a cheese ripens, the drier the texture and the sharper the flavor — usually.

3. Some unripened cheese are: cottage cheese, cream cheese, farmer cheese.

4. Some soft cheeses are: Brie and Camembert from France as well as the triple cream cheeses from France.

5. Some semi-firm cheeses are: Swiss cheese, Port Salut, Monterey Jack, Mozzarella and most of the blue-veined cheeses.

6. Some firm cheeses are: Cheddars, Gouda, Edam, Provolone.

7. Some hard cheeses are: Parmesan, Romano and Asiago. These cheeses are usually referred to as grating cheeses.

8. Generally, you should serve all cheeses at room temperature.

9. Always wrap cheese well in plastic wrap and keep it refrigerated between use.

10. If mold forms on cheese, just scrape it off — it is harmless. *Except* on the unripened cheeses. If mold forms on cottage cheese, cream cheese, etc., discard that cheese.

I am constantly learning about cheeses. It's a very interesting (and delicious!) subject. One of the joys of traveling to new places is to sample the local foods — particularly cheese as far as I am concerned!

USEFUL ADDRESSES

Wherever I go to talk about herbs, there are a few questions I'm *always* asked. Such as, "where do I get certain seeds or plants?", "where do I get my bottles for herb vinegars?", "where do I get the little corked bottles for dried herbs?", etc. After looking up addresses here and there for 2 or 3 years, I decided to put those addresses I use most frequently together in one place. Here is that place:

1. Williams-Sonoma
P.O. Box 7456
San Francisco, CA 94120-7456
   Ask them to send you "A Catalog for Cooks." My herb vinegars and liqueurs are in bottles from Williams-Sonoma.

2. White Flower Farm
Litchfield, Connecticut 06759-0050
   Ask for their catalog. One will come for Spring and one for Fall. They have wonderful plants. They also have Tellicherry Peppercorns.

3. Johnny's Selected Seeds
Foss Hill Road
Albion, Maine 04910
   Ask for their catalog. They have many hard-to-find seeds.

4. Park Seed Co.
Cokesbury Road
Greenwood, S.C. 29647-0001
   I order many of my herb seeds from their catalog.

5. Nichol's Garden Nursery
1190 North Pacific Highway
Albany, Oregon 97321
   Ask for their catalog called "Herbs and Rare Seeds." A wonderful selection of seeds, herb seeds, herb plants, potpourri oils, potpourri supplies, etc. I use this catalog a lot — it's great!

6. Wayside Gardens
Hodges, South Carolina 29695-0001
   Another excellent seed catalog — similar to Park Seed Catalog.

7. Burpee's Seeds
W. Atlee Burpee Co.
300 Park Ave.
Warminster, PA 18991-0001

8. Shepherd's Garden Seeds
7389 West Zayante Road
Felton, CA 95018
   Hard-to-find seeds, new varieties, etc. They have some basils, for example, that I haven't seen listed anywhere else.

9. Crate and Barrel
P.O. Box 3057
Northbrook, IL 60065
   Good source for containers for dried herbs, bottles, cookware, etc. Reasonably priced.

10. The Lebermuth Company, Inc.
P.O. Box 4103
South Bend, IN 46624
   Their speciality is fragrances, essential oils and other potpourri supplies.

11. Well Sweep Farm
317 Mt. Bethel Road
Port Murray, NJ 07865
   They have just about any herb plant you're looking for.

12. Frontier Herbs
1 Frontier Road
Box 299
Norway, IA 52318
   Over 500 herbs and spices. Ask for catalog.

   Of course there are many other good catalogs available. This is only intended as a guide.
   Go to your local nursery man or greenhouse *first*. He often has just what you need. If he doesn't and if he can't get it, that's when I use the resources listed here.

COOKING CLASS FAVORITES

As I said in my Farm Progress Show speech, one thing has certainly led to another — my 1) herb garden led me into thinking more about cooking, recipes, etc., which led me into 2) writing *Take a Little Thyme,* with my friend Ann S. Harrison, which led us into 3) herb talks and demonstrations, and inevitably into 4) cooking classes. Ah — cooking classes — sounds like fun, doesn't it? It *is* for the person that goes! It also is for the person that cooks, but what a lot of work! But I have to tell you, I improved lots of cooking skills with those classes — out of necessity! The last thing you want to happen is have your beautiful soufflé fall in front of 50 people! I can't guarantee all or any of the above things will happen to you if you plant an herb garden, but some of them probably will!

So with all this in mind, here are the recipes I have used in my cooking classes. Only one of the following recipes appears in the book, *Take a Little Thyme* — that's Cranberry Conserve. Some of these recipes are my own creations and most are variations of recipes I have collected. The first cooking classes consisted only of recipes from *Take a Little Thyme,* so they are not in this book.

Of all the recipes I've prepared for cooking classes, the favorites are 1) pasta making and pasta recipes and 2) any recipe using fresh herbs.

Chicken Breasts With Tarragon Wine Sauce

This is a McCall's Cooking School recipe. It's a wonderful dish to add to your chicken recipe file.

4   whole large chicken breasts
2   tablespoons oil
2   tablespoons butter
6   shallots, chopped, OR 6 green onions
2   peeled carrots, sliced into ¼" rounds
¼   cup Cognac or brandy
1   cup dry white wine
¼   cup chopped fresh French tarragon, OR 2 teaspoons dried
1½ tablespoons chopped fresh chervil, OR ½ teaspoon dried
1   teaspoon salt
⅛   teaspoon fresh ground pepper
1   cup light cream (Half and Half)
1   egg yolk
1   tablespoon flour
¼   pound mushrooms, washed and sliced
2   tablespoons butter

Bone and skin chicken breasts. Cut into halves. In a heavy pan or Dutch oven, heat oil and butter. Add chicken breasts to cover bottom of pan. Sauté, turning until browned on all sides. Remove chicken and add rest of breasts to brown. To drippings in pan, add shallots or chopped green onions and carrots. Sauté, stirring 5 minutes, or until golden. Now return chicken to Dutch oven and keep warm. Slightly heat brandy, then ignite. When flames die down, pour over chicken. Add wine, tarragon, chervil, salt and pepper. Bring to a boil. Reduce heat and simmer gently, covered, 30 minutes. Remove chicken to serving platter. Strain drippings from Dutch oven, then return drippings to the pan.

In a small bowl, combine cream, egg yolk and flour. Mix well with a wire whisk. Stir the cream-egg mixture into the drippings. Stir constantly with wire whisk and bring just to a boil. If sauce is too thick, add a little more white wine. Now, last, sauté mushrooms in hot butter until tender, 3 or 4 minutes. Add sautéed mushrooms to the sauce. Spoon sauce over breasts. Garnish with fresh tarragon, if you have it, or parsley will do. Serves 8 for lunch or 4 for dinner.

Glazed Cranberry Chicken Breasts

1 or 2 boneless chicken breasts per serving
¼ cup flour
½ teaspoon salt
1 teaspoon ground ginger
4 tablespoons butter
2 tablespoons chopped onion
4 tablespoons orange juice
2 tablespoons honey
   about 2 cups cranberry conserve

Mix flour, salt and ginger. Lightly coat chicken breasts with flour mixture (save flour). Heat butter in a skillet. Sauté onions and chicken (remove skin from breasts as well as the bones) until chicken is golden brown. Remove chicken from skillet and set aside.

In a small bowl, slowly add orange juice to the reserved flour mixture. Stir until blended and strain if necessary to remove lumps. Mix orange juice mixture with cranberry conserve (recipe follows) and honey in skillet. Heat, stirring constantly, until thickened. Put chicken pieces into an attractive baking dish. Spoon sauce over chicken. Put into a 350° oven and bake for 30 minutes or until chicken is tender. (May not need 30 minutes, depending on thickness of chicken.) *Do not overbake* or the sauce will lose its beautiful color. Serves 4.

Cranberry Conserve

ঽ *From* Take A Little Thyme, *by Marge Clark and Ann S. Harrison.*

In a large, heavy saucepan, combine 1 - **12 to 16 ounce package of raw cranberries** (picked over and rinsed) and **1½ cups water**. Bring to a boil over moderately high heat and simmer for 5 to 8 minutes, or until berries pop and are tender. Stir in **3 cups sugar**, **1 cup crushed pineapple**, undrained, **½ cup light raisins***, **1 seedless orange**, peeled and pith removed, then chop orange. Simmer this mixture, stirring occasionally, for 20 minutes. Stir in **½ cup chopped walnuts or pecans***. Store in refrigerator. Serve with turkey, chicken, or pork. Makes about 5 cups. Wonderful at holiday time, but good anytime!

*For the Cranberry Glazed Chicken Breasts, I leave out the raisins and nuts. You may substitute a good brand of cranberry conserve for this homemade version in the Cranberry Glazed Chicken Breasts recipe, if you wish.

Fragrant Herb Bread

1½ cups milk, scalded
4 tablespoons sugar
4 tablespoons oleo
3 teaspoons salt
1 teaspoon ground nutmeg
2 teaspoons ground sage
4 teaspoon caraway seeds
1 tablespoon poppy seeds
1 tablespoon dried onion
2 packages dry yeast
½ cup warm water
2 eggs, beaten
about 6 cups bread flour

After milk is scalded, add next 8 ingredients while milk is still warm. Stir and set aside to cool. Add yeast to warm water. Add the eggs. Beat into the milk mixture. Gradually beat in 4½ to 5 cups of flour — 1 cup at a time. Put about 1 cup of the flour on work surface and dump dough mixture onto it. Start kneading and knead until smooth. Sorry, this takes 5 minutes!

Put dough into a large, greased bowl. Cover with a clean cloth and let rise until doubled. Punch down dough and knead again for a minute or so to make a smooth ball. Divide dough into half and place in 2 greased 5½" x 9½" x 2½" pans. Cover loosely with a clean towel and let rise again to just above pans — 30 minutes to 1 hour. Bake at 350° for 30 to 35 minutes. If not done and browning too much, lay a piece of foil over loaves the last few minutes of baking. As soon as loaves come out of oven, brush tops with melted, unsalted butter. You may cool this bread thoroughly, wrap very well and freeze.

Thaw an hour or two in wrappings. Then remove wrapping, wrap loaves loosely in a clean towel and finish thawing. No moisture collects on loaves this way. This is really delicious!

*A Thymely Footnote . . . Speaking of fragrant, **sweet woodruff** is a wonderful low-growing, shade-loving perennial that has a very distinct smell of new-mown hay when it's dried. Use it to flavor May wine (page 105).*

Apple Strudel

This strudel recipe was my first attempt to make something with phyllo dough. It was surprisingly easy to work with! This recipe will make 3 nice strudels. Each strudel will serve 5 or 6.

6   or 7 tart apples (Granny Smith or McIntosh)
⅔   cup ground pecans
15   vanilla wafers
1   cup sugar
    heaping ¼ cup raisins
1   teaspoon ground cinnamon
2   or 3 sticks unsalted butter (may need another one)
1   1 pound package frozen phyllo dough (each package contains about 20 sheets of dough)

(1) The day before you make strudels, remove dough from freezer and place unopened package in the refrigerator.

(2) In a bowl, thinly slice the peeled and cored apples. Sprinkle a few drops of lemon juice over slices to keep them from turning dark. Cover bowl with a piece of plastic wrap while you prepare the crumbs.

(3) In food processor bowl fitted with the steel blade, put the vanilla wafers, sugar and cinnamon. Put lid on and process on and off until crumbs are formed. Do *NOT* overprocess. Put chopped pecans in a small bowl. Put crumb mixture in a small bowl. Add raisins to the apple bowl.

(4) Melt butter.

(5) Remove phyllo dough from the refrigerator and carefully remove from the package. Have a dampened cloth on your work surface (not wet, just dampened). Lay all sheets of dough out on the dampened cloth. Take melted butter and butter each sheet with a very soft-bristled pastry brush — try to find a 2″ or 3″ wide one to speed up this job. Butter a sheet, lay that sheet onto another dampened clean cloth. Keep buttering until you have a stack of 7 phyllo leaves.

(6) Now put ⅓ of apples down middle of the dough; sprinkle on ⅓ of apple-raisin mixture; sprinkle fruit with ⅓ of crumb mixture. Carefully fold leaves in to make an envelope, and roll strudel into a neat 10″ to 12″ roll.

(7) Brush melted butter all over the rolled-up strudel.

(8) Repeat steps 5, 6 and 7 to make 2 more strudels, using about 7 leaves of dough for each, ⅓ of ingredients for each, and brushing each with melted butter.

(9) Bake now or wrap well and freeze individually for later use.

(10) To bake, carefully lay a strudel (if frozen, no need to thaw) on a well-greased cookie sheet with sides. Bake in a pre-heated 350° oven for 40 to 45 minutes or until nicely browned and apples are tender. Dust lightly with powdered sugar.

These are best if served warm from the oven.

Brie In Phyllo

This is spectacular to serve. A big hit in a cooking class.

1 **1 pound package frozen phyllo dough, thawed**
   about 1 pound butter, melted
1 **small whole Brie cheese (about 1 pound size if you can find it, or even larger)**

Butter a baking sheet (a jelly roll pan is a good choice — it *must* have sides on it or the butter will drip off into the oven!). Remember to put unopened, frozen dough into refrigerator the day before you want to use dough. Brush 10 or 12 sheets of dough with butter, one sheet at a time (follow procedure for handling dough in apple strudel recipe). Set Brie (rind on) on top of buttered phyllo and fold edges of dough up around the cheese. Cover top of Brie with another buttered 10 or 12 sheets (use up the 1 pound package, *except* save 1 sheet for top-knot). Tuck ends of pastry under the cheese. Make into a neat round package.

Brush top and all sides with more melted butter. Fold the 1 last sheet of buttered dough in a knot, or form into a rosette. Lay this on top of dough and butter again. Preheat oven to 350°. Bake for about 30 minutes, or until golden brown. Let stand for 20 to 30 minutes before serving. Cut into small wedges to serve. This is gooey and flaky and wonderful! Serve on a small plate — provide a fork and napkin.

Chicken In Phyllo

You can make the chicken rolls ahead of time and freeze. If you do this, put frozen rolls in oven and bake according to directions below. You may need to bake an extra 3 to 5 minutes if starting with frozen rolls. This is a combination of 3 or 4 recipes. I love to work with phyllo dough! There are about 20 sheets of phyllo in a 1 pound package. Put package of frozen phyllo in refrigerator a day before using. This recipe makes 8 rolls. Will serve 8.

6   tablespoons butter
1   cup broccoli flowerets, cut small
2   small onions, diced
1   cup sliced, fresh mushrooms
1   cup diced zucchini
2   pounds cooked, diced chicken breast
½   pound cooked, diced ham
2   cups grated Cheddar cheese
    dash of curry powder
1   teaspoon dried basil
    pinch of dried thyme
    salt and freshly ground pepper
½   to 1 cup Amaretto-Tarragon Sauce (recipe follows)
1   1 pound package phyllo pastry (20 to 24 sheets)
    about 1½ to 2 sticks butter, melted

Heat butter in a large saucepan and add the broccoli, onion, mushrooms and zucchini. Cook over medium heat, stirring until vegetables are crisp-tender. *Do not overcook.* Add the chicken, ham, cheese, seasonings and herbs and mix well. Add ½ cup to 1 cup of the Amaretto-Tarragon Sauce to the chicken mixture. Taste and correct seasonings. Preheat oven to 400°. Heavily butter a cookie sheet. Set aside.

Remove thawed phyllo from refrigerator. Lay 2 clean towels on counter. Put phyllo sheets on 1 towel. Cover sheets with a damp piece of paper towel (or towels). Lay a sheet of dough on the second towel. Quickly brush with melted butter (use a soft-bristled pastry brush for this). Do this 5 more times for a total of 6 sheets. (Keep the reserved phyllo sheets covered as they will dry out quickly.) Cut sheets in half. Place a portion of the chicken-vegetable mixture in the center of each half. Working quickly, tuck in sides and roll up. Place the rolls, seam side down, on the cookie sheet and brush tops with melted butter. Repeat above process until the chicken mixture is gone. At this point you may wrap well and freeze. To bake now, bake in the 400° oven for 15 to 20 minutes, or until brown and crisp. Serve one per person with Amaretto-Tarragon Sauce.

Amaretto-Tarragon Sauce For Chicken In Phyllo

1   stick butter
1   cup sliced mushrooms
¼   cup Amaretto liqueur
1   tablespoon chopped, fresh French tarragon OR 1 tea-
    spoon dried
¼   cup minced onion
2   tablespoons flour
2   cups light cream (Half and Half)
    salt and freshly ground pepper

Heat butter in a heavy skillet (do not let it brown). Add onion and mushrooms and cook a minute or two, stirring all the time. Stir in flour and cook until completely absorbed. Stir in Amaretto and cook another minute. Add the cream and tarragon and simmer over *low* heat about 5 minutes. Add salt and pepper to taste.

Place baked chicken rolls on each person's plate. Top with a spoonful or two of above sauce and serve immediately. The secret is to *not* use too much sauce or you'll lose the wonderful crispness of these rolls.

This sauce is terrific! Try it on baked chicken breasts another time.

Baklava

🍂 *Baklava is a classic Greek dessert. It is very rich, so serve small portions. This recipe will make 3 dozen or more pieces, depending on how big you cut the diamonds. Baklava is tradionally always cut in diamond shapes. Read recipe through before starting.*

2   pounds coarsely chopped walnuts
1   pound coarsely chopped almonds
¾   cup sugar
3   tablespoons ground cinnamon
1   pound phyllo dough (Located in freezer section of grocery. There are 20 to 24 sheets of phyllo per pound of dough.)
    about 2 pounds unsalted butter, melted
¾   cup fresh breadcrumbs (make in your blender or food processor)
¾   cup vanilla wafer crumbs

Preheat oven to 375°. Heavily grease a 10″ x 15″ baking pan with sides. Combine nuts, sugar and cinnamon in a bowl. Combine breadcrumbs and wafer crumbs in another bowl. Have phyllo dough thawed (take out of freezer day before use and thaw in the refrigerator). Unwrap dough. Lay sheets on a piece of waxed paper. Cover sheets with more waxed paper, then with a damp towel (sheets must not dry out, or you won't be able to work with them). Uncover dough, one sheet at a time. Lay first sheet in pan. Brush generously with melted butter. Sprinkle a few crumbs on top. Lay another sheet on top and proceed until you have used 6 or 7 sheets of dough (butter each, add crumbs to each). On the 7th sheet of buttered dough, put ⅓ of the nut mixture evenly over dough. Now use 6 or 7 more sheets and proceed as above. On the 12th or 14th sheet, put another ⅓ of the nut mixture. Use up rest of dough, *except* save 1 sheet for the top. Use up rest of dough (except the reserved sheet) and proceed again as above, buttering each sheet and putting a few crumbs on each sheet. Put rest of nut mixture on. Add last sheet of dough and butter it, covering all of sheet thoroughly with melted butter.

Using a sharp, serrated knife, make 5,6 or 7 lengthwise cuts in the baklava (number depends on size of pieces you desire). Keep knife straight, use your free hand to help hold phyllo behind the knife, and be sure to slice *carefully* through *all* the layers. After all lengthwise cuts are made, slice diagonally, beginning at an upper corner of the pan. Continue until all pastry has been cut into diamonds, trying to keep rows straight and diamonds the same size, if possible.

Brush entire surface one more time with melted butter. Bake 30 minutes, basting every 10 minutes with the butter on top. Reduce heat to 350° and bake another 30 minutes, or until golden, basting several times with butter that accumulates on top. (Cover loosely with foil if top is browning too much.) While pastry bakes, prepare syrup (recipe follows). Pastry is done when it's nicely browned and crisp. Spoon the *cooled* syrup evenly over the *hot* baklava. Cool completely in pan before removing pieces to serve.

Syrup

Combine **4 cups sugar, 2 cups water, 1 lemon slice**, seeds removed, and **1 cinnamon stick** in a saucepan and bring to a boil over medium-high heat, stirring constantly until sugar dissolves. Boil gently for about 20 minutes. Remove from heat and let syrup cool while baklava finishes baking. Remove lemon slice and cinnamon stick. Spoon all the syrup over the baked baklava. When it is all thoroughly cooled, wrap well in plastic wrap.

This is not difficult to make. It does take some time, obviously, and all the steps have to be followed, but it's a dessert you'll be proud to serve.

Phyllo Cups

Stack **4 sheets of phyllo dough** on top of each other. With a sharp knife, cut into 16 equal pieces. Carefully brush each piece with **melted butter**. Stack 4 of the small buttered pieces together and carefully put into a glass custard cup and form into a cup-shape. Use all 16 pieces to fill 4 custard cups. (These are very fragile!) Put the cups on a cookie sheet and bake in a 375° oven for 10 to 12 minutes. Cool. Remove shells from glass cups. Put a shell on a dessert plate, fill with ice cream and a favorite fruit sauce, such as raspberry, strawberry, rhubarb, etc. Fabulous!

Pasta Dough

𝒆 *This is a basic pasta dough recipe that is super-easy to make in the food processor. This is Carol Sermersheim's pasta dough recipe.*

1   teaspoon salt
2   large eggs
1   to 2 tablespoons olive oil (must be good quality)
2   cups all-purpose flour
3   or 4 tablespoons water (usually 3 tablespoons)
    additional flour for kneading, rolling and cutting

In work bowl of processor, break eggs. Add 1 teaspoon salt and process until eggs are well beaten. Add the flour, all at once, and process until mixture resembles coarse cornmeal. Add olive oil and process on and off 2 or 3 times. Now add water slowly until a ball of dough forms in the bowl. If dough looks too dry, add a little water. If dough looks too sticky, add a little more flour. Remove dough from bowl and cover with plastic wrap. Let rest 30 minutes for easier rolling. This makes about 1 pound of dough.

After about 30 minutes, put dough on a heavily floured surface and roll with hands into a long cylindrical shape. Cut dough in half. Pat cut dough until it is soft and smooth.

Flour both sides of dough and put through the pasta machine* on setting #1. Fold dough into thirds. Flour again and run through #1 again. Do not fold into thirds again. Run dough through #1 for the third time. Set machine on #2 and roll dough on this setting 3 times. Do the same for #3 and #4 settings. (You'll need to lightly flour the sheet of dough each time before rolling.) Let sheets dry 15 to 30 minutes before cutting. When sheet of dough is ready, put it through proper cutting attachment**. Dry the pasta on a rack or on paper towels until cooking time.

When you're ready to cook pasta, bring about 4 quarts of water to a boil. Add 1 teaspoon salt and 1 tablespoon or so of olive oil to the water. Add half of pasta and cook approximately 30 seconds. (usually 45 seconds at the most.) For wider-cut noodles, cook a little longer, but watch. When done, drain immediately to stop the cooking. Rinse or not — depends on your preference. If you need the whole pound of dough, cook second half as above, or obviously, you can cook *all* the pasta at once in an 8 to 10 quart pot of water. Do *not* overcook.

I don't profess to know a lot about pasta, but what I do know, I must credit my friend, Carol Sermersheim of Danville, Illinois. I went to one of her all-day pasta classes one Saturday and learned so many basic things. I've been very enthused about pasta since!

*I use an Atlas hand-cranked pasta machine.

**My attachments are for angel hair, fettucine and spaghetti.

Quick Pasta Dinner

Sauté **4 or 5 chopped green onions** and **2 or 3 cloves of garlic**, chopped, in **2 tablespoons olive oil**. Use a heavy, large skillet or sauté pan. Do not brown onion and garlic. Remove casings of **1 pound of Italian sweet sausages** and crumble sausage into sauté pan. Sauté until sausage is lightly browned. Remove all with a slotted spoon and keep warm. Now add to pan ½ **to 1 pound sliced, fresh mushrooms, 1 red pepper**, cut into thin strips and **1 green pepper**, cut into strips. Sauté until tender-crisp. Do *not* overcook. Put sausage-onion mixture back into sauté pan. Add **1 quart of home-made or good-quality, store-bought Italian pasta tomato sauce**, and **a few hot red pepper flakes**. Simmer all together for 5 to 10 minutes.

Lastly, add about **2 tablespoons of chopped fresh herbs** — oregano, basil, sweet marjoram, parsley — I use a combination of these four when I have them fresh. If I don't have fresh herbs to use, I use ½ teaspoon of dried of each of the four herbs mentioned.

After adding the herbs, simmer sauce for another 2 or 3 minutes — no more. Pour immediately over cooked and drained fettucine (fresh is best, but store-bought is good too). Sprinkle a little fresh-grated Parmesan cheese on top. Serves 4 to 6, depending on how much fettucine you cook.

These kinds of dishes don't have to have exact recipes. There are basic rules to follow, then add your own meat, seafood, etc., to the sauce. If you can't find a red pepper, for example, just leave it out. If you love mushrooms, add a pound. If you're so-so on mushrooms, add less. Create your own!

Look for the fresh pasta doughs in the refrigerated section of the grocery. These are marvelous and like homemade. My favorite brand of store-bought pasta sauce is "Classico". I love the tomato-basil one and the new one called "Spicy Red Pepper". They come in quart glass jars.

Pasta With Italian Sausages In Diablo Sauce

❧ *(The Diablo Sauce recipe is from Carol Sermersheim.) Read recipe through before starting.*

	homemade pasta cut into fettucine noodles (make 1 recipe Pasta Dough — see Index)
½	pound small mushrooms
2	tablespoons olive oil
	salt
1½	pounds sweet Italian sausages
1	large green pepper
1	large red pepper
1	large yellow pepper (if available)
1	small onion
½	cup good quality olive oil
½	stick butter
1	cup minced fresh parsley leaves
2	cloves minced garlic
½	teaspoon to 1 teaspoon hot red pepper flakes
1	teaspoon salt
4	cups pureed tomatoes*

In a large, heavy Dutch oven, over medium-high heat, in hot olive oil, cook mushrooms and ¼ teaspoon salt until mushrooms are slightly browned, stirring often. Remove mushrooms to a bowl. Prick sausages several times with a fork. Use the same Dutch oven and heat sausages and ¼ **cup water** to boiling. Reduce heat. Cover and cook about 5 minutes. Remove cover and cook about 20 minutes longer until sausages are browned, turning often. Remove sausages to paper towels to drain. Cut each sausage into ½" wide chunks.

Now cut peppers into bite-size pieces. Mince the onion. In the same Dutch oven, cook peppers and onion and about ¾ teaspoon salt for 5 minutes, stirring often. Add ⅓ **cup water**. Cover and cook about 5 minutes or until vegetables are just tender. Combine the mushroom-sausage mixture with the pepper and onion mixture in the Dutch oven. Heat thoroughly over medium heat, stirring often. Don't cook anymore, but keep this mixture warm.

To make the Diablo Sauce, heat ½ cup olive oil in another heavy pan. Add the butter and melt. Add the cup of minced parsley leaves and the minced garlic. Sauté all together, but be very careful *not* to brown the garlic. Add the hot pepper flakes and sauté a few seconds. Add 4 cups puréed tomatoes and the 1 teaspoon salt. Let this all simmer very slowly for about 30 minutes, uncovered. Next add contents of first Dutch oven to the Diablo Sauce. Stir and heat well together, but don't cook anymore at this point.

Have a large pot of boiling water ready (6 quarts or so). Add the pasta dough cut into fettucine noodles to the boiling water. Stir gently to separate the noodles. Heat back to boiling. Reduce heat to medium and cook 30 to 45 seconds until tender, but firm. Do *not* overcook this or *any* pasta! Drain. Add noodles to Diablo Sauce pan and using a rubber spatula, mix all together. This will serve 8 hungry people. This is also a combination of 2 or 3 of my favorite pasta recipes. You may also serve the pasta separately and pass the sauce. I have also made this in advance (put pasta and sauce together), refrigerated it and baked in a 325° oven just until warmed through thoroughly.

*I have found that the canned puréed tomatoes are best for this recipe. I have puréed my own fresh ones and found the sauce to be too watery with them. If you do want to use fresh tomatoes, be sure to squeeze out as much juice and seeds as you can before puréeing.

Fruit-Flower-Herb Topiary

I often put one of these together during a cooking class - herb demonstration. Pile seasonal fruits on the glass tiers (I use antique cake stands). Fill in bare spots with herb sprigs and small flower blooms (such as pansy blooms, Siberian iris, daisy blooms, small carnations) in filled, small water tubes. These tubes are available at your florist. Beautiful on a tea table or on the sideboard.

Vegetable-Herb Lasagna

about 3 cups chopped zucchini
about 2 cups broccoli flowerets
about 2 cups cleaned and dried spinach leaves
butter
2 teaspoons fresh oregano leaves or ½ teaspoon dried
salt to taste
1 pound package ricotta cheese
2 eggs
12 lasagna noodles
¼ cup flour
2½ cups milk
½ cup grated Parmesan cheese
2 cups shredded Mozzarella cheese

In a large sauté pan, melt 4 tablespoons butter. Sauté zucchini and broccoli and a little salt until vegetables are tender-crisp, 3 or 4 minutes. Add spinach leaves and fresh oregano and stir until spinach is wilted. In a small bowl, mix together ricotta cheese and eggs, set aside. Prepare lasagna noodles as label directs. Drain.

Preheat oven to 350°. In a saucepan, melt 3 tablespoons butter. Stir in flour and ¼ teaspoon salt until smooth. Gradually stir in milk. Cook, stirring constantly, until sauce boils and thickens. Remove pan from heat and stir in Parmesan cheese.

In a large, greased baking pan (at least 9" x 13") lay 6 lasagna noodles. Spread half of ricotta mixture on noodles, half of vegetable mixture and half of the Mozzarella. Top with half the sauce, then rest of noodles, ricotta and vegetables. Spread with the rest of the sauce, then sprinkle rest of Mozzarella on top. Bake lasagna 45 minutes until hot and bubbly. Let lasagna stand for 10 minutes before cutting into squares. Will serve about 8. Serve this with broiled or outdoor-grilled chicken, steak, or chops, a good crusty bread and a good bottle of wine — a wonderful summer meal!

A Thymely Footnote . . . French sorrel is a hardy perennial that could take over your garden — it grows very easily. It is rather sour tasting with a hint of lemon. The French love it in soups and also for fish sauces. Your Grandmother probably considered it a weed!

Pasta With Fresh Herbs

Cook **pasta** (I like fettucine) according to directions (or make your own!). Drain **pasta**. Melt **3 or 4 tablespoons butter** in a large sauté pan. Add about **1 cup heavy cream**, **½ cup grated Parmesan cheese**, **1 tablespoon chopped fresh parsley**, **1 tablespoon chopped sweet marjoram**, **1 tablespoon chopped sweet basil** and **a little freshly grated pepper**. Stir all together and simmer a little while to thicken sauce. Add pasta to sauté pan and toss all together to coat the pasta with this wonderful sauce. Serve immediately and pass more grated Parmesan cheese. For a great summer meal, add some sautéed boneless, skinless chicken breast pieces, or some cooked shrimp, crab meat or lobster.

I'm afraid only the fresh herbs will do for this recipe. I can't tell you how good this is! Serves 4 to 6.

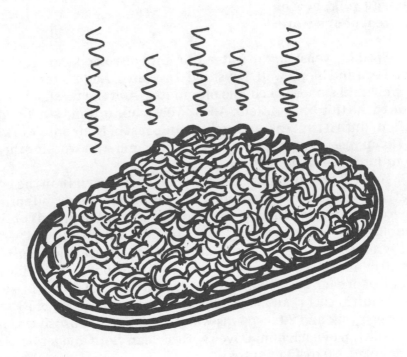

Easy Hot Cross Buns

What would Good Friday and Easter be without Hot Cross Buns? These are especially good. Next time, leave out the cinnamon and raisins or currants and bake these as dinner rolls. A professional baker told me we don't use enough yeast in our recipes, so we took care of that little problem here! Makes about 24 buns.

3	packages active dry yeast (I like Rapid Rise)
2	cups lukewarm water
¼	cup oil
1	egg
1	teaspoon ground cinnamon
½	cup sugar
1¼	teaspoons salt
6	to 7 cups bread flour
½	to ⅔ cup raisins or currants

To brush on dough:

1	egg yolk, beaten
2	teaspoons water

Sprinkle yeast on the water. Stir until dissovled. Add sugar, oil, salt and egg and blend well. Let stand 5 minutes. Add 2 cups flour and beat well until smooth, a couple of minutes. Add the teaspoon of cinnamon to the third cup of flour. Add to yeast mixture and stir. Keep adding flour until it isn't easy to mix in. Dump rest of flour onto work surface. Dump yeast-flour mixture onto the flour and start working the rest of flour into the dough.

You will probably have from ½ to 1 cup of flour left on the board — that's okay. Knead for 4 or 5 minutes. Flatten out dough and sprinkle raisins or currants on dough. Knead the raisins into dough and continue kneading 4 or 5 minutes more. Place dough in a greased bowl — turn over to grease top. Cover with a clean towel and let rise in a warm place about 45 minutes, or until doubled. Punch down dough and divide into 4 parts. Out of each part, shape 6 balls. Put each ball of dough in a well-greased muffin tin or put all 24 balls into a well-greased 9″ x 13″ pan. Mix the egg yolk and 2 teaspoons water together and brush this mixture on the top of each bun. Cover with a clean cloth and let buns rise until doubled, 30 to 45 minutes.

Bake in a preheated 350° oven for 15 to 20 minutes or until nicely browned. (I start with 15 minutes, and then add another minute or 2 at the end.) If baked in muffin tins, remove hot rolls from tins and let cool on rack. You don't need to remove rolls from the 9″ x 13″ pan. When nearly cool, mix about 1 cup sifted powdered sugar with just enough water to make a fairly stiff icing. With a sharp-tipped spoon or pastry bag, pipe icing in the shape of a cross onto each bun. To freeze, cool un-iced buns completely. Wrap well and freeze. To serve, thaw. Then put icing crosses on.

Maple Wheat Bread With Maple Butter

2   cups flour
2   teaspoons baking powder
2   teaspoons baking soda
1   teaspoon salt
1⅓ cups maple syrup (real - no substitute)
2   cups whole wheat flour
2   eggs
1½ cups buttermilk
1½ cups sour cream

Have all ingredients at room temperature. Grease 2 loaf pans — 8½″ x 4½″ x 2½″. Line bottom and sides with waxed paper and grease again.

Combine flours, baking powder, baking soda and salt. Set aside. Beat eggs; blend in buttermilk, sour cream and maple syrup. Pour into dry ingredients and stir well. Pour batter into prepared pans. Preheat oven to 325° (a little less if using glass pans). Bake about 1 hour or until a wooden pick comes out clean. As soon as bread comes out of oven, spread tops with some maple butter (recipe follows). Let loaves cool in pans 10 to 15 minutes, then carefully remove bread from pans. Peel off waxed paper. Let cool thoroughly. Wrap well and freeze or slice now. Refrigerate any left over (be sure to keep it well-wrapped).

Maple Butter
To approximately ⅓ cup softened butter, stir in ¼ cup pure maple syrup.

Maple Walnut or Pecan Muffins
❧ Simply superb!

1½ **cups chopped walnuts or pecans**
3 **tablespoons unsalted butter, softened**
2 **eggs**
1 **cup whipping cream**
1¼ **cups pure maple syrup (no substitute)**
1 **teaspoon maple or vanilla extract**
1½ **cups flour**
1½ **cups old-fashioned rolled oats**
1 **tablespoon ground cinnamon**
2 **teaspoons baking powder**
1 **teaspoon baking soda**
1 **cup chopped dates**

Preheat oven to 350°. Line 18 muffin cups with paper liners. Grease spaces between cups on muffin tins so the side of the muffin doesn't stick to the pan. Mix nuts and butter together on a baking sheet and toast in the oven for 5 minutes, stirring a time or two. Remove from oven.

Beat eggs, cream, 1 cup maple syrup and extract together in a mixing bowl. Combine flour, oats, cinnamon, baking powder, baking soda. Stir into the egg mixture just until combined. Stir in the dates and 1 cup of the toasted nuts.

Fill each muffin cup ¾ full with the batter. Sprinkle the tops with the rest of toasted nuts and drizzle each muffin with part of the remaining ¼ cup maple syrup. Bake for 20 minutes, or until it tests done. Makes 18 muffins.

A friend gave me this recipe. She though it might go over well in a class — it did!

A Thymely Footnote ... Monarda (bee balm, bergamot, Oswego tea) belongs to the mint family. It has nice red or purple blooms on long stems. Hummingbirds like this plant, but bees especially like it. It is a native American herb.

Chocolate Black Walnut Bon Bons

🍂 *These are great on your holiday cookie tray or in a gift box.*

6 ounces semisweet chocolate
5 tablespoons butter
½ cup sugar
2 eggs, slightly beaten
½ cup flour
½ teaspoon baking powder
1 teaspoon vanilla
1 cup chopped nuts (almonds, pecans, walnuts,
    especially black walnuts)
    Creamy Frosting

Preheat oven to 375°. Line miniature muffin tins with bon bon papers. Melt chocolate and butter in top of double boiler over hot water. Remove from hot water and stir in sugar. Add eggs, mixing well. Stir in flour, baking powder, vanilla and nuts. Spoon a small amount of mixture into each cup, filling ½ to ¾ full. Bake 8 minutes *only*. Cool in muffin cups. Spoon a little Creamy Frosting over each bon bon. Makes about 4 dozen.

Creamy Frosting
½ cup whipping cream
¾ cup sugar
2 ounces semisweet chocolate
1 egg yolk, beaten
2 tablespoons butter
1 teaspoon vanilla

Mix cream and sugar in a small, heavy saucepan. Bring to a boil, stirring constantly. Simmer over medium heat for about 5 minutes. Add chocolate and stir to melt. Stir a spoonful of chocolate mixture into the egg yolk to warm it slightly. Add egg yolk mixture to saucepan. Add butter and stir until melted. Stir in vanilla.

A Thymely Footnote . . . Anise is an annual that is very licorice in taste. It is used to flavor many liqueurs. It takes a long summer to ripen anise seed. You'll be lucky if 1 plant will produce 1 tablespoon of seed.

Cherries Jubilee

2   **cups sweet black cherries, drained, but reserve 1 cup of juice**
1   **tablespoon sugar**
1   **tablespoon cornstarch**
½   **cup brandy**
    vanilla ice cream

Mix the 1 tablespoon sugar and 1 tablespoon cornstarch together. Slowly add the 1 cup black cherry juice, a little at a time. Put in a heavy, small saucepan and cook slowly, stirring constantly, for 2 or 3 minutes, or until thickened and clear. Add the drained black cherries. Warm the brandy (see note below). Pour it over the cherries and light with a long match. Stir the brandy into the cherries. Have ice cream in serving dishes and spoon the flaming cherries over the ice cream. Serve immediately. Serves 4.

A note on Flaming: If you don't heat brandy or liqueur, you can not ignite it. On the other hand, if you heat it too hot, when you light it, flames will shoot high! So, just heat the brandy to *warm*. The alcohol all burns off and you're left with the flavor only. As you spoon the sauce on the ice cream, the flames will extinguish.

Peach Glaze For Ham

🍂 *A wonderful glaze for a holiday ham, or for anytime.*

Heat about **1 cup peach preserves** until they become liquid (stirring constantly). Remove from heat and using a rubber spatula, work preserves through a strainer. Throw away pulp left in the strainer. Add **2 or 3 tablespoons of peach schnapps** or **peach brandy** to the peach syrup. Mix well. Brush on ham before and during baking.

A Thymely Footnote ... Salad burnet and lovage are 2 interesting herbs because of the way each tastes. Salad burnet is a low-growing perennial that tastes and smells like cucumbers. It is a beautiful, lacy-leafed plant. Lovage, on the other hand, grows very tall and tastes and smells like celery.

Homemade Mayonnaise

≈ Everyone is always so surprised to learn how easy it is to make mayonnaise! Try this in the next potato or chicken salad you make.

> 2 egg yolks
> 1 whole egg
> 1 tablespoon prepared Dijon mustard
>   pinch of salt
>   freshly ground black pepper
> ¼ cup fresh lemon juice, remove 1 tablespoon
> 2 cups corn or vegetable oil

Combine yolks, whole egg, mustard, salt and pepper to taste and half of the lemon juice in bowl of your food processor fitted with the steel blade. Process for 1 minute.

While motor is running, dribble in oil in a slow steady stream. This will take a little time. When all of oil has been added, shut off motor and scrape sides of bowl with rubber spatula. Put top back on and turn on motor. Add rest of lemon juice and process a few seconds. If mayonnaise is too thick, add a little of the reserved 1 tablespoon of lemon juice, but probably won't need it. Put in a covered jar and refrigerate. Good for 2 or 3 weeks. Makes about 3 cups.

Herbed Mayonnaise

> 1 cup homemade mayonnaise (or store-bought is of course okay)
> 1 cup watercress leaves, rinsed and blotted dry
> ¼ cup chopped Italian or curly parsley
> ¼ cup snipped fresh chives

Combine all of the above in work bowl of the food processor fitted with the steel blade. Process until smooth, but don't overprocess. Makes about 1 cup.

I wouldn't attempt this with dried herbs, it just wouldn't be as good. Supermarkets often have watercress. If you don't have chives in your garden, plant one. It will come up every spring (it's one of the very first things to come up!) and rewards you with fresh chives until a hard freeze late in the fall. If you don't have Italian (flat leaved) parsley, the regular supermarket parsley will do.

English Date Pudding

This is a good, rich date pudding.

    1 cup plus 1 tablespoon flour
    1 teaspoon baking powder
    7 tablespoons butter, divided
    ¾ cup sugar
    1 egg, slightly beaten
    1 teaspoon baking soda
    1 teaspoon vanilla
    1 cup pitted dates
 1¼ cups boiling water
    5 tablespoons brown sugar
    2 tablespoons whipping cream
       whipped cream

Preheat oven to 350°. Butter an 8" x 8" broiler-proof baking dish. Sift the 1 cup flour and the baking powder into a bowl. Set aside. Chop dates rather fine and toss with the 1 tablespoon flour in a small bowl. Beat 4 tablespoons butter and ¾ cup sugar in a large bowl until mixture is light and fluffy. Beat in the egg, along with a little of the flour mixture. Beat for 1 minute. Beat in remaining flour mixture. Add dates, baking soda and vanilla to the 1¼ cups boiling water, stirring to combine. Add date mixture to the batter, stirring to combine. Pour batter into prepared pan. Bake until set and browned, about 35 to 40 minutes. Remove from oven.

Heat broiler. Heat the other 3 tablespoons butter, the brown sugar and the 2 tablespoons heavy cream in a small, heavy saucepan over medium heat until it simmers. Simmer until thickened, about 2 or 3 minutes. Remove from heat and pour over the hot pudding. Place pudding under broiler, about 4" from heat, and broil until topping bubbles, less than 1 minute. Serve pudding warm with whipped cream. Serves 6 or 8.

*A **Thymely Footnote** . . . This English pudding is probably served on Boxing Day. In Great Britain, Boxing Day is the first week day after Christmas when boxes or presents are given to deliverymen, postmen, etc.*

Fresh Herbed Tomato Sauce

꒰ This is simply wonderful and a cooking class favorite.

> 2 tablespoons good olive oil
> ¼ cup chopped green onion (white part)
> 3 cups peeled, seeded, chopped ripe tomatoes
> ¼ cup white wine or water
>   salt and freshly ground pepper to taste
> 2 tablespoons chopped fresh basil
> 1 tablespoon chopped fresh oregano
> 1 teaspoon chopped fresh thyme

Heat oil in a heavy saucepan. Add onions and sauté briefly, but do not brown. Add chopped tomatoes, wine, salt and pepper and cook, stirring often, for about 15 minutes. Add the herbs and cook and stir for another 3 to 5 minutes. Transfer mixture to a blender or food processor and purée until smooth. Return sauce to pan and simmer gently 10 to 20 minutes to thicken a little. This is a classic herbed Italian sauce. Will make about 2 cups of cooked sauce. Double or triple recipe, if desired.

Zucchini Provencal

꒰ If you have a garden, and if you grow zucchini, you probably have more than you know what to do with. This is a great way to use some.

> 1 to 2 tablespoons good olive oil
> 2 to 3 green onions, chopped
> 1 clove garlic, finely chopped
> 4 or 5 smallish zucchini, sliced
> 2 ripe tomatoes, peeled, seeded and chopped
> 1 tablespoon chopped fresh parsley, or 1 teaspoon dried
> 1 tablespoon chopped fresh oregano, or 1 teaspoon dried
> 1 tablespoon chopped fresh basil, or 1 teaspoon dried
> 1 or 2 cups shredded Mozzarella cheese

Sauté onion and garlic in olive oil, but do not brown. Add sliced zucchini and stir fry with a wooden spoon *only* until tender-crisp. *Do not overcook!* Add chopped tomatoes and stir a minute or so. Turn off heat. Sprinkle cheese over top and let set until cheese melts. Serve from the skillet. It's stringy and messy, but delicious! As you can tell, the secret of this recipe is to *NOT* overcook any of it. Serves 4-6.

SOME OLD, SOME NEW, SOME MOTHER'S, SOME FAR AWAY

We all lose or misplace recipes. Some that I wanted in *Take a Little Thyme* didn't get in because of sentence #1 above! One day I cleaned out all the kitchen drawers and any other place that I might have stashed away recipes, and got all the strays and lost ones together again. From those, I gleaned many for this chapter.

If you ever write a cookbook of your own, you'll find that *everyone* wants to give you his or her favorite recipe! This is great, because I figure it's really special or they wouldn't want to pass it on. So, lots of the recipes in this chapter have been given to me by wonderful cooks and wonderful new-found friends I've met as I go around giving my herb talks and demonstrations.

One day in Summer, 1984, my Father appeared at my door, shopping bag in hand. The bag was stuffed full of Mother's 60 or more years of recipes she had collected. Ann's and my cookbook was already in the process of being printed, so it was too late to include more of Mother's recipes in that book. It took me nearly a year to go through all those recipes and papers. In the process, I found many of her favorites and many of my childhood favorites that I hadn't been able to locate for *Take a Little Thyme*. Mother was a great one to scribble down the ingredients for a recipe, but often eliminated the name — Oatmeal Cookies, Cream Pie, for example — and she *never* wrote down the method for putting it all together! So most of Mother's recipes I used in this chapter have been re-constructed from her notes. Since I did have to re-construct them, I also tested them in the process. Out of literally hundreds and hundreds, I have chosen a few to put in this book. I will designate each of Mother's recipe with the following symbol —

⊂══⟩ MOTHER ♡

Dick and I have been fortunate to get to travel a great deal. I have collected many recipes and ideas from these far-away (and not so far-away) places, so I am sharing some of those also.

I hope you'll enjoy these old, new, Mother's, and far-away recipes as much as I do.

APPETIZERS
AND
DRINKS

Stanley Griggs' Mushrooms

🍂 *My friend Anne from Florida gave me this recipe. It's very simple and very good.*

    2 pounds fresh mushroom caps, wiped clean
    1 stick butter
    ¼ cup Worcestershire sauce
    ¼ cup Teriyaki sauce
    ½ to ¾ teaspoon garlic powder
       freshly ground pepper to taste

Melt butter; add remaining ingredients, except mushrooms. Sauté mushroom caps on high heat for about 5 minutes, stirring constantly. Reduce heat to medium high and cook until liquid is gone — watch closely. Serve with toothpicks as an appetizer or wonderful with roast beef or pork.

Easy Swiss-Bacon Squares

     1 8 ounce package refrigerated crescent roll dough
     8 to 10 slices bacon, fried, drained, crumbled
    12 ounces shredded Swiss cheese
     3 eggs, beaten
     ¾ cup milk
     1 tablespoon minced green onion (or onion)
     ½ teaspoon salt

Press the roll dough into a 9" x 13" baking pan. Combine remaining ingredients and pour over the dough. Bake at 375° for 30 to 35 minutes. Remove from oven and let set for about 5 minutes, then cut into 1½" squares to serve. Makes about 48 squares. Tastes like little quiches, only easier.

*A Thymely Footnote . . . Besides garden **thyme** and **lemon thyme**, I also grow **caraway thyme** and **oregano thyme**. They are loaded with flavor. I especially like these thymes in my herb butters. **Caraway thyme** is a thing of beauty when it is covered with rosy-purple blooms.*

Cheesy Triangles

1½   cups shredded sharp Cheddar cheese
1   cup chopped ripe olives
½   cup mayonnaise
½   cup green onions, finely chopped
½   teaspoon salt
½   teaspoon curry powder
8   plain English muffins

Combine the first six ingredients and set aside. Split and toast muffins. Spread about 2 tablespoons cheese mixture over each muffin half. Arrange these on a broiler pan. Broil until cheese melts, 2 or 3 minutes, but don't burn. Cut each muffin half into three or four wedges. Serve immediately. A good hot appetizer. Makes about 5 dozen.

Party Cheese Ball

1   8 ounce package cream cheese, softened
1   3 ounce package cream cheese, softened
1   4½ ounce can deviled ham
2   cups (8 ounces) shredded sharp Cheddar cheese
2   tablespoons pimiento - stuffed olives, chopped fine
1   tablespoon prepared mustard
1   teaspoon chopped fresh chives (or freeze dried)
¼   teaspoon dry mustard
¼   teaspoon celery seeds
¼   teaspoon cayenne pepper
⅛   teaspoon salt
½   cup chopped pecans

Combine all ingredients, except pecans. Mix well. Shape into a ball and roll in chopped pecans. Chill well. Best if made and chilled several days before serving. You can wrap cheese ball well and freeze it, if desired.

Salmon-Cheese Ball

1   7¾ ounce can red salmon, best quality
1   8 ounce package cream cheese, softened
½   cup shredded Cheddar cheese
¼   cup pimiento - stuffed green olives, chopped
4   slices bacon, cooked crisp and crumbled
2   tablespoons minced onion
1   or 2 dashes bottled hot pepper sauce
⅓   cup fresh parsley, chopped fine

Drain salmon; remove skin and bones. Flake salmon. Combine gently with remaining ingredients, except the chopped parsley. Chill the mixture thoroughly. Shape into a ball and roll in the parsley. Serve with crackers. Keep refrigerated, or you may freeze the ball. Thaw in the refrigerator overnight before serving. Makes about 2 cups.

Boursin

🍃 *This is the real thing. A purist will tell you one can't make Boursin with dried herbs — only fresh ones. Well, maybe he's right.*

8   ounces cream cheese, softened
1   tablespoon fresh lemon juice
1   minced clove garlic
½   teaspoon Worcestershire sauce
½   teaspoon dry mustard
1   tablespoon fresh parsley, finely chopped
1   tablespoon fresh chives, finely chopped
4   tablespoons minced fresh herbs*

Combine all ingredients, but don't beat — just mix gently and thoroughly. Cover tightly and refrigerate. When ready to serve, bring to room temperature. Makes about 1 cup.

*I use at least four of the following herbs in my Boursin — the more, the better! Rosemary, thyme, dill, Greek oregano, marjoram, summer savory, basil, sage.

Herbed Cheese Spread

🥬 *This is terrific on bagels, on a hot baked potato, on a chicken or turkey sandwich. You'll think of lots of ways to use this spread.*

>2 8 ounce packages cream cheese, softened
>1 cup unsalted butter, softened
>2 to 3 cloves garlic, minced fine
>1 teaspoon dried oregano or 1 tablespoon chopped fresh
>½ teaspoon dried thyme or 1½ teaspoons chopped fresh
>½ teaspoon dried basil or 1½ teaspoons chopped fresh
>½ teaspoon dried dill or 1½ teaspoons chopped fresh
>½ teaspoon freshly ground pepper

Cream the butter and cheese together. Add all the other ingredients and mix well — thoroughly but gently. Cover and chill for a day before using. Will keep for a week or more if covered and refrigerated. Serve at room temperature. Makes 3 cups.

Roquefort Spread

🥬 *You may substitute bleu cheese if Roquefort is not available.*

>1 stick unsalted butter, softened
>2 or 3 ounces Roquefort cheese, softened
>3 ounces cream cheese, softened
>½ cup walnuts, chopped fine
>2 tablespoons unflavored brandy

Blend thoroughly the first 3 ingredients. Stir in the walnuts and brandy. Refrigerate until ready to use, but serve at room temperature. Fabulous on crusty French bread slices.

*A **Thymely Footnote** . . . There are several wonderful herbs in the artemesia family. One of them is **southernwood**, a beautiful ornamental plant with lacy, gray-green leaves that have the scent of lemon. **Wormwood** is a bitter herb used to make the potent liqueur called absinthe. **Southernwood** is often called "Old Man". **Wormwood** is often called "Old Woman".*

Roasted Pecans

4 tablespoons butter
1 pound shelled pecan halves
1 to 2 teaspoons salt (start with 1 teaspoon and taste — if not enough, add more)

Preheat oven to 350°. Melt butter in a shallow roasting pan. Add pecan halves and stir well to coat nuts with the butter. Bake for 20 minutes, stirring every 5 minutes. Remove from oven and sprinkle with salt. Let cool completely. Store in a tightly covered tin.

Smoked Salmon Dip

🍃 *This is wonderful on dark pumpernickel bread, on crackers, or with raw vegetables. Don't substitute canned salmon here — use only smoked.*

8 ounces cream cheese, softened
½ cup sour cream
1 tablespoon fresh lemon juice
¼ to ⅓ pound smoked salmon (remove any skin or bones and discard; chop salmon fairly fine)
1½ tablespoons chopped fresh chives or chopped green onion
freshly ground white or black pepper

Use a food processor and blend the cheese, sour cream and lemon juice until mixture is smooth. Scrape mixture into a medium bowl. Add the salmon, chives and pepper and mix gently with a wooden spoon. (I like for bits of salmon to be seen so I don't use the processor for this step.) Makes about 2 cups of delicious dip. It if lasts, it's good for a week in the refrigerator.

A Thymely Footnote . . . Sweet Cicely is a very tall perennial that loves a shady growing spot — one of a few herbs that prefers the shade. It is in the parsley family and has a distinct licorice flavor. Its most famous use is in the making of Chartreuse liqueur.

Salmon Dip

Put in mixer bowl:
- **2 8 ounce packages cream cheese, softened**
- **½ teaspoon celery salt**
- **½ teaspoon garlic salt**
- **½ teaspoon onion salt**
- **½ teaspoon Accent (MSG), optional**
- **2 tablespoons mayonnaise**
- **1 tablespoon fresh lemon juice**

Mix the above ingredients thoroughly. With a wooden spoon, stir in a **7 to 8 ounce can of red salmon** (pick out the bones and skin and discard). Another time, use crab meat or drained tuna. Serve with crackers, cocktail rye bread slices, or small French bread slices. Makes about 2 cups of delicious dip or spread. Best served at room temperature.

Taco Dip

- **1 cup chopped onion**
- **2 tablespoons butter**
- **1 10 ounce can tomatoes, seasoned with green chilies (look in Mexican food section of grocery), mashed**
- **½ teaspoon cumin seed**
- **1 pound diced American cheese**
- **12 ounces cubed Cheddar cheese**
- **1 1 pound can chili without beans**
- **4 tablespoons taco sauce (bottled)**
- **1 4 ounce can chopped green chilies**

Sauté onion in butter. Add mashed tomatoes and juice. Add all other ingredients and simmer until cheese melts. Serve hot with corn chips or tortilla chips. Makes about 3 cups. Men love this dip.

Chicken and Chicken Liver Pâté

1 cup chopped onion
2 cloves garlic, minced
2 tablespoons butter
1½ pounds boneless pork roast
1 pound boneless and skinless chicken breast
1 pound chicken livers
½ cup heavy (whipping) cream
2 eggs
1 tablespoon salt
1 teaspoon dried thyme (or 1 tablespoon fresh)
½ teaspoon pepper
½ teaspoon ground allspice
¼ cup unflavored brandy
1 pound bacon
4 bay leaves

Sauté onion and garlic in butter until soft but not brown. Cut pork and chicken into 2 inch pieces. Put sautéed onion, pork, chicken and chicken livers into food processor, fitted with steel blade. Process on and off until mixture is smooth, but do not overprocess. Combine this ground mixture with the cream, eggs, salt, thyme, pepper, allspice and brandy in a large bowl. Beat mixture with a wooden spoon until it is smooth and well mixed. Line two 9" x 5" loaf pans with strips of bacon. Don't overlap bacon or it will make ridges in the pâté. Each pan will take about 7 strips of bacon. Cut to fit if necessary and let ends hang down over sides of the pans. Divide the pâté mixture between the pans. Press down firmly and smooth the tops. Press 2 bay leaves on top of each loaf. Fold bacon ends over the mixture, then add additional strips to completely cover the mixture. Cover pans tightly with heavy-duty aluminum foil. Put pans in a larger pan and place on oven shelf. Pour boiling water into the outer pan to come halfway up the sides. Bake in a 350° oven for 2 hours, or until juices show no tinge of pink. Remove pans from the oven. Remove the foil and cool pans on a wire rack. When cool, wrap in fresh foil and refrigerate. Pâté will keep, refrigerated, for a week. Makes 2 loaves. To serve, unwrap and remove bacon strips and any solid fat from the top of each loaf. Serve with thin slices of French bread which have been buttered and toasted. The best pâté this side of France!

Herbed Chevre (Goat Cheese)

🍂 *I may be putting this recipe in just for me. I have developed a taste for fresh goat cheese (called chevre - pronounced "shev-er"). Many people don't like goat cheese, and if it's too old (aged), I'm one of them. But fresh chevre is mild, smooth and delicious. The aged chevre, which many people do like, is sharp, tangy and aromatic. At any rate, slices of a good chevre that have been marinated for several hours are delicious on small rounds of crusty French bread. Here is the way I like this cheese.*

½   cup extra virgin olive oil
1   tablespoon fresh chopped rosemary OR 1 teaspoon dried
1   tablespoon fresh chopped thyme, OR 1 teaspoon dried
1   log of fresh, mild goat milk cheese (usually less than a pound in size)
    freshly ground black pepper
    loaf of crusty French bread to serve cheese on

Slice the cheese into ½" thick slices. Place slices in a single layer in a glass baking dish. Combine the olive oil, rosemary and thyme. Drizzle dressing over the cheese slices. Grate black pepper over the top to your taste. Cover tightly with plastic wrap and refrigerate overnight or for several hours. Serve a cheese slice on a bread slice. If slices are too large, cut in half.

Spiced Sun Tea

4   quarts cold water
3   inches of cinnamon stick
1   teaspoon whole cloves
8   tea bags

Pour water into a gallon glass jar with a screw-on lid. Put cinnamon stick (broken up) and cloves in a coffee filter. Draw up and tie with kitchen string. Add tea bags and spice bag to the jar. Put on lid and let jar stand in full sun for eight hours or until tea is of desired strength. Remove spice bag and tea bags. Refrigerate. Serve with plenty of ice.

Minted Iced Tea

    4 cups strong tea
    2 cups fresh orange juice
  1½ cups sugar
   ½ cup water
    2 tablespoons grated orange rind
   ½ cup fresh mint leaves, chopped fine
       orange slices, for garnish
       fresh mint leaves, for garnish

Put tea and orange juice in a two quart pitcher. In a small saucepan, combine sugar, water and orange rind. Heat to boiling over high heat. Boil 5 minutes and remove from heat. Add mint leaves to hot mixture. Stir, then cover and let mixture cool to room temperature. Strain this mixture into the pitcher of tea and orange juice. Refrigerate. Serve with an orange slice and fresh mint leaves, if desired. Makes about 1½ quarts.

Fruit Tea

Combine **2 tea bags** and **1 cup boiling water.** Let steep for 3 minutes. Remove tea bags and let set until cool. Then add: **½ cup lemon juice, ¾ cup grape juice, ¼ cup orange juice, 1 cup cold water** and **¼ to ½ cup sugar.** Mix well. Chill. Just before serving, add **1 cup gingerale.** Stir. Pour over ice. Delicious. Makes 1 quart.

Christmas Cran-Raspberry-Peach Drink

❦ *One of the best, easiest and prettiest drinks I serve at Holiday time is this one. Everyone loves it.*

Use your prettiest Champagne glasses. Pour 2 or 3 tablespoons peach schnapps in bottom of each glass. Mix a pitcher of cranberry-raspberry frozen juice cocktail (I like Welch's) as package directs. When ready to serve, pour *cold* juice over the schnapps. Stir gently and serve. This is a delightful blend of fruit flavors.

Herbed Tomato Juice

🍃 *If you're tired of plain old tomato juice, this herbed juice made with fresh tomatoes is wonderful. You can freeze or can this juice.*

      2 **gallons ripe tomatoes, peeled and quartered**
      1 **cup chopped fresh parsley**
      1 **cup chopped fresh basil**
      1 **cup chopped onion**
      ½ **cup chopped celery**
         about ½ cup sugar, or to taste
      2 **teaspoons salt, or to taste**

Put all ingredients together except sugar and salt. Cook in a large kettle on medium heat until tomatoes are soft. Stir often — do not burn. Remove from heat and put a cup or so at a time into blender container. Blend until smooth. Pour out into a large clean container. Continue to blend batches until all of mixture is blended. Add sugar and salt to taste. Stir well. Put in clean, sterilized jars and refrigerate, freeze or can (according to canning directions for tomato juice). Makes about 8 pints.

Luau Refresher

      1 **46 ounce can of pineapple juice**
      1 **12 ounce can thawed orange juice concentrate**
      1 **12 ounce can thawed lemonade concentrate**
      1 **12 ounce can thawed limeade concentrate**
      5 **cups cold water**
      4 **cups chilled club soda**

Combine all ingredients, except club soda. Mix well and refrigerate. Just before serving, add club soda and ice or an ice ring if you're using a punch bowl. Makes 30 servings (½ cup each). This is the best and easiest punch I make. It is not sweet, so it's very refreshing.

Champagne Wedding Punch

• *A wedding isn't necessary! This is wonderful anytime for a large crowd. It will make 60 to 80 punch cup servings.*

  6 **oranges (save juice for below)**
  6 **lemons (save juice for below)**
 ½ **cup white corn syrup**
  4 **cups sugar**
  2 **cups water**
 ¼ **teaspoon salt**
  1 **quart pineapple juice**
  1 **quart fresh or frozen orange juice**
  2 **cups fresh lemon juice**
  2 **bottles medium dry to dry white wine**
  2 **bottles Champagne**
  2 **16 ounce bottles soda water**

Peel oranges and lemons. Cut peel into thin strips. Add sugar, water, corn syrup and salt. Bring to a boil, stirring to dissolve sugar. Lower heat and simmer for 15 minutes. Cover and cool. Remove peel and discard. Add this cooled syrup to the fruit juices and white wine. Pour over a ring of ice in a large punch bowl. Let mixture stand for 30 minutes. Stir well and just before serving, add the Champagne and the soda water.

For ice ring, slice a navel orange into ¼" thick round slices; stand slices up around edge of ring mold; carefully add about 1" of water; freeze. When frozen, fill ring mold with water and put back in freezer. This method will hold the slices in place. You can use lemon slices, cherries, kumquats, crab apples, etc., for the fruit.

Easiest-Of-All Fruit Punches

  2 **6 ounce cans frozen orange juice concentrate, thawed**
  2 **6 ounce cans frozen lemonade concentrate, thawed**
  6 **cups water**
  1 **46 ounce can pineapple juice**
  1 **cup sugar**
  2 **16 ounce bottles ginger ale, chilled**

Combine the thawed concentrates. Add water and pineapple juice. Stir in sugar. Refrigerate. At serving time, add the ginger ale. Makes about 30 punch cup servings.

White Sangria

🍂 *Sangria is the national drink of Spain — they serve it with everything. Every household has its own recipe! I particularly like this one.*

2   750 milliliter bottles good dry white wine
¼   cup Grand Marnier liqueur
½   cup sugar (superfine is easiest to stir in)
1   cup strawberries, washed, dried, cut in half
1   ripe peach, peeled, pitted, sliced
1   ripe pear, cored and sliced
1   navel orange, unpeeled and sliced
1   lemon, unpeeled and sliced
1   cup seedless white grapes, cut in half
3   cups chilled sparkling water
    mint sprigs, for garnish

Use a very large *glass* pitcher (this isn't only good to drink, you *must* look at it also!). Mix wine, liqueur, and sugar together and stir until sugar dissolves. Add all the fruits. Cover with plastic wrap and refrigerate several hours. When ready to serve, add the sparkling water and stir gently. Pour over ice and mint sprigs in large glasses or goblets. Serves 6 to 8.

Champagne-Orange Cocktail

🍂 *Beautiful and delicious for a brunch.*

3   cups chilled fresh orange juice
2½ cups chilled Champagne
1   cup Grand Marnier liqueur
    orange slices

Combine orange juice, Champagne and Grand Marnier in a pitcher. Pour into Champagne glasses. Garnish each glass with an orange slice and serve immediately. Will make about 6 drinks.

Champagne Framboise

🍃 *Framboise, of course, means raspberries in French. Chambord is a marvelous raspberry liqueur made in France. This is another beautiful and delicious drink.*

1 **1 pound can whole raspberries in heavy syrup**
   Chambord liqueur
   chilled Champagne

Divide raspberries and syrup among ice cube trays and freeze. Place one frozen cube in each Champagne glass. Add 1 tablespoon Chambord to each glass, then fill with chilled Champagne. Serve immediately.

Champagne-Strawberry Cooler

🍃 *Wonderful to serve for a brunch.*

1 **10 to 12 ounce package frozen strawberries in syrup**
1 **cup orange juice**
1 **375 milliliter bottle of Champagne or sparkling white wine**

Let frozen berries stand at room temperature for about 15 minutes. In blender at low speed, blend berries and syrup and orange juice until smooth. Pour this mixture into a large pitcher or bowl. Gradually pour in Champagne or wine and stir gently. Serve immediately. About 8 four ounce servings.

Spiced Apple Cider

Break **16 cinnamon sticks** into 1" or smaller pieces. Tie **2 tablespoons whole cloves, 2 tablespoons whole allspice, 1 teaspoon ground mace**, and **1 teaspoon salt** in a coffee filter to make a spice bag. Add spice bag and **2⅓ cups brown sugar** to **2 gallons cider**. Heat all together and bring slowly to a boil. Simmer about 15 minutes. Remove spice bag. Serve hot. Makes about 30 cups.

May Wine Punch

🍃 *May wine is an old European drink and was popular here in colonial days. If you have sweet woodruff, do make this punch for a beautiful bridal shower or luncheon, or anything you want to celebrate in May or June. Sweet woodruff has no aroma when it's fresh and green, but dried, it smells like clover hay — very interesting.*

For the punch:
   1 **bottle May wine (recipe follows)**
   1 **13 to 15 ounce can pineapple chunks, drained**
   ¼ **cup Grand Marnier (orange flavored liqueur)**
   1 **bottle dry sparkling wine, chilled**
       fresh ripe strawberries

Put a block of ice in your prettiest crystal or glass punch bowl. Add pineapple chunks, the bottle of May wine, and the orange liqueur. Stir well. When ready to serve, add the sparkling wine and stir only once. Garnish each punch cup with a fresh, ripe strawberry (leave green stem on).

May Wine

Dry the herb, sweet woodruff, on an old screen for several days, or until leaves are crispy dry. Strip off leaves and crush slightly. For one bottle of wine, you'll need ⅓ **to ½ cup of the dried woodruff leaves**. Put the dried woodruff in a coffee filter. Gather up and tie with white kitchen string. Place in a wide mouthed glass canning jar. Pour **1 bottle of Riesling or Chenin Blanc wine** over the woodruff (save wine bottle and cork). Screw lid on the jar and let it set for 2 to 4 hours. Remove the bag of woodruff and strain the wine back into the wine bottle (use another coffee filter for this). Cork the bottle and chill it until ready to use in the punch. Good to drink as is also. The punch serves 12.

*A Thymely Footnote . . . I have found wonderful labels for vinegar bottles. They are called **Gifted Labels** and they can be ordered from: The Gifted Line, John Grossman, Inc., 2656 Bridgeway, Sausalito, CA 94965.*

Chocolate Black Walnut Fudge ⊂▭[MOTHER ♡]▭⊃

🍂 *If two things were ever meant to go together it is chocolate and black walnuts! If you don't have black walnuts, of course you can substitute other nuts. This is an old-fashioned, rich candy.*

    2 cups sugar
    2 tablespoons butter
    5 tablespoons cocoa
    ⅔ cup milk
       dash of salt
    1 teaspoon vanilla
    1 cup chopped black walnuts, or other nuts

Combine in a heavy saucepan the sugar, butter, cocoa, milk and salt. Bring to a boil. Boil to soft-ball stage (234° to 238°). Add vanilla. Cool to room temperature without stirring. Use electric mixer and beat until thick and creamy. Add walnuts and stir in by hand. Pour into a well-greased 9″ square pan and cut into squares. Or drop teaspoons of candy into tiny paper muffin cups to add to your homemade candy gift.

Double Fudge ⊂▭[MOTHER ♡]▭⊃

🍂 *Another of Grandma Clem's recipes.*

    2 cups white sugar
    ½ cup heavy cream
    2 squares unsweetened chocolate
    1 tablespoon butter

Mix together above ingredients and boil gently for 7 minutes. Beat until thickened and spread in a buttered 9″x9″x2″ pan. Set aside to cool.

    2 cups light brown sugar
    ½ cup cream
    1 teaspoon vanilla
    ⅓ cup butter

Mix above ingredients and boil gently for 10 minutes. Beat until it begins to thicken. Add 1 cup chopped walnuts or pecans (black walnuts are especially good) and continue to beat until thickened. Spread this layer over first layer. Cool thoroughly. Cut into small squares. (Use a sturdy wooden spoon to beat with.)

SOUPS,
SALADS,
SALAD
DRESSINGS

Creamy Chicken Soup

       about 3 cups diced, cooked chicken
¾   **cup butter**
¾   **cup flour**
2   **cups Half and Half cream, warmed**
       salt and pepper to taste
4   **cups rich chicken broth (saved from cooking the chicken)**

In a saucepan, melt the butter. Add flour and stir until very smooth. Cook and stir over *low* heat for 4 or 5 minutes. Warm the cream and gradually add it to the broth, stirring constantly. Stir or whisk the cream-broth mixture into the cooked flour mixture. Stir until very smooth. *Simmer* for 30 minutes or so. Add salt and pepper to taste and add the diced chicken. Heat another 5 minutes, then serve. Serves 6 or 7.

Canadian Cheese Soup

¼   **cup onion, finely chopped**
¼   **cup carrot, finely chopped**
¼   **cup celery, finely chopped**
2   **tablespoons butter or oleo**
⅓   **cup flour**
2   **cups chicken broth**
2   **cups light cream**
8   **ounces sharp Cheddar cheese, shredded**

In a sauté pan, cook vegetables in melted butter until tender, but do not brown. Stir flour into broth until smooth. Add broth and cream to vegetables. Cook and stir until thickened and bubbly. Add the cheese. Season with a little salt and pepper, if desired. Cook, stirring constantly, until cheese is melted and soup is hot, but do not boil. Will serve 4. This recipe is easy to double or triple. It's a good, very simple and easy to make soup. I went to the Tulip Festival in Ottawa one spring (beautiful!) and brought this recipe home with me.

Vegetable-Cheese Chowder

1 clove garlic, minced
1 cup finely chopped onion
2 tablespoons butter
1 cup cooked ham or Canadian bacon, chopped fine (or more, if desired)
1 cup mushrooms, sliced
2 cups chicken broth
1 pound sharp Cheddar cheese, grated
2 tablespoons cornstarch
1 teaspoon Worcestershire sauce
2 cups half and half cream
1 cup cooked broccoli flowerets
½ cup cooked sliced carrots

In a sauté pan, cook the garlic and onion in melted butter over low heat for about 10 minutes, stirring often. Add the ham and mushrooms. Cook mixture over medium heat for 3 minutes, stirring. In a large saucepan bring the chicken broth to a boil. In a bowl, toss the cheese with the cornstarch and add the mixture to the broth, a little at a time, over low heat. Stir the mixture all the time and stir until smooth. Stir in the Worcestershire sauce, the half and half, the broccoli, carrots and onion mixture. Add salt and pepper to taste and heat the chowder over moderate heat until it is very hot, but do not boil. Serves 5 or 6. This chowder is delicious. It makes a marvelous Sunday night supper or a holiday eve supper or lunch. Serve with bread sticks and fruit for dessert. Or for a little heavier meal, serve with a fruit pie. This will become one of your favorite soups.

Nancy Fisher's Zesty Tomato Soup

Combine a **10½ ounce can of zesty tomato soup**, a **10½ ounce can of beef broth** and **1½ to 2 cans of water**. Heat to simmering. Nancy served this wonderfully easy soup to the Old Church Garden Guild of Attica, Indiana, along with already-made sandwiches. She served the soup in mugs — no bowl, no silverware, no fuss!

Chicken Soup

   1 **large frying chicken or a stewing hen**
   1 **whole onion**
   1 **carrot, scraped**
   2 **ribs celery with leaves**
  10 **whole peppercorns**
     salt to taste (1 to 2 teaspoons or more)
     bouquet garni (use ½ of Garni #1 on page 32)

Cover chicken with water. Add rest of ingredients. Bring to a boil. Skim broth. Reduce heat and simmer until chicken is fork tender. Strain broth into a clean pot. Throw away vegetables and garni. Cool broth a little and skim off fat. Cut up chicken meat into desired size pieces and add to broth. Throw away bones and skin. Add **4 or 5 chopped green onions, 2 or 3 sliced carrots**, and **chopped celery** — a cup or so. I usually add **½ cup rice** (not instant) or **1 cup broken noodles**. Five minutes before serving, add **1 cup frozen peas** and **1 tablespoon dried parsley flakes**. Taste and correct seasonings. Add a couple of dashes of **seasoned pepper**.

Beef Vegetable Soup

   2 **or 3 meaty beef bones (I like cross-cut shank bones)**
   1 **whole onion**
   1 **whole carrot, scraped**
  10 **whole peppercorns**
   1 **Spice Island bay leaf**
   2 **ribs celery with leaves**
  ½ **teaspoon seasoned pepper**
   1 **to 2 teaspoons salt, or to taste**

Put bones in a large pot. Cover with water. Add rest of ingredients. Bring to a boil. Skim broth if foam rises. Lower heat and simmer until beef is very tender. Lift meat out of kettle — spread in a flat pan to cool. Meanwhile, strain broth into a large clean pot. Cool broth and skim off fat. Throw away the vegetables and spices. Cut meat into desired size pieces and add to the broth. Add a **28 ounce can whole tomatoes**, chopped; **1 large onion**, chopped fine; **3 carrots**, sliced; **3 medium potatoes**, diced. You can add chopped **celery, cabbage, cut corn** or **green beans** at this point. Simmer until vegetables are tender. Ten minutes before serving, add **1 cup frozen peas** and **¼ cup dried parsley**. Correct seasonings.

Tomato, Onion, Mozzarella and Basil Salad

๛ *My favorite of all salads.*

Use only the freshest, best ingredients. Peel ripe **tomatoes** and slice rather thick. Slice **sweet onions** and separate into rings. Slice a block of good **Mozzarella cheese** into about ¼" slices. Wash and dry large, tender **green basil** leaves. Use a rectangular tray or platter. Lay down a tomato slice, overlap 2 or 3 onion rings on top of the tomato, a slice of cheese, a basil leaf. Follow this order and cover the platter with rows, in this order. Cover with plastic wrap and refrigerate. Make a dressing of ⅔ **cup good quality olive oil** and ⅓ **cup mixed herb vinegar** (or basil vinegar or just plain vinegar). When ready to serve, remove tomato-onion platter from the refrigerator, remove plastic wrap. Drizzle the dressing over all. Add a grating or two of **fresh ground pepper**. Sprinkle a couple of table-spoons of **fresh chopped parsley** over the top. Serve immediately. Beautiful to serve.

Fresh Tomatoes with Herbs

  6 **or 8 nice ripe fresh tomatoes, peeled and cut into wedges**
  2 **green onions, diced (tops too)**
  1 **tablespoon Worcestershire sauce**
  1 **teaspoon Dijon mustard**
  1 **teaspoon dried dill, or 1 tablespoon fresh**
  1 **teaspoon dried parsley, or 1 tablespoon fresh**
  1 **teaspoon salt**
     freshly ground pepper
  2 **cloves garlic, fincly minced**
     juice of 1 lemon
 ¼ **cup good olive oil**
 ⅓ **cup vinegar (herb is great here)**

Put tomato wedges in a large bowl. Combine remaining ingredients to make a dressing. Drizzle dressing over tomato wedges. Serve on lettuce leaves as a salad. Will serve 6 or 8.

Overnight Cauliflower Salad

1 head lettuce, shredded
1 small head cauliflower, broken into flowerets
1 Bermuda onion, sliced thin
12 to 15 slices bacon, fried crisp, drained and crumbled

Put all the above ingredients into a large salad bowl. Make a dressing of **1 cup mayonnaise or salad dressing, 2 tablespoons sugar**, and **⅓ cup grated Parmesan cheese**. Spread dressing over the salad ingredients, completely covering the surface. Cover with plastic wrap to seal and refrigerate overnight. To serve, toss dressing with the salad ingredients. Serves 8 or more.

Favorite Christmas Salad

🍋 *This is a delicious, as well as beautiful, salad to serve at holiday time. It's such a nice change from the usual gelled salads served that time of year.*

1 head lettuce, shredded
   segments of 2 pink grapefruit
   segments of 3 navel oranges
   the juicy seeds of ½ pomegranate
   Poppy Seed Dressing

Shred lettuce into a large serving or salad bowl. Peel grapefruits and oranges very close to flesh so that no white remains on outside. With a sharp knife, cut down toward center of fruit between each membrane to make perfect segments. Scatter these segments on top of lettuce. Now scatter the pomegranate seeds over the fruit. Add dressing and toss very gently to distribute fruit with lettuce. Serves 8 or 10.

Bobbie Shilling's Poppy Seed Dressing

Combine in a bowl: **1½ cups sugar, 2 teaspoons dry mustard, 2 teaspoons salt, 3 tablespoons poppy seeds, ⅔ cup cider vinegar, 1 tablespoon grated onion, 2 cups salad oil** and **2 or 3 drops red food coloring**. With electric beater, beat until smooth and until sugar is dissolved. You may not need to use the full recipe of dressing on this salad — **don't** wilt the salad, or **any** salad, with too much dressing!

A Special Shrimp Salad

1   bunch fresh spinach
1   head butter lettuce (Bibb)
1   head red leaf lettuce
½   head romaine

Wash all the greens above. Pat dry. Mix together and chill.

Now combine:
2   tablespoons chopped fresh chives
2   tablespoons chopped fresh parsley
1   teaspoon chopped fresh tarragon
1   teaspoon Dijon mustard
1   teaspoon salt
1   whole egg
    juice of 1 lemon

Whisk these together. Slowly add ½ **cup oil** and beat until dressing thickens.

Blend in:
1   cup sour cream
    dash of bottled hot pepper sauce

Refrigerate dressing until ready to use. Put greens in a large serving bowl. Add **2 cups cooked, peeled and deveined shrimp.** Pour dressing over all and toss gently. Sprinkle with freshly ground pepper and serve. Serves 6 or 8.

Marinated Green Beans

Cook **2 pounds of fresh green beans** (leave them whole) in a little salted water. Cook only until beans are tender-crisp. Drain beans and put them into a bowl. Dice **2 or 3 green onions** (tops too) and add to the green bean bowl. Add **2 tablespoons chopped fresh parsley.** Grate some **fresh pepper** over all and stir well. Combine ½ **cup dill vinegar** and ⅓ **to ½ cup good quality olive oil.** Drizzle dressing over beans and toss. Cover and refrigerate for several hours. You may want to add a little more salt. This will serve 6 or 8 as a salad. You could also add a little diced red pimiento for color. This is a wonderful cold summer salad.

Marinated Antipasto

&🙧 *You've noticed by now, I'm sure, that I love marinated salads, especially fresh ones. Here is yet another one.*

2 cups cauliflowerets
2 small zucchini, sliced
2 cups cherry tomatoes, halve some of them
1 cup pitted ripe olives, drained, halved
1 ¾ ounce package Good Seasons Herb Salad dressing mix
4 ounces good salami, sliced
4 ounces sliced Prosciutto (If Prosciutto is not available, use a good, lean ham.)*
6 round slices Provolone cheese, cut into fourths
6 round slices Colby or mild Cheddar cheese, cut into fourths

Cook cauliflowerets and zucchini in boiling water for about 2 minutes, or until tender crisp. Drain. Put cauliflowerets, zucchini slices, tomatoes and ripe olives in a zip plastic bag. Prepare the dry dressing mix according to package directions (I use my herbed vinegar here) and pour this dressing over the vegetables. Zip up the bag and marinate for 4 to 6 hours in the refrigerator. To serve, drain the marinade (save for another use) and arrange the vegetables on a platter. Surround with rolled-up salami and ham slices and quartered cheese slices. Drizzle a little of the marinade over the meat and cheese. Serve on lettuce-lined plates. Serves 4 for lunch or several for an appetizer. If served as an appetizer, provide picks and napkins.

*Prosciutto is a wonderful ham from Italy, always rather dry and lean, and *always* sliced paper thin! It is illegal to import it into the United States, so if you see Prosciutto in your store, it *didn't* come from Italy!

THYME UPDATE . . .

As of late 1989, Prosciutto is **now** legally shipped into the U.S. from Italy. Parma, Italy, is famous for its Parmesan cheese, Prosciutto and Balsamic vinegar. A wonderful place to visit!

Dilled Cucumbers and Onions

🍃 *I can't imagine summer without this cold, tart salad.*

1 large red or white onion, sliced thin and separated into
   rings
2 or 3 cucumbers, washed, unpeeled, and sliced thin
   about 1 cup dill vinegar
2 to 4 tablespoons sugar (depends on your taste)
½ to 1 teaspoon salt
   freshly grated black pepper
1 tablespoon (or more to taste) chopped fresh dill

Put onions and cucumbers into a bowl. Mix vinegar, sugar, salt and pepper. Stir until sugar is dissolved. Pour over vegetables. Sprinkle with the fresh, chopped dill. Refrigerate several hours. Serves 4 to 6.

Sanibel Salad

🍃 *This is our favorite salad when we go to Sanibel. I guess I don't make it much at home because I seldom find the beautiful big avocadoes that are essential for this salad.*

For four people:
3 or 4 fresh ripe tomatoes
1 large ripe avocado
3 slices of red onion, separated into rings (or sweet white
   onion)
   chopped fresh parsley
   Good Seasons Classic Herb or Old Fashion French salad
   dressing mix (I use my Mixed Herb Vinegar for the
   vinegar part of the recipe, but regular vinegar will do)

Peel tomatoes and avocado. Remove pit from avocado. Slice tomatoes into rather thick slices. Slice avocadoes into ½" slices. Put tomato slices, avocado slices, and red onion rings into a glass serving bowl. Sprinkle fresh chopped parsley over top. Prepare the dressing and drizzle about ⅓ to ½ cup over the vegetables. Do not toss or the avocado slices will break. Cover dish with plastic wrap and refrigerate for an hour before serving.

Fresh Herbed Tomato Salad

½ cup fresh parsley leaves
1 tablespoon fresh tarragon leaves, or 1 teaspoon dried
1 clove garlic, chopped
1 egg
½ cup good olive oil
¼ cup red wine vinegar
½ teaspoon salt
    freshly ground pepper
4 or 5 tomatoes, peeled, cored, sliced

Mince parsley, tarragon and garlic in a blender or food processor. Add the egg, oil, vinegar and salt and pepper. Process on-off 5 or 6 times to blend. Arrange tomato slices on a serving platter. Pour the dressing over. Serve to 6 or 8 people. If you happen to have some wonderful cheese on hand (don't need much — ¼ to ½ cup) crumble it on top of the salad. I use Roquefort if I have it, or bleu, or Feta, or even a little shredded Mozzarella.

Mediterranean Salad

≥ *This mixed salad is good with most any dressing, but try the Buttermilk Ranch-Style on page 122 sometime on it. There are no exact measurements.*

Combine in a large salad bowl: chopped **iceberg lettuce** (or other fresh lettuces), chopped **fresh ripe tomatoes**, halved **ripe olives**, cubed, good quality **Feta cheese**, chopped **green onions**, sliced fresh **cucumber**, cubed, good quality **salami**, chopped **fresh parsley**. Toss all together and serve with your favorite dressing.

A Thymely Footnote . . . Angelica is a spectacular tropical-looking herb with huge leaves and flowers. It is a biennial that produces flowers the second year. It likes cool, moist conditions. Angelica stems can be candied and used in fruitcakes. All parts of Angelica are aromatic and edible.

Budapest Salad

I got this wonderful recipe from a hotel dining room overlooking the Danube River. Did you know that Budapest is really two cities divided by the Danube River? Buda is on one side of the river and Pest is on the other side. Buda is the pretty side.

2	or 3 firm cucumbers, peeled and sliced very thin
1½	teaspoons salt
1	cup sour cream
1	tablespoon red wine vinegar
1	tablespoon chopped green onion
1	teaspoon sugar
1	teaspoon chopped fresh dill
	Hungarian (of course!) sweet paprika to sprinkle on top

Combine cucumbers and salt in a bowl. Cover with plastic wrap and refrigerate for an hour or two. Drain the cucumber slices and pat dry with paper towels. In another bowl, combine the sour cream, vinegar, onion, sugar and a little freshly ground pepper. Add cucumbers to this sour cream mixture and toss gently to distribute the cream mixture. Cover salad and refrigerate two hours or more until serving time (but probably no more than four or five hours, or salad might get watery). At serving time, sprinkle salad with the fresh, snipped dill and then a good dash of paprika. Distribute salad on four lettuce leaves and serve to 4 lucky people.

Sugared Grapes

I use these little clusters of grapes to decorate the turkey platter at Thanksgiving time, or to decorate a gelatin salad.

Wash small, firm **clusters of grapes (white or purple)** and let them dry completely. Whip **one egg white** with **2 tablespoons of water.** Brush this egg white mixture all over the grape clusters, a few at a time. Roll clusters in **granulated sugar.** Lay in a single layer on waxed paper and let them dry thoroughly. For a beautiful centerpiece, fill a glass bowl with these grape clusters (handle them carefully so you don't knock off the sugar coating). Tuck a grape leaf or two into the bowl — pretty.

Walnut & Roquefort Salad

Southern France is famous for many wonderful foods. Two of them are Roquefort cheese and walnuts. The French put the two together in a terrific salad. The best salad of this kind I ever had was in a little outdoor café in the medieval walled town of Sarlat. If I could, I'd go there every summer!

- **4 ounces walnut halves**
- **3 tablespoons white wine vinegar, or white vinegar**
  freshly ground pepper to taste
  dash or two of salt
- **½ cup good olive oil**
- **1 head romaine lettuce, cleaned, dried and torn into pieces (If head isn't large, use 2 medium sized ones)**
- **6 or 8 green onions, chopped (use green tops, too)**
- **4 ounces Roquefort cheese, crumbled (only the real will do)**

Toast walnuts in a heavy skillet for about 5 minutes over direct heat on top of the stove. Shake skillet occasionally. Remove nuts and cool. Make a dressing of the vinegar, salt and pepper. Whisk in the olive oil, a little at a time. Combine the romaine, green onions, cheese and walnuts in a large bowl. Pour dressing over salad and toss gently. Serve immediately. Serves 4.

For this salad, you *must* toast the walnuts. You *must* use real Roquefort cheese, and you *must* use romaine for the greens.

Fluffy Cranberry Salad

- **2 cups raw cranberries, ground**
- **3 cups tiny marshmallows**
- **¾ cup sugar**
- **2 cups diced Red or Yellow Delicious apples, unpeeled**
- **½ cup seedless green grapes**
- **½ cup chopped walnuts or pecans**
- **¼ teaspoon salt**
- **1 cup whipping cream, whipped**

Combine cranberries, marshmallows and sugar. Cover and chill overnight. Add apples, grapes, nuts and salt. Fold in whipped cream. Chill several hours or overnight. Serve in your prettiest glass or crystal bowl, or serve in lettuce cups. Beautiful! Serves 6.

Frosted Apricot Salad

🍃 *This was a favorite of Mother's. Be sure to save the drained juices for the dressing.*

1 6 ounce package orange gelatin
3 cups boiling water
½ cup apricot juice
2 cups miniature marshmallows
1 1 pound, 13 ounce can apricot halves, drained and
     chopped
1 9 ounce can pineapple tidbits, drained

Add boiling water to the gelatin. Stir well. Add miniature marshmallows and stir until marshmallows are melted. Add the ½ cup apricot juice. Stir and set aside to cool. When cool, add chopped apricots and pineapple tidbits. Pour into a 9" x 13" pan or dish and chill in refrigerator until salad is gelled.

Make the following topping:
1½ tablespoons cornstarch   ½ cup apricot juice
¼ cup sugar   ½ cup pineapple juice
1 beaten egg

Combine ingredients and cook slowly, stirring constantly. Cover and refrigerate. When cool, add **1 cup whipped cream** to topping. Spread on top of salad. Delicious!

Easy Frozen Fruit Salad

1 8 ounce package cream cheese, softened
¾ cup sugar
1 20 ounce can crushed pineapple, drained
1 10 ounce package frozen strawberries, thawed
2 bananas, diced
1 8 ounce container Cool Whip or La Creme dessert
     topping

Mix together cream cheese and sugar. Add drained pineapple, the strawberries, bananas and Cool Whip. Stir together gently. Put in a loaf pan or into individual molds. Freeze. Remove from freezer 10 minutes before serving.

Pat's Heavenly Apple Salad

1   6 ounce package lemon gelatin
2   cups boiling water
2   cups miniature marshmallows
1   cup cold water
1   9 ounce can crushed pineapple, drained
2   large apples, peeled and diced (I like Red or Yellow Delicious)
½   cup chopped pecans

Dissolve gelatin in boiling water. Add marshmallows and stir until melted. Sir in 1 cup of cold water. Chill until the mixture is the consistency of unbeaten egg whites. Add diced apples, drained pineapple and nuts. Pour into a 9" x 13" pan or dish and chill until firm.

For the dressing: combine ¾ **cup sugar, 2 tablespoons fresh lemon juice** and **2 beaten eggs** in the top of a double boiler. Cook over simmering water, stirring constantly until mixture thickens. Cover and cool. Whip **1 cup heavy cream** and fold into the cooled cooked mixture. Spread on salad.

Favorite Cranberry Salad

🍃 *I've worked on this recipe for years — it's finally just right!*

1   10 ounce package fresh cranberries, picked over and washed
4   cups water
¼   teaspoon baking soda
2   cups sugar
3   3 ounce boxes strawberry gelatin
4   cups miniature marshmallows
2   cups apple, peeled and diced
1   cup chopped nuts, optional
1   9 ounce can crushed pineapple, drained
2   navel oranges, peeled and sectioned
1   or 2 cups seedless green or red grapes, halved

Cook cranberries in the 4 cups water to a boil. Add soda and stir. Simmer 10 minutes. Stir in sugar, gelatin and marshmallows. Stir until melted. Let mixture cool. Add apples, nuts, pineapple, orange sections and grapes. Pour into one 9" x 13" pan and one 8" x 8" pan. Chill until firm. Will serve 20 or more.

Nicoise Salad (Greek Salad)

Several have asked for this recipe, so I thought I'd include it here.

3   cups potato slices (boil potatoes and slice ¼" thick)
1   pound fresh green beans, cooked whole (only until barely tender, then drained)
1   7 ounce can best quality white tuna
4   ounces good olive oil
4   ounces vinegar
1   teaspoon salt
    freshly ground black pepper
2   teaspoons Dijon mustard
3   tomatoes (fresh), quartered
¼   cup sliced black olives

Mix the cooked potatoes, beans and drained tuna in a bowl. Make a dressing of the next five ingredients. Pour over the potatoes, beans and tuna and mix gently. To serve, put a mound of salad on 4 to 6 lettuce-lined salad plates. Sprinkle a few sliced olives over the top and add the tomato quarters. Serves 4 to 6. Use only fresh green beans.

Fruit Salad in Orange Cups

6   large navel oranges
1   cup miniature marshmallows
1   cup diced pineapple
1   cup sliced bananas
1   cup mayonnaise
⅓   cup orange juice
    whipped cream
    candied cherries

Cut oranges in half. Scoop out the pulp and cut into small cubes. To the orange cubes add marshmallows, pineapple, bananas and any other fresh fruit you desire (such as grapes, peaches, etc.). Thin the mayonnaise with orange juice and fold the fruit into the mayonnaise. Heap the fruit in orange cups. Top each cup with a dollop of whipped cream and a candied cherry. Serve with plain sugar cookies. Serves 12. If there isn't enough fruit to fill the twelve orange halves, just add more fresh fruit. Prepare these ahead of time, cover each orange with plastic wrap and refrigerate. Serve orange half on a lettuce leaf.

The Real Waldorf Salad

&a From the kitchen of the Waldorf-Astoria Hotel in (what else?) the Big Apple!

 4   **cups cubed Red Delicious apples**
 2   **cups sliced celery**
 4½ **teaspoons fresh lemon juice, divided**
 ½   **cup sliced pitted dates**
 ½   **cup chopped walnuts, toasted***
 ½   **cup heavy or whipping cream**
 2   **tablespoons mayonnaise**
 ½   **teaspoon honey**

Combine apples and celery (do not peel the apples). Toss with 3 teaspoons lemon juice. Add dates and toasted walnuts. In a small bowl, whip cream until soft peaks form. Fold in mayonnaise, 1½ teaspoons lemon juice and honey. Toss with the fruit and nuts. Serve on lettuce leaves to 6 or 8 people.

*To toast walnuts: Drizzle about 1 tablespoon melted butter over the ½ cup chopped walnuts. Toss all together. Spread on a cookie sheet and toast in a 350° oven for 4 or 5 minutes, stirring a time or two. Anytime a recipe calls for toasted nuts, follow this method. For 1 cup nuts, use 1 to 2 tablespoons melted butter.

Please do *not* use a whipped dairy topping in this salad. Use only *real* whipped cream and *real* mayonnaise, not salad dressing. The Waldorf-Astoria would never forgive you!

Buttermilk Ranch-Style Salad Dressing

Blend together in a blender or food processor:
 1   **cup buttermilk**
 1   **cup cottage cheese**
 2   **tablespoons chopped green onion**
 2   **tablespoons lemon juice**
 1   **teaspoon salt**
 1   **tablespoon chopped fresh chives**
 1   **to 2 cloves garlic, chopped (depends on your taste)**

Store dressing in a covered container in the refrigerator. This dressing is good on the Mediterranean Salad.

Hot Spinach Salad

🍃 *The first spinach from the garden goes here!*

1 pound fresh spinach, washed and stems removed
1 pound fresh mushrooms, cleaned and sliced
1 small red onion, sliced thin

Put spinach , mushrooms and onion slices into a large salad bowl. Make a dressing of:

10 or 12 slices bacon, diced
½ cup cider vinegar
⅓ cup water
3 to 4 tablespoons sugar
½ teaspoon salt
  dash of pepper

Fry bacon until crisp. Reduce heat. Add vinegar, water, sugar, salt and pepper. Simmer about 5 minutes. Adjust seasonings. To serve, add hot dressing to bowl ingredients and toss. Serve immediately. Serves 4 to 6. Sometimes I'll add a couple of sliced hard boiled eggs to the salad ingredients.

Russian Salad Dressing

½ cup sugar
2 teaspoons paprika
2 teaspoons celery salt
1 teaspoon salt
1 small onion, grated
1 cup salad oil
½ cup cider vinegar

Mix all ingredients thoroughly. Make sure sugar is dissolved. Store in a covered pint jar in the refrigerator. Stir or shake well before using.

Herb Salad Dressing

ઈ *This is an unusual mixture of a fresh dressing and a store-bought dressing. The combination is really delicious.*

1   cup vegetable oil
6   tablespoons tarragon vinegar, your homemade mixed herb vinegar, or as a last resort, cider vinegar
½   teaspoon salt
½   teaspoon dry mustard
    dash of freshly ground pepper
3   cloves garlic, minced
1   tablespoon chopped fresh sweet marjoram , or 1 teaspoon dried
1   tablespoon chopped fresh sage, or 1 teaspoon dried
1   tablespoon chopped fresh thyme, or 1 teaspoon dried
1   ¾ ounce package Good Seasons Garlic and Herbs salad dressing mix

Mix the first 9 ingredients together in a quart jar. Mix the Good Seasons package according to package directions — be sure to use the **same vinegar** that you used in the fresh herb dressing. Combine the 2 dressings and mix thoroughly. Put dressing in the prettiest corked bottle you have (a wine bottle is fine). Shake well before using each time. It gets better and better as it sets in the refrigerator. The addition of the Good Seasons dressing mix adds just the right zip to this dressing. Everyone asks for this recipe!

Honey-Mustard Salad Dressing

ઈ *There is a great seafood restaurant on Sanibel Island, Florida, called Mc T's. Their house dressing is one of the best I've tasted. It was printed in the newspaper food section one day and a friend was lucky enough to see it. Thanks to Vivian Gruber for passing it on to me!*

¼   cup cider vinegar
¼   cup puréed onion
¼   cup sugar
1   cup honey

1   6 ounce jar Gulden's Spicy Brown Mustard
1½ cups mayonnaise
1¼ cups buttermilk

Combine all ingredients and mix well. Refrigerate between uses.

Roquefort Dressing

½ cup crumbled Roquefort*
1½ cups sour cream
¼ cup Half and Half cream
2 tablespoons mayonnaise
1 tablespoon olive oil
2 tablespoons white wine vinegar, or distilled white vinegar if you don't have white wine vinegar
a little cayenne pepper

In a blender or food processor, blend first six ingredients together until the dressing is smooth. Add a dash of cayenne pepper and stir. Store in a covered jar in the refrigerator. Makes about 2 cups dressing.

*Did you know that *real* Roquefort cheese *only* comes from certain caves in a mountain in France? We have many bleu cheeses that are similar to Roquefort in looks and taste, but there is only one true Roquefort. There are several brand names, but they all age in these same caves. I think this helps to explain why *real* Roquefort cheese is so expensive. There are always red lambs (or lamb) imprinted on real Roquefort packages. So, if you see a cheese in your store that says Roquefort, but has no red lambs on the package, it isn't the real thing! A good brand to look for is the Society brand. I was fortunate to get to go through the Society caves in southern France. It was a wonderful day!

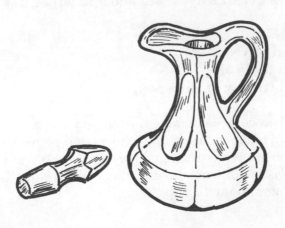

Bleu Cheese Dressing

2   garlic cloves, peeled
2   cups mayonnaise
1   cup sour cream
¼   cup chopped fresh chives
2   teaspoons Worcestershire sauce
2   teaspoons fresh lemon juice
½   teaspoon freshly ground pepper
4   ounces bleu cheese, crumbled

Mince the garlic in a blender or food processor. Blend in rest of ingredients except the cheese. Pour blended ingredients into a bowl. Stir in the crumbled bleu cheese. Store in a covered container in the refrigerator. Makes about 3 cups. There are lots of good bleu cheeses from the U.S. An especially good one to look for is Maytag Bleu, made in Newton, Iowa. To learn a little more about cheeses, see the article on "Cheese," in *A Potpourri of Ideas* section.

Basil Mayonnaise with Lemon

🍃 *If you ever tasted this dressing on poached chicken breasts or cooked shrimp, you would plant some basil for sure. It is wonderful!*

5   tablespoons fresh lemon juice (*only* fresh)
2   cups fresh basil leaves, washed and wiped dry
1   egg
1   egg yolk
1   cup good olive oil
⅓   cup vegetable oil
    salt and freshly ground pepper

In a food processor, combine the lemon juice, basil leaves, whole egg, egg yolk, 1½ teaspoons salt and ½ teaspoon pepper. Process until smooth. With the machine running, slowly add both oils until the mayonnaise forms and is smooth and creamy. May need to add a little more salt and pepper. Makes about 1½ cups.

Herbed Salad Dressing

1⅓ cups French tarragon vinegar
1   cup safflower oil, or other light oil
⅔ cup olive oil
4   teaspoons mayonnaise
3   cloves garlic, minced fine
2   teaspoons Dijon mustard
1   teaspoon salt
1   teaspoon brown sugar
1   teaspoon dried thyme, OR 1 tablespoon fresh, chopped
½ teaspoon dried tarragon, OR ½ tablespoon fresh, chopped

Combine all ingredients in a one quart jar with a lid. Screw on lid and shake well. Store in the jar, tightly covered, and keep refrigerated until ready to use. Shake or stir well before each use. Do not make in blender or processor because the herb leaves shouldn't be pulverized. Makes about 3 cups.

Herbed Cream Cheese Salad Dressing

1   8 ounce package cream cheese, softened
½ cup sour cream
½ cup chopped fresh parsley leaves
½ cup fresh dill sprigs (no coarse stems)
½ cup chopped green onion
1   tablespoon white-wine vinegar, or dill vinegar
¼ cup vegetable oil
2   teaspoons Worcestershire sauce
2   tablespoons milk

In a food processor or blender, blend the first five ingredients until the mixture is smooth. With the motor running (on processor), add rest of ingredients and salt and pepper to taste. Blend until it is all combined well. Makes about 2 cups of *marvelous* creamy salad dressing.

Basic Oil and Vinegar

Combine:
- 3 cups light, good oil
- 1 cup red wine vinegar
- 4 teaspoons Dijon mustard
- 2 teaspoons sugar
- 2 teaspoons salt
- 1 teaspoon pepper

This makes a quart of good dressing to have on hand in the refrigerator. In the summer, chop some favorite fresh herbs into your green salad, then dress with this simple dressing. Very good. The French probably shudder at what we call "French" dressing. A *real* French dressing is *only* oil, vinegar or lemon juice, salt and freshly ground pepper.

Vinaigrette for Tomatoes or Asparagus

- 1 cup good quality olive oil or vegetable oil
- ⅓ cup wine vinegar (or if you've made herb vinegar, now's the time to use some!)
- 2 teaspoons dried oregano leaves, or 2 tablespoons fresh
- 1 teaspoon salt
- ½ teaspoon pepper
- ½ teaspoon dry mustard
- 1 teaspoon dried basil, or 1 tablespoon fresh
- 2 cloves garlic, minced

Combine all ingredients in a quart jar. Shake well. Pour vinaigrette over thick tomato slices (fresh garden tomatoes are best) or tender-crisp cooked fresh asparagus spears. Let marinate in refrigerator for 2 hours before serving. Drain and arrange tomatoes or asparagus on a platter lined with lettuce leaves. Sprinkle a little chopped onion and chopped fresh parsley on top. (Save the dressing for a great tossed salad.) Makes 1⅓ cups vinaigrette.

FISH
AND
SEAFOOD

Fettucine and Salmon

¼ cup oil
1 garlic clove, sliced thin
1 bunch fresh broccoli, cut into flowerets
½ pound fresh mushrooms, sliced
2 carrots, sliced
2 or 3 green onions, chopped coarsely
¾ teaspoon salt
12 ounces fettucine noodles
2 tablespoons butter or oleo
2 tablespoons flour
2½ cups milk
1 chicken flavor bouillon cube, or 1 teaspoon granules
¼ cup grated Parmesan cheese
1 7½ ounce can red salmon, best quality, drained, bones
and skin removed, and flaked

In a skillet over medium heat, sauté garlic in hot oil until it is brown. Remove garlic and discard it. Add the prepared vegetables and salt and cook and stir until they are tender-crisp, 4 or 5 minutes. Prepare the fettucine. Drain it and put it back in the cooking pot with lid on to keep it warm. Make the sauce. In a saucepan, melt the butter. Stir in the flour and cook a minute or so. Stir in the milk and bouillon and cook, stirring constantly, until the sauce thickens. Remove from heat and stir in the cheese. Stir again. Toss fettucine with the salmon, cheese sauce, and vegetables in the fettucine pot. Gently and carefully heat all together until it's warmed through — don't cook anymore here, just warm it. Will serve about 6, or 4 hungry ones.

This basic fettucine, cheese sauce and vegetable mixture can be used as the basis for other dishes. Another time, omit the salmon and use sautéed chicken breast pieces. Add some chopped fresh herbs in the summer time — I use a little basil, a little Greek oregano, a little thyme, a little parsley.

A Thymely Footnote . . . A nice ornamental clump for the garden is comfrey. It is a perennial. It used to be favored for teas, but has recently been discovered to be harmful if taken internally.

Seafood Fettucine

೩ This is a pure, unadulterated pasta dish — just like you might have in a fine Italian restaurant.

  about 1 pound fettucine noodles
2 tablespoons butter
2 or 3 cloves garlic, chopped fine
1 small onion, chopped fine
1 pound fresh seafood (shrimp, scallops, crab, etc. use one or a combination)
2 cups whipping cream
½ cup grated Romano cheese
½ cup grated Parmesan cheese

Cook fettucine to al dente stage (just done — *not* overcooked) in boiling salted water. Rinse well and set aside. In a heavy large sauté pan, melt butter. Sauté onion and garlic until onion is transparent. (Do not brown). Stir all the time. Add seafood and sauté. Add whipping cream and stir until cream is warm. Add grated cheeses and heat over low heat until cheese melts and sauce thickens. You can increase heat a little, but you must stir all the time. Add cooked fettucine and lift and toss until noodles are coated with the sauce. Serve to 4 or 5 lucky people.

Marinade for Shrimp

1 cup good olive oil
1 teaspoon salt
2 or 3 cloves garlic, chopped very fine
  juice of 1 lemon
  about 1 teaspoon Tabasco sauce (or to taste)
1 teaspoon dried oregano OR 1 tablespoon chopped fresh
½ cup chili sauce

Shell and devein 2 pounds of fresh, uncooked shrimp. Mix marinade ingredients together. Add shrimp to marinade and refrigerate several hours. Thread shrimp on skewers and grill over hot coals for 2 or 3 minutes on each side, or broil in the oven, if desired. Save marinade and use again within a week or so. It keeps well in the refrigerator. (If olive oil congeals in the refrigerator, zap it a few seconds in your microwave, or just let it set at room temperature until you can shake it). These are incredibly good. Serves 4 to 6.

Paella

This is a wonderful dish from Spain. The closer to the ocean, the better the Paella (the more fresh seafood). If I can't get all the fresh seafood necessary for this dish, I add more chicken or more shrimp. Saffron is also native to Spain and it is the dominant seasoning in Paella. It's what makes the rice yellow.

5	tablespoons good olive oil
1	large onion, coarsley chopped
2	cloves garlic, finely chopped
1	green pepper, cut into strips
1	red pepper, cut into strips
6	chicken thighs
6	chicken breast halves (3 whole breasts)
2	cups uncooked rice
½	cup dry white wine
1	cup baked ham, cut into cubes
1	pound sweet Italian sausage, broiled and then sliced*
1	teaspoon saffron threads
3½	cups chicken broth, heated
½	teaspoon sweet paprika
½	teaspoon dried thyme, or 1 teaspoon fresh
1	dozen mussels, cleaned (optional)
16	medium shrimp, shelled and deveined
1	cup frozen peas
	chopped fresh parsley

Heat 3 tablespoons olive oil in a very large sauté pan. Sauté onions and peppers over moderately high heat until they are soft. Stir in garlic and heat through. Use a slotted spoon and remove sautéed vegetables from pan to a bowl. Add other 2 tablespoons olive oil and sauté chicken over fairly high heat until it is golden. Remove and add to vegetables. Add rice to the skillet and stir well over high heat to coat rice. Immediately add wine and stir well. Return chicken and vegetables to pan. Add ham and prepared sausages. In a small saucepan, dissolve the saffron in hot chicken broth. Add to the sauté pan. Bring to a boil. Stir in paprika and thyme. Cover and simmer for 15 to 20 minutes, until chicken is tender. Add shrimp, mussels (if you have them) and peas. Continue to cook until shrimp are pink and mussel shells have opened and rice is tender. Taste. May need to add salt and pepper and even more saffron.

Sprinkle fresh chopped parsley over the top and serve to 8 or 10. You can add cherrystone clams or small lobster tails or pieces of firm cooked fish to your Paella. It's an interesting combination and a delicious one. Toss a good salad, add crusty bread and a good bottle of white wine (or Sangria) and enjoy a fabulous meal!

*The true Spanish Paella calls for Chorizo sausages. They are not readily available where I live, so I substitute the sweet Italian.

Linguine with Scallops and Herbs

  ½ **pound linguine**
  ½ **cup (1 stick) unsalted butter**
  1 **pound bay scallops, halved crosswise if they're large**
  ½ **cup dry white wine**
  1 **cup chicken broth**
  2 **tablespoons fresh lemon juice**
  ⅓ **cup minced green onions**
  ⅓ **cup minced fresh parsley**
  3 **tablespoons snipped fresh dill**
  1 **to 2 tablespoons drained capers, optional**

      In a large kettle of boiling salted water, cook linguine for 7 to 10 minutes, or until al dente, and drain it well. For the sauce: In a large skillet, heat the butter over moderately high heat. Sauté scallops for only about 2 minutes. Transfer the scallops with a slotted spoon to a plate. Add white wine, broth and lemon juice to the skillet and boil until the liquid is reduced by half. Add the onion, parsley, dill and capers and simmer for about 1 minute. Add scallops and the linguine and cook mixture over fairly high heat, stirring constantly, until all is heated through, 2 or 3 minutes at most. Serves 4.

*A Thymely Footnote . . . A great ornamental herb is **lamb's ear**. It is a perennial and will multiply rapidly. It has silvery, wooly foliage that is ideal for the border. It produces tall purple flower stalks which I keep cut out — I think this keeps the foliage nicer. Lamb's ear is not culinary.*

Wild Rice with Shrimp and Mushrooms

⊱ A nice luncheon dish.

2½ cups chicken broth
1½ cups wild rice, rinsed
½ teaspoon salt
2 tablespoons butter
½ cup finely chopped onion
½ cup finely chopped celery
1 cup sliced fresh mushrooms
1 to 2 cups cooked, shelled and deveined medium shrimp
½ cup chopped fresh parsley

Bring broth to a boil in a two quart saucepan over high heat. Stir in rice and salt. Reduce heat to medium low. Cover and simmer until rice is tender and all the liquid is absorbed, 50 minutes to 1 hour. Melt butter in a large skillet or sauté pan over fairly high heat. Add onion and celery and sauté about 5 minutes. Reduce heat and add mushrooms and cook, stirring often, another 5 minutes. Add shrimp and cook until they are heated through, 1 to 2 minutes. Add the fresh parsley. Stir into the cooked rice. Serve with a wonderful green salad and a crusty bread. Serves 4.

Broiled Salmon with Herbed Lemon Butter

8 nice salmon fillets, fresh is best
¼ cup butter, melted
2 tablespoons lemon juice
2 tablespoons chopped fresh parsley
¼ teaspoon dried dill weed, OR 1 teaspoon fresh chopped
¼ teaspoon dried marjoram, OR 1 teaspoon fresh chopped
¼ teaspoon salt
   freshly ground pepper to taste

Line broiler pan with foil. Grease the rack. Lay fillets on greased rack. Combine remaining ingredients. Baste salmon with the butter mixture. Broil 4″ from heat, allowing 10 minutes cooking time per inch of thickness, or until salmon flakes easily with a fork. Do not turn salmon. Baste several times during broiling. Serves 8.

Shrimp Creole

    3 tablespoons butter
    1 medium size green pepper, chopped
    3 medium onions, chopped
  ¾ cup celery, chopped
    1 28 ounce can tomatoes
    1 16 ounce can tomato sauce
    1 to 1½ teaspoons salt
  ½ teaspoon (or less) pepper
       few dried red pepper flakes
    4 cups cooked and cleaned shrimps

Lightly sauté green pepper, onions and celery in butter in a large heavy skillet. Add tomatoes, tomato sauce and seasonings. Add shrimps and heat thoroughly, but don't overcook. Serve over cooked white rice. Serves 4.

Shrimp de Jonghue

    2 pounds cooked, deveined shrimps
    4 cloves garlic, diced fine
    1 cup butter
  ½ teaspoon dried tarragon, or 2 teaspoons chopped fresh
  ½ teaspoon dried parsley flakes, or 2 teaspoons chopped
       fresh
  ½ teaspoon dried chives, or 2 teaspoons chopped fresh
    1 tablespoon minced onion
  ¼ teaspoon dried thyme, or 1 teaspoon chopped fresh
  1½ teaspoons salt
  ¼ teaspoon pepper
       dash of nutmeg
  ½ cup Sherry (not cooking Sherry)
    1 cup dry bread crumbs

Heat oven to 400°. Divide shrimps into 6 or 8 individual greased baking dishes. Cook garlic in butter just until brown. Remove garlic pieces and discard. Add herbs, seasonings and Sherry. Turn off heat. Stir to combine well. Remove about ⅓ cup of the butter mixture and toss with the bread crumbs. Pour rest of butter over shrimps. Top each baking dish with buttered crumbs. Bake 15 minutes. Do not brown — just bake to a golden toasty brown. Especially good served with the Pilaf, page 175. Serves 6 or 8.

Treasure of the Sea

&ℴ *Here are 2 of the best seafood salads you'll ever eat. They are not inexpensive to make, but you'll be glad you splurged on these!*

1 **cup cooked lobster meat, diced**
1 **cup cooked crab meat**
1 **cup cooked shrimps (cut shrimps in half)**
1 **cup mayonnaise**
2 **tablespoons chili sauce**
1 **hard boiled egg, chopped**
½ **teaspoon salt, or to taste**
1 **tablespoon fresh lemon juice**
2 **tablespoons sweet pickle, chopped**
   lettuce leaves

Combine the seafood in a bowl. To make the dressing, blend together the mayonnaise, chili sauce, chopped hard boiled egg, salt, lemon juice and chopped sweet pickle. Gently combine dressing with the seafood. Divide the salad among 4 lettuce-lined salad plates. Garnish with a little **chopped fresh parsley** and **tomato wedges**. Serves 4.

Crab Louis

4 **lettuce leaves plus rest of head of lettuce**
3 **cups cooked crabmeat**
2 **tomatoes, cut into wedges**
2 **hard boiled eggs, cut into wedges**
   Louis dressing

Line 4 salad plates with lettuce leaves. Shred the remainder of the lettuce and put about 1 cupful on each plate. Divide crabmeat onto the 4 plates. Circle crabmeat with tomato and egg wedges. Sprinkle with a little salt. Pour ¼ cup (or more) Louis dressing over each salad.

Louis Dressing: Combine **1 cup mayonnaise, ¼ cup sour cream, ¼ cup chili sauce, ¼ cup finely chopped green onion** and **1 teaspoon fresh lemon juice**. Add **salt** to taste. Make dressing ahead of time and chill. Makes about 2 cups of dressing.

Easy Scampi

1½ sticks butter
¼   cup onion, chopped fine
3   garlic cloves, chopped fine
4   or 5 sprigs of parsley, leaves chopped
1   pound shrimp, shelled and deveined, but uncooked (or
    use 1½ pounds shrimp for five or six people)
⅓   cup dry white wine
2   tablespoons fresh lemon juice
    salt and pepper

Melt butter in medium skillet over low heat. Add onion, garlic and parsley and sauté 4 or 5 minutes. Do *not* brown the onion or garlic. Add shrimp to the skillet and stir and sauté until shrimp are pink. Remove shrimp and put them on a warm serving platter. Cover lightly to keep warm. Add wine and lemon juice to skillet and bring to a boil. Simmer for 2 or 3 minutes. Season with salt and pepper, if needed, and pour sauce over shrimp. Serve immediately. Serves 3 or 4.

Sanibel Fish

This is a great way to fix fresh fish. The lime juice marinates and tenderizes the fish as well as gives it a little zip. The fillets I use are grouper, red snapper, or shark (yes, shark — it's good!).

To serve four:
    About 2 pounds of fresh fish, cut into small fillets or
    strips about 1½" wide
¼   cup fresh lime juice
1   egg
¼   cup milk
1   cup or more flour
    oil
    salt and pepper

Put fish pieces into a bowl. Add lime juice and toss to coat all pieces. Marinate 15 to 30 minutes. Put about an inch of oil in a large skillet. Mix egg and milk together. Dip fish pieces into the egg mixture, then dredge in the flour. Shake off excess flour. Fry in hot oil until golden brown on all sides (won't take long). Drain pieces on paper towels. Salt and pepper to taste. Serve hot with tartar sauce.

Outdoor Grilled and Herbed Shrimps

1 stick unsalted butter, melted
¼ cup olive oil
¼ cup minced fresh herbs (parsley, or thyme, or
    marjoram, or Greek oregano — I use a combination of
    all four)
3 tablespoons fresh lemon juice
3 large garlic cloves, crushed
1 tablespoon minced shallot, or green onion
    salt and freshly ground pepper
2 pounds medium-large shrimps, shelled and deveined

Combine all ingredients, except shrimps, in a large bowl. Mix in shrimps. Marinate several hours in the refrigerator, stirring occasionally. (Butter will harden, so heat a few seconds in microwave so you can stir it.) Prepare outdoor barbecue with medium-hot coals. Thread shrimps on 8 narrow skewers. Grill about 2 minutes on each side. Do not overcook. Garnish with lemon, if desired. These are *wonderful* on the outdoor grill. Serves 6 or 8.

Herbed Shrimps in Garlic Butter

Shell and devein **36 large shrimps**, leaving the tails intact. Put shrimps in a large bowl and toss them with **1 teaspoon salt, 1 teaspoon dried oregano** (or 1 tablespoon chopped fresh) and **1 teaspoon dried thyme** (or 1 tablespoon chopped fresh). Cover and chill shrimps for an hour.

In another bowl, cream together ½ **cup butter**, softened, **4 garlic cloves**, minced, and **1 tablespoon fresh chopped parsley**. In a skillet, sauté ¼ **pound fresh mushrooms**, sliced, in ½ **cup butter** for 3 or 4 minutes. Divide the shrimps among 6 individual buttered baking dishes and top each with some of the sautéed mushrooms. Dot the mushrooms with the garlic butter and bake the shrimps in a 375° oven for about 12 minutes — 15 minutes at most. Serve with rice or wild rice. Absolutely delicious! Serves 6.

CHICKEN
AND
MEAT

Scalloped Chicken ⊂▭MOTHER♡▭⊃

🍂 *This is another recipe of mother's that I was so happy to find. Mother knew someone who worked in the old Chestnut Room in the Purdue University Memorial Union. This person gave mother (after much begging on mother's part!) the Chestnut Room's Scalloped Chicken recipe, which is really excellent. Notice that the recipe calls for a stewing hen — a fryer just isn't fat and rich enough.*

4½ to 5 pound stewing chicken, cooked, boned and cut up
1 quart white sauce (recipe follows)
3 cups buttered fresh bread crumbs (plus a few more for the top)

White Sauce
½ cup fat from the stewed chicken
½ cup flour
2 cups milk
2 cups rich chicken broth
2 teaspoons salt
dash or two of pepper
¼ teaspoon or more ground sage or poultry seasoning

Heat chicken fat in top of double boiler until fat is liquid. Stir in the flour until well-blended. Add milk and broth, stirring until smooth. Cook and stir until sauce thickens. Add seasonings. Spread a layer of buttered fresh bread crumbs in bottom of a greased casserole. Add a layer of chicken, then half the white sauce. Add the second layer of crumbs, chicken and sauce. Lastly, sprinkle top with more bread crumbs. Bake at 350° for 30 to 40 minutes, or until hot and bubbly. Serves 8. It's delicious!

Buttered Fresh Bread Crumbs (Food Processor)

For about 4 cups of crumbs, process slices of white bread until you can measure 4 cups of crumbs. (Difficult to tell how many slices of bread because of differences in size of slice, thickness of slice, etc.) Put the 4 cups crumbs in a large bowl (these will be nice soft and fluffy crumbs). Melt 1 stick butter, pour over crumbs and toss well.

Chicken Normandy

❧ *I think the best food in all of France is from the Normandy region. The area is particularly famous for apples — Calvados is their apple brandy. Ciders, fresh and hard, are served everywhere. The area is also famous for its seafood, especially oysters and mussels, and for rich dairy products. So, it's not surprising that these products show up in much of their cooking.*

For four servings:
- 1 **frying chicken, about 3 pounds, cut up**
- 3 **tablespoons oil**
- ½ **teaspoon salt**
   freshly ground pepper
- 12 **small white onions, peeled**
- 1 **cup apple juice**
- 1 **small bay leaf**
- 3 **small apples, cored and sliced**
- 2 **or 3 tablespoons butter**
- ¼ **cup apple brandy (your homemade would be good here) OR cider**
- 1 **tablespoon flour**
- ½ **cup whipping cream**

Brown chicken in hot oil in a large heavy saucepan. Brown about 5 minutes on each side. Salt and pepper to taste. Remove chicken pieces to a platter. In same skillet, brown onions 3 or 4 minutes, shaking pan to brown all sides. Pour off excess fat. Return chicken to pan with onions. Add apple juice and bay leaf. Bring to a boil. Cover and lower heat. Simmer until chicken pieces are done and tender. Meanwhile, sauté apple slices in the butter in another skillet for 3 to 4 minutes, or until tender, but not mushy. Put chicken and onions in serving dish — I usually use a 9″ x 13″ Pyrex glass dish. Cover and keep warm. Skim any fat from skillet and remove the bay leaf. Measure out ¾ cup of the pan juices. Combine the ¾ cup juices with the apply brandy. Boil hard for 3 minutes. Reduce heat to low. Stir flour into the cream in a small bowl. Stir into the brandy mixture and whisk until smooth. Add the apple slices and cook gently for 1 minute to heat through. You want to heat it thoroughly, but don't let it boil. Spoon sauce over chicken and put into a 350° oven for 5 minutes. Serve immediately. Be sure each person gets chicken, onions and apple slices. Serves 4.

Chicken Wild Rice Casserole

1 6 ounce package long grain and wild rice
¼ cup butter
¼ cup flour
1 13 ounce can evaporated milk
½ cup chicken broth
2½ to 3 cups chopped, cooked chicken
1 4 to 6 ounce can sliced mushrooms, drained
⅓ cup chopped green pepper
1 small jar diced pimiento
¼ cup slivered almonds, toasted

Prepare rice according to package directions and set aside. Melt butter in a heavy saucepan over low heat. Add flour and stir until smooth. Cook 1 minute, stirring all the time. Gradually add milk and broth and cook over medium heat, stirring constantly, until thickened and bubbly. Combine in a large bowl, the sauce, rice, chicken, mushrooms, green pepper and pimiento. Pour into a greased 9″ x 13″ baking dish. Sprinkle the top with almonds. Cover and refrigerate until ready to bake — several hours or overnight. Bring to room temperature, then bake at 350° for 35 to 45 minutes. Serves 6 or 8.

Madeira Sauce

Serve this delicious sauce over baked chicken breasts.

After you have browned 4 to 6 chicken breasts, pour the grease out of the skillet but do not wipe skillet out — leave crusty bits. Add ½ **cup Madeira** wine and boil it, scraping up the brown bits. Boil until skillet contents are reduced to about two tablespoons. Add ¾ **cup chicken broth** and bring mixture to a boil, stirring for 1 minute. Dissolve **2 teaspoons cornstarch** in about **a tablespoon of water** (may need a few drops more) and stir this mixture into the skillet. Use a whisk and simmer the sauce, whisking for a minute or so. Strain, if desired. Will serve 4 or 6.

Champagne Sauce

In a three quart saucepan over low heat, in **1 tablespoon but-ter,** cook **1 shallot,** minced, until tender, stirring occasionally. Increase heat to medium high. Add ½ **cup Champagne or sparkling white wine.** Heat to boiling and boil for 5 minutes. Reduce heat to medium and stir in **1 cup whipping cream** and a **dash of salt.** Heat to boiling and boil gently for 2 minutes. Another good sauce to dress up plain broiled or baked chicken breasts. Also good on baked pork tenderloin.

Thyme-Lime Chicken

2   **whole large chicken breasts (cut in half to make 4 pieces)**
4   **chicken thighs**
2   **limes**
2   **tablespoons olive oil**
2   **tablespoons butter or oleo**
1   **teaspoon dried thyme OR 1 tablespoon chopped fresh**
½   **to ¾ teaspoon salt**
    freshly ground pepper
1   **clove garlic, minced fine**

Grate about 1 teaspoon peel from the limes. Squeeze 2 table-spoons juice from limes. In a small pan, combine over low heat, the peel, the juice, olive oil, butter, chopped thyme, salt, pepper and garlic. Stir and heat until butter melts. Wipe chicken pieces dry. Put chicken in a broiler pan, without the rack, and brush some of the butter mixture over all sides of chicken. Broil 8 or 9 inches from source of heat 15 to 20 minutes per side, basting frequently with the butter. Finish the broil-ing with skin side up. It may take less time, or more time, depending on your broiler, thickness of chicken meat, etc. Serve a breast half and a thigh to each person. Garnish with fresh thyme sprigs. Serve this with wild rice (or any rice) and a fresh green vegetable. Serves 4. The first fresh thyme of the season goes into this dish at my house!

Chicken Cashew

1 to 1½ pounds chicken breast (remove the skin and
   bones and cut meat into ½" strips)
2 tablespoons Sherry
2 tablespoons soy sauce
1 tablespoon cornstarch
2 tablespoons salad or peanut oil
2 cloves garlic, chopped
½ teaspoon salt
1 pound fresh mushrooms, cleaned and sliced
1 4 ounce can water chestnuts, sliced and drained
1 4 ounce can bamboo shoots, optional
1 cup snow peas
1 cup cashews
1½ cups chicken broth
2 tablespoons cornstarch
1 tablespoon soy sauce

Mix the 2 tablespoons Sherry, 2 tablespoons soy sauce and 1 tablespoon cornstarch together in a bowl. Add chicken strips. Cover and marinate about 2 hours. Heat oil in a wok or large electric skillet. Add the garlic and salt and cook until golden. Drain the chicken strips, save the marinade. Add chicken to the hot oil and stir — be sure not to overcook. Cook and stir about 2 minutes. Add mushrooms, water chestnuts, bamboo shoots, snow peas and cashews and cook and stir over high heat for 3 or 4 minutes. To the first marinade the chicken strips were in, add the 1½ cups chicken broth, the 2 tablespoons cornstarch and the 1 tablespoon soy sauce. Blend all together until smooth and add to the wok mixture. Continue to cook until sauce thickens and bubbles, but do *not* overcook. Serve with white rice. Serves 4 generously. Very good. Carol Sermersheim gave me this recipe.

*A Thymely Footnote . . . Two very showy, new basils are **Purple Ruffles basil** and **Green Ruffles basil**. They aren't the best basils to cook with, but the Purple Ruffles makes the most beautiful and fragrant ruby red vinegar you've ever seen! I particularly like this vinegar in marinades. Purple Ruffles was an All-America Selection plant winner in 1987.*

Oriental Chicken with Peaches

For four persons:
- 8 pieces of chicken (4 chicken breast halves and 4 legs or thighs, for example)
- 2 tablespoons butter or oleo
- 1 1 pound can sliced peaches in heavy syrup
- 1 tablespoon cornstarch
- 1 teaspoon grated fresh gingerroot (available at most supermarkets — store unused gingerroot in refrigerator)
- 1 cup water chestnuts, drained, or cashews (I love the cashews!)

Rinse and dry chicken pieces. In a large sauté pan, cook chicken in hot butter over medium heat until it is tender enough to pierce with a fork, 10 to 15 minutes or longer. Remove chicken from pan and keep it warm. Drain peaches. Add water to the reserved syrup to make ¾ cup. Stir cornstarch and gingerroot into the peach juice. Add this to the sauté pan and cook and stir until sauce thickens. Add peaches and water chestnuts or cashews and heat through. Salt and pepper, if needed. Spoon peaches and sauce over the chicken. Serve with white rice. Delicious!

Old Fashioned Oyster Dressing ⊂ MOTHER ○

- 2 1 pound loaves of bread
- 1 quart oysters
- 4 cups chicken or turkey broth
- 4 eggs, beaten
- 1 teaspoon salt, or to taste
   pepper to taste
- ½ cup celery, chopped fine
- ½ cup onion, chopped fine
- 2 or 3 tablespoons butter
- 2 to 3 tablespoons ground sage
- ½ teaspoon poultry seasoning

Tear or cut bread into pieces. Sauté celery and onion in butter. Add to the bread. Add all other ingredients. Mother always said good dressing should be soupy, so you may need to add more broth. Bake in a big casserole (greased) or a roaster pan at 350° for 1½ hours, or until browned and set. I think oyster dressing is best cooked *outside* the bird. Will serve 10 or 12.

Country Style Chicken Kiev

⅓ cup dry bread crumbs
2 tablespoons grated Parmesan cheese
1 teaspoon dried basil
1 teaspoon dried oregano
½ teaspoon garlic salt
¼ teaspoon salt
2 whole chicken breasts, split
⅔ cut butter, melted
¼ cup white wine or apple cider
¼ cup chopped green onion
¼ cup chopped fresh parsley

Combine first 6 ingredients. Set aside. Dip chicken pieces into melted butter. Set remaining butter aside. Roll buttered chicken pieces in the seasoned crumbs. Place, skin side up, in a shallow casserole. Bake at 375° for about 45 minutes. To leftover butter, add the remaining ingredients. Pour over the chicken. Return to oven for 5 minutes or so. Serves 3 or 4.

Mom's Noodles

&❧ *She never had an exact recipe — she just knew when it was right. Mother never used an egg white in her noodles!*

Combine in a bowl, **1¼ cups flour** and ½ **teaspoon salt**. Make a well in the center. Add **6 egg yolks** and **2 tablespoons half and half cream** (or more) to the well. With fingertips, stir yolks and cream together and start pulling flour into the center. Mix with fingertips until dough forms — you may need to add a few more drops of cream. Divide the ball of dough into 2 parts. Roll each part out very thin on a floured surface. Sprinkle the rolled dough very lightly with a dusting of flour. Roll up tightly and cut with a sharp knife. Unroll each coil and spread out to dry. When no longer tacky, package to use soon or put in freezer. When ready to use, drop noodles (if frozen, no need to thaw) into boiling rich chicken broth. Season broth to taste. Cook until tender — won't take long.

Mom's Chicken Noodle Casserole

& *An old standby. Always delicious. Freezes well — make and freeze.*
Thaw overnight in the refrigerator, then bake according to directions.

    1 large frying chicken (or 1 hen — Mom preferred the hen)
    1 10 ounce can cream of chicken soup
    1 10 ounce can cream of celery soup
    1 10 ounce can cream of mushroom soup
    1 4 ounce can sliced mushrooms
    1 4 ounce jar diced pimento
    2 to 4 cups shredded mild Cheddar cheese
    1 cup chicken broth
    1 7 to 8 ounce package dry noodles, cooked and drained

Cover chicken with water in a large pot. Bring to a boil. Lower heat
and simmer until chicken is fork tender. Remove from heat and cool.
Remove chicken from bones and cut meat into chunks. Combine the
soups, mushrooms, pimento and cheese. Stir in chicken pieces and
noodles. Add broth slowly and mix well. Mixture should be slightly soupy,
so may need to add a little more broth. Bake at 350° for about 1 hour.
Serves 8 or more. You may use leftover turkey in place of chicken.

Sue Rigg's Lemon-Basil Chicken in Pita Bread

    16 ounces boneless, skinless chicken breast pieces
        vegetable cooking spray or vegetable oil
     4 tablespoons reduced-calorie or regular mayonnaise
     2 teaspoons fresh lemon juice
    ½ teaspoon grated lemon rind
     2 6" whole wheat pita bread rounds, halved crosswise
        fresh basil leaves (12 or more, depending on size)

Place each piece of chicken inside a zip-lock bag (do not close
bag). Lay bag on a breadboard and flatten to ⅛" thickness, using a
meat mallet or rolling pin. Coat a large skillet with the cooking spray,
or a thin coat of vegetable oil. Heat oil and add chicken. Cook 2
minutes on each side, or until done. Remove chicken and cut into 2" x
1" strips. Set strips aside. Combine mayonnaise, lemon juice and rind
in a medium bowl. Stir well. Add chicken and toss gently to coat.
Cover and refrigerate. To serve, line the pita pockets with fresh clean
basil leaves. Spoon chicken mixture into the bread. Serves 4.

Sour Cream Baked Chicken Breasts

Make a sauce of the following:

- 1¾ **cups sour cream**
- ⅛ **cup fresh lemon juice**
- 2 **tablespoons Worcestershire sauce**
- 1 **teaspoon celery salt**
- 1½ **teaspoons paprika**
- 1 **teaspoon salt**
- ½ **teaspoon pepper**

Combine above ingredients and mix well. Bone and split **6 large chicken breasts.** Wipe breasts with paper towel to dry well. Put breasts in large glass bowl. Cover with the sour cream mixture. Put plastic wrap on top of bowl and refrigerate overnight. Next day, remove chicken pieces from sour cream mixture. Roll each piece in **dry bread crumbs** — will take 1½ to 2 cups of crumbs. Lay each piece in buttered 9" x 13" glass baking dish. Dribble a little sour cream sauce over each chicken piece. Melt **6 tablespoons butter** and drizzle butter over all. Bake at 350° for 1 hour.

Raspberry Vinegar Sauced Chicken Breasts

&. *Have you made or bought a bottle of raspberry vinegar and then wondered what to do with it? Here is a great recipe to use some.*

- 4 **chicken breasts, boneless and skinless**
- 2 **tablespoons vegetable oil**
- 2 **tablespoons butter or oleo**
- 2 **tablespoons raspberry vinegar**
- ½ **cup whipping cream**
-   **salt and pepper**
-   **fresh chopped chives**

Heat oil and butter in a large skillet. Sauté chicken over medium to high heat for 8 to 10 minutes per side, or until cooked through. Do not, however, overcook. Remove chicken to a warm platter. Stir in the vinegar and the cream and bring to a boil. Boil for 1 minute. Add salt and pepper to taste. Spoon sauce over the chicken breasts and sprinkle fresh chopped chives over the top. Serves 4.

Another time, use one of your scented basil vinegars in place of the raspberry vinegar.

Day Later Turkey

🍂 *Finally! A leftover turkey recipe that is delicious.*

    4   cups leftover turkey breast, sliced or cut into large
        chunks
    4   tablespoons butter
    2   tablespoons flour
    2   cups half and half cream
        salt and pepper to taste
    4   egg yolks
    ¼   cup dry Sherry or apple cider

In a large heavy saucepan, brown turkey pieces lightly in butter. When lightly browned, sprinkle flour over the turkey. Turn gently. Gradually add 1 cup half and half cream, stirring gently. Meanwhile, lightly beat the egg yolks. Add the second cup of half and half, then salt, pepper and Sherry. Add this gradually to the turkey mixture. Stir carefully and slowly until it thickens. Taste for seasonings. Serve over crisp buttered toast or hot split biscuits. Serves 4 to 6.

The Best Barbecued Chicken

Brown **chicken pieces** in hot **vegetable oil**. Transfer pieces to 9" x 13" baking dish or dishes. Pour the following sauce over pieces and bake at 325°, uncovered for 1 hour.

In the chicken skillet, sauté **1 chopped onion**, and **½ cup chopped celery** until transparent. Do not brown. Add **1 cup catsup**, **⅔ cup water**, **3 tablespoons lemon juice**, **⅓ cup brown sugar**, **2 tablespoons Worcestershire sauce**, **2 tablespoons vinegar** and **2 tablespoons prepared mustard**. Add **salt** and **pepper** to taste. Now add **2 cups of any good bottled barbecue sauce**. Simmer for about 15 minutes. This is enough sauce for 3 chickens. Whatever isn't used, store in the refrigerator for later use.

Roast Pork with Cinnamon Apple Brandy

❧ *Make Apple Brandy, page 296, sometime in October or early November. When it is ready to use, take a cup of it to use in this recipe.*

3½ to 4 pounds pork roast, at room temperature
    salt and pepper
1 cup apple brandy (homemade or otherwise)
1 cup water

Season roast all over with salt and pepper. Put roast in a shallow roasting pan. Pour the brandy and water around roast. Cover pan with heavy foil and put in a 450° oven for about 30 minutes. Reduce heat to 250° and continue to roast 3 to 4 hours, but don't overcook.* When it is nearly done, remove foil, raise heat to 350° and roast another 15 to 30 minutes or until it's done. Baste two or three times with pan juice the last few minutes. Serves 8.

*Use your meat thermometer. Cook only until meat is done. It may take 2 hours, or it may take 4 hours. Watch thermometer closely.

Ham-Noodle Casserole ⊂▇[MOTHER ⌀]▇⊃

1 6 to 8 ounce package noodles
1½ cups diced cooked ham
1 cup shredded sharp cheese
1 10½ ounce can condensed cream of chicken soup
½ cup milk
2 tablespoons butter or oleo

Cook noodles as directed on package. Drain. Combine ham and cheese. Alternate layers of noodles and ham in greased 1 to 1½ quart baking dish. Mix soup and milk. Pour over noodles and ham. Can sprinkle another ¼ cup cheese over top if desired. Dot with the 2 tablespoons butter. Bake in a 375° oven for about 30 minutes. Serves 4 to 6. Good way to use up left-over ham from a holiday dinner.

Old Fashioned Cider Baked Ham

1   12 to 14 pound bone-in cooked ham
2   quarts apple cider, unsweetened if possible
1   tablespoon whole black peppercorns
2   bay leaves
    whole cloves
2   cups applesauce
½   cup dark brown sugar, packed
⅓   cup sherry wine or apple cider
2   tablespoons prepared horseradish
1   tablespoon coarse grained Dijon mustard

Put ham in a large pot. Pour cider over ham and add enough water to cover ham completely. Bring to a boil. Reduce heat and add bay leaves and peppercorns. Cover partially and simmer for about 4 hours. Do not boil — just simmer. Keep liquid level to cover ham at all times. Let ham cool in the liquid until you can handle it. Remove ham from pot and put it in a large shallow baking pan. Preheat oven to 350°. Remove the rind from the ham, but leave a layer of fat on. Score the fat in diamonds and stud each diamond with a whole clove. Pour 3 cups of the cooking liquid around base of ham. Roast the ham at 350° for about 30 minutes, basting two or three times with pan liquid. While ham is baking, blend the applesauce, brown sugar, sherry or cider, horseradish and mustard. Spread over the ham and put back in oven to roast another 30 to 40 minutes, or until ham is beautifully glazed and golden brown. Remove from oven and let ham set for several minutes before carving. Serves 12 or more.

Mother's Ham Patties ⊂═▭ MOTHER ♡ ▭⊃

🍃 *A great way to use left-over ham.*

2   cups ground ham
1   egg, slightly beaten
¼   cup milk
½   cup dry bread crumbs

Mix all together and shape into patties. Sauté in a little butter until nicely browned. Makes 3 or 4 patties.

Herb Rubbed Roast Pork

    1 tablespoon sugar
    2 teaspoons ground sage
    2 teaspoons dried marjoram
    1 teaspoon salt
   ½ teaspoon celery seed
   ½ teaspoon dry mustard
   ⅛ teaspoon pepper
    1 5 pound (or larger) boneless pork loin roast
    1 tablespoon chopped fresh parsley

In a small bowl, combine the first 7 ingredients. Thoroughly rub the roast with this mixture. Cover and let stand at least 4 hours or overnight in the refrigerator.

Set meat on a rack in a shallow roasting pan. Insert meat thermometer. Roast, uncovered, in a 325° oven for 2 to 2½ hours or until thermometer registers 165° to 170°. Remove roast from oven. Put on serving platter. Sprinkle the fresh chopped parsley on top. Serves 8 or 10. Note: Do not overbake. This roast is juicy and succulent.

Margaret's Sausage and Egg Soufflé

   1½ pounds bulk pork sausage or omit the salt
        and use 2 cups ground raw ham
    9 eggs, slightly beaten
    3 cups milk
   1½ teaspoons dry mustard
    1 teaspoon salt
    3 slices white bread, cut into ½ inch cubes
   1½ cups shredded Cheddar cheese

Brown meat and drain off fat. Set aside. Mix eggs, milk, dry mustard and salt. Stir in bread cubes, sausage or ham and cheese. Pour into a greased 9" x 13" pan. Cover and refrigerate overnight. Bake at 350° for 1 hour. We often have this Christmas morning. Wonderful because it's do-ahead.

Spaghetti Bake

🍂 *One of the best carry-in dishes I know of. Everyone loves this.*

    2 **pounds ground beef**
    1 **cup chopped onion**
    1 **clove garlic, minced**
    1 **28 ounce can tomatoes, cut up**
    1 **16 ounce can tomato sauce**
    1 **6 ounce can tomato paste**
    1 **6 or 8 ounce can mushroom pieces**
    2 **teaspoons sugar**
  1½ **teaspoons dried oregano**
    1 **teaspoon salt**
    1 **teaspoon dried basil**
    8 **ounces spaghetti, cooked and drained**
    2 **to 4 cups shredded Mozzarella cheese (depending on how cheesy you like it)**
   ½ **cup grated Parmesan cheese**

In a large pan, cook ground beef, onion and garlic until meat is browned. Drain off fat. Stir rest of ingredients into the pot except the spaghetti and the cheeses. Simmer, uncovered, for about 30 minutes. Stir in drained spaghetti. Put half of spaghetti mixture in a greased 9" x 13" pan. Cover with half the Mozzarella cheese. Add rest of spaghetti mixture. Top with other half of Mozzarella and sprinkle all with the Parmesan cheese. Bake at 375° for about 30 minutes. Serves 10 to 12. You can make this dish ahead of time and either freeze or refrigerate it. It must, however, be at room temperature when you put it in the oven. By the way, I use 4 cups of Mozzarella.

All-Purpose Marinade

🍂 *This marinade is equally good with beef, pork and chicken. I got tired of looking for this recipe — now I can find it! You can too.*

    1 **cup soy sauce**
   ½ **cup light brown sugar**
   ¼ **cup cooking oil**

   ¼ **cup Sherry**
    1 **or 2 cloves garlic, chopped**

Combine all ingredients. Pour over your choice of meat. Cover and refrigerate 2 or 3 hours, stirring occasionally. When you broil the meat or chicken, brush frequently with the marinade. Makes 1½ cups.

Ham and Cheese Soufflé

8	slices white bread, cubed
1½	cups ham, cut into small dice
1½	cups grated Cheddar cheese
2	or 3 green onions, chopped fine
	salt and pepper
10	eggs
2½	cups milk
½	stick butter, melted
	1 teaspoon dry mustard
	grated Cheddar cheese

Butter a two quart soufflé dish. Layer ⅓ of bread cubes, half the ham, half the cheese, half the onions, and salt and pepper. Repeat layers and end with bread cubes on top. Beat eggs. Add milk, melted butter, and dry mustard. Mix well. Pour over bread in the dish. Cover and refrigerate overnight. Bake uncovered at 350° for 45 to 50 minutes. Sprinkle some grated Cheddar cheese on top. Return to oven for 10 to 15 minutes or until cheese is melted and bubbly, but do not brown cheese. Easy and delicious. Serves 6.

Mustard Glaze

🍃 *Try this on grilled outdoor meats, such as ribs, pork chops or chicken.*

½	cup Dijon mustard
2	tablespoons vinegar
2	tablespoons brown sugar
2	tablespoons honey
2	tablespoons ketchup
½	teaspoon red pepper flakes, optional

Combine all ingredients. Brush on meat during grilling. Makes about 1 cup.

Baked Ham with Mandarin Oranges and Amaretto

❧ I clipped this recipe from a liqueur ad. It's really good and it's beautiful to serve.

- 1   **10 to 12 pound bone-in ham, cooked**
- 1   **cup Amaretto liqueur (an almond flavored liqueur)**
- 1⅓ **cups orange marmalade**
- ½   **teaspoon Tabasco sauce, or hot sauce**
- 1   **11 ounce can mandarin oranges, drained**
- 1   **small jar maraschino cherries, drained**

Remove rind and most of fat from ham, but leave a thin layer of fat. Score surface in a diamond pattern. Put ham, fat side up, in an open roasting pan. Insert meat thermometer in center away from bone and bake in a 325° oven until thermometer reads 140°. Heat Amaretto liqueur, orange marmalade and Tabasco sauce together. Remove ham from oven. Remove thermometer. Brush glaze thickly all over ham. Put ham back in oven for 15 minutes to glaze. Remove ham and arrange mandarin orange slices in a daisy or pinwheel design. Stud the center of the design with a cherry. Use 6 orange slices and 1 cherry per design. Reheat glaze and carefully brush hot glaze over the fruit. Return ham to oven and bake another 5 to 10 minutes or until well glazed. Take the ham to the table to carve so your guests can see how beautiful it is. Serves 12 or more.

Apricot Glaze for Ham or Ham Loaves

- 2   **12 ounce jars apricot preserves**
- 2   **tablespoons lime juice**
- 2   **teaspoons whole cloves**
- ½   **cup Galliano or other orange-flavored liqueur, or ½ cup orange juice**

Heat ingredients in a saucepan — use low heat. Prepare ham or ham loaves for the oven. Completely cover the surface with the warm glaze. Let ham set with glaze on it for 1 hour before baking. As ham is baking, brush it with the glaze several times.

Marinade for Leg of Lamb

🐑 Ask your butcher to bone and butterfly the leg of lamb.

- 1 **cup good quality olive oil**
- 1 **cup red wine**
- 6 **whole cloves**
- 12 **whole peppercorns**
- 3 **cloves garlic, chopped**
- 1 **teaspoon dried rosemary, OR 1 tablespoon fresh**
   salt and pepper

Put butterflied **leg of lamb** in a large glass or ceramic bowl. Slowly add wine to olive oil and whisk until blended. Add all the seasonings. Pour this marinade over the meat. Cover and refrigerate for 24 hours before cooking, turning several times. Remove lamb from marinade and roast at 350°. Use a meat thermometer and do *not* overbake — 165° for rare and 180° for well done. Serves 10 or more.

Broiled Lamb Chops with Thyme

🐑 Most of us don't cook enough lamb. I wonder why? It is so delicious! Here are two good lamb chop recipes — one to cook inside, one to cook outside. This one is inside —

- 1 **tablespoon good olive oil**
- 1 **tablespoon salad oil**
- 2 **cloves garlic, finely minced**
- ½ **teaspoon dried thyme, OR 1½ teaspoons chopped fresh**
   salt and freshly ground pepper
- 4 **rib lamb chops, 1 inch thick (or if small use 8 chops —**
   serve 2 per person)

Preheat broiler and broiler rack. In a large bowl, combine all marinade ingredients and mix well. Submerge the chops in the marinade, turning often to coat all sides. Cover bowl loosely and let chops marinate for 15 to 20 minutes. Broil the chops four to six inches from heat 4 to 5 minutes per side for medium rare. Serves 4. Cooking time depends on heat, distance from heat and thickness of chops, so watch closely.

Grilled Lamb Chops

🍃 *This one is for outside.*

   8 **rib lamb chops, 1" to 1½" thick**
   1 **or 2 garlic cloves, cut in half**
   2 **teaspoons dried herbes de Provence***
  ½ **cup dry red wine**
   1 **tablespoon butter**
      salt and pepper to taste
      sprig of parsley, thyme or rosemary for garnish

Have the outdoor grill ready with medium coals. Rub the chops on all sides with the cut garlic. In a small pan combine the herbes, wine and butter. Heat until butter melts. Brush some of the butter mixture on each chop. Put chops on grill and broil 4 inches from heat source, turning once and basting often with the butter mixture. Grill 4 to 8 minutes per side, but this depends on several things — how well done you like the meat, the temperature, the thickness of the chops. So, watch closely. Sprinkle chops with salt and pepper and serve immediately. Garnish with fresh herb sprigs, if you have them. Serves 4.

*Herbes de Provence is a marvelous blend of herbs from the south of France (the Provence area). It's hot and dry there and the area is famous for its herbs and its local cooking. The cooks use lots of herbs, cheeses, tomatoes, fresh vegetables, etc. You might almost think you were in Italy. At any rate, wonderful foods and seasonings come from the Provence. Dominant herbs in herbes de Provence are thyme and rosemary. You can buy this blend at specialty food stores or some large supermarkets.

Pizza Sauce

Combine **one 15 ounce can tomato sauce**, **½ cup chopped onion, 1 clove garlic, minced, 2 tablespoons chopped fresh parsley**, or 1 tablespoon dried, **¾ teaspoon dried oregano, ¾ teaspoon dried basil** and **a few red pepper flakes**. Bring to a boil and simmer, uncovered, for 15 minutes. Store in refrigerator. Makes about 1½ cups.

Sirloin Tips

🍃 *This recipe has a great garlic butter with it. There is butter left over, so refrigerate it and use to dress fresh cooked vegetables, or spread onto bread slices to toast in the oven. You can also freeze the butter.*

Garlic Butter
- 4 **sticks butter, softened**
- 2 **to 4 cloves garlic, finely minced (depends on how well you like garlic)**
- ¼ **cup dry white wine**
- 1 **tablespoon chopped parsley**
- ¼ **teaspoon freshly ground pepper**

Combine above ingredients in a bowl and mix until thoroughly blended. Melt **2 tablespoons of the garlic butter** in a large skillet over medium high heat. Add **1 large onion** which has been sliced and sauté until onion is golden. Now add ½ **to ¾ pound fresh mushroom slices** and sauté lightly for 2 or 3 minutes. Remove to a plate and keep mushrooms and onions warm. Clean out pan and wipe with paper towels — no need to wash it. Season **1 to 1½ pounds of beef sirloin or tenderloin tips** (cut into ½" strips) with **salt and pepper** to taste. Melt about **2 tablespoons of the garlic butter** in the wiped out skillet. Put over medium high heat and add beef tips and sauté to desired doneness.* Return mushrooms and onions to the skillet and stir to blend. Splash a little Sherry into the pan and stir again. Serve immediately. Serves 4.

*If you like the meat rare, it doesn't take long to sauté the sirloin — depends on the thickness of meat, temperature, etc. The Sherry is optional, but adds a nice flavor.

A Thymely Footnote . . .Some of the most beautiful geraniums have little or no bloom! They are scented geraniums and they are unmatched in the garden for fragrance and beauty. They have a wide range of growing habits — some are tall, short, spreading, upright, vining, etc. There are well over 50 varieties. They range in "flavor" from peppermint to rose to coconut to apple and the list goes on! I make rose geranium jelly with the leaves. These plants are a true joy in the garden.

Herbed Standing Beef Ribs

1   4, 5 or 6 rib standing rib roast, or rib eye roast, or other tender cut of roast

1   clove garlic, cut into slivers

3   tablespoons fresh lemon juice

Spices

1   teaspoon dry mustard

1   teaspoon ground ginger

1   teaspoon onion powder

1   teaspoon salt

½   teaspoon cayenne pepper

Mixed Herbs

1   tablespoon dried savory

1   tablespoon dried sweet basil

1   tablespoon dried celery flakes

1   tablespoon dried parsley

1   tablespoon dried marjoram

1   tablespoon dried rosemary

1   tablespoon dried tarragon

Use a sharp knife to make little slits in the beef. Insert slivers of garlic into the beef. Sprinkle lemon juice over the beef. Sprinkle with the combined spices. Combine the dried herbs and sprinkle beef with 1 tablespoon of this mixture. (Save the rest for other uses.) Put roast on a foil-lined pan and broil several inches from heat for about 10 minutes per side. Wrap roast tightly in foil. Bake at 400° for 18 minutes per pound for rare. Slice thin to serve. Juicy and delicious.

Vivian's Marinade

¼   cup water

1   chicken bouillon cube or 1 teaspoon granules

¼   cup sugar

¼   cup ketchup

2   tablespoons soy sauce

1   teaspoon molasses

2   teaspoons salt

¼   teaspoon pepper

Boil water. Add bouillon and stir to dissolve. Add remaining ingredients. Blend well. Remove from heat and cool. Put a beef roast or brisket in a zip-type plastic bag. Pour marinade over meat. Zip bag and marinate several hours. Grill meat over charcoal. Slice meat thin across the grain.

Baked Steak

Use **1 to 2 pieces good quality cubed round steak** per person. Flour steaks and brown in a little hot oil in a heavy skillet. **Salt and pepper.** Lay browned steaks in a large casserole. Pour fat from skillet, leaving 2 to 3 tablespoons in the skillet. Add **2 to 3 tablespoons of flour** to fat. Stir and brown flour until flour is all absorbed. Slowly add **2 to 3 cups of water** and stir to make a smooth, brown gravy. Add **a little Worcestershire sauce** if you like. **Salt and pepper** to taste. You may add a **4 to 8 ounce jar of sliced, drained mushrooms**, if desired. Pour gravy over steak (gravy should be relatively thin). Cover casserole and bake at 350° for 1 hour, or until meat is tender and gravy is bubbly. There is nothing much better!

Hamburger Cheese Bake

A very good carry-in supper dish for school and church suppers.

- 1 **8 ounce package noodles, cooked and drained**
- 2 **pounds ground beef**
- 1½ **teaspoons salt**
- ¼ **teaspoon pepper**
- 1 **medium onion, chopped**
- 2 **tablespoons green pepper, chopped**
- ½ **teaspoon garlic salt**
- 2 **8 ounce cans tomato sauce**
- 1 **teaspoon dried oregano**
- 1 **8 ounce package cream cheese, softened**
- ½ **cup sour cream**
- 1½ **cups cottage cheese**

Brown beef with salt, pepper, onion, green pepper and garlic salt. Drain off any fat. Combine beef mixture with tomato sauce and oregano. Set aside. Blend softened cream cheese with sour cream and cottage cheese. Mix well. Put half of noodles in a large greased baking pan. Cover noodles with all of cheese mixture. Put remaining noodles on top of cheese. Spread beef mixture over all. Refrigerate if desired. To bake, bring to room temperature, then bake in a 350° oven for 35 to 45 minutes. Serves 12.

Veal Parmesan

4   veal cutlets, pounded thin between sheets of plastic
wrap, then each cutlet cut in half
1   cup fresh bread crumbs (make your own crumbs in
blender or food processor with day-old bread)
1   tablespoon grated Parmesan cheese
1   tablespoon fresh parsley, chopped
2   eggs, beaten
salt and pepper
½   cup good olive oil
1   teaspoon dried oregano, or 1 tablespoon chopped fresh
1   cup best quality tomato sauce (or 1 cup of Fresh
Herbed Tomato Sauce on page 89)
8   slices Mozzarella cheese

Prepare the cutlets. Prepare the bread crumbs in blender or
processor. Add the Parmesan cheese and oregano to the work bowl
and process a few seconds only to mix well. To prepare the batter, add
salt, pepper and parsley to the eggs and beat thoroughly. Heat olive
oil in a large skillet or sauté pan. Dip the veal pieces in the egg batter,
then into the bread crumb mixture. Fry quickly in the hot oil until
golden brown. Turn only once and do *not* overcook. Butter a large
casserole (one that will hold all eight pieces). Lay cutlets in the dish or
pan. Top each with some tomato sauce and top each with a slice of
Mozzarella cheese. Slip under preheated broiler and broil until cheese
is bubbly and is just starting to brown. Watch closely. Serve immediately. Serve two cutlets to each of 4 people. Serve with a green salad,
Italian bread, a side dish of pasta (a little spaghetti dressed with the
same tomato sauce used in the recipe, or dress the spaghetti with a
little butter and fresh chopped herbs). Serve a dish of Almond Creme
(on page 272) for dessert. These dinner guests will beg to come back!

*A **Thymely Footnote** . . . One of the most beautiful edging or border
plants is **lady's mantle**. It is a beautiful low perennial that has large
pleated leaves that were thought to resemble the folds of a medieval
cloak. In the spring, the plant has small yellow flowers. It is lovely
planted around a sun dial or armillary.*

Taco Burgers

1   pound ground beef
1   1 pound can tomatoes, cut up
1   teaspoon chili powder
1   teaspoon Worcestershire sauce
¾   teaspoon garlic salt
½   teaspoon sugar
¼   teaspoon dry mustard
6   or 8 hamburger buns, split, lightly buttered and toasted
2   cups shredded lettuce
1   cup shredded American OR taco cheese
    bottled taco sauce

Brown meat in a skillet. Drain off fat. Add tomatoes, chili powder, Worcestershire sauce, garlic salt, sugar and dry mustard. Stir well to blend. Bring to a boil. Reduce heat and simmer gently, uncovered, for 12 to 20 minutes. Spoon onto the toasted buns. Top with lettuce and cheese. Spoon on a little taco sauce, if desired. Will fill 6 or 8 buns. Kids love these.

Barbecue Sauce, Colorado-Style

A ranch wife from Colorado gave me this recipe. Wonderful on chicken or ribs.

1   cup ketchup
½   cup dark molasses
½   cup finely chopped onions
½   cup packed brown sugar
2   tablespoons cider vinegar
1   tablespoon A-1 Steak sauce
1   teaspoon chili powder
½   teaspoon cayenne pepper
3   dashes hot pepper sauce
    salt and pepper
½   cup raisins

Combine all ingredients, except raisins, in the food processor. Blend until smooth. Add raisins and mix using five on/off turns. Use now or refrigerate for several days before using. If you don't tell anybody about the raisins, they'll *never* guess what they are! Makes about 2 cups.

FRUITS
AND
VEGETABLES

Fresh Peaches with Apricot Glaze

4   ripe freestone peaches
2   teaspoons fresh lemon juice
½   cup apricot preserves
¼   cup crumbled macaroon cookies
    apricot brandy, optional

Blanch peaches in a large pot of boiling water for 30 seconds. Rinse under cold water and slip skins off. Cut peaches in half and put them in a pretty bake-proof dish, cut side up. Sprinkle halves with the lemon juice. In a small pan, heat the apricot preserves with **2 tablespoons water** OR **2 tablespoons apricot brandy.** Stir over low heat to blend. Spoon some into each peach half and out over peaches to glaze them. Put in a 325° oven for 15 minutes to heat through. Remove from oven and sprinkle the crumbled macaroons over peaches. Serve immediately as a meat side dish or as a light dessert. Another time, spoon cranberry conserve, heated with cranberry liqueur, into peach halves and follow rest of directions. Delicious! Serves 4.

Hot Fruit Casserole

1   1 pound can pitted Bing cherries (sweet)
1   1 pound can sliced peaches
1   1 pound can pear halves
1   1 pound can apricot halves
1   1 pound can pineapple chunks
1½   cups syrup — any juice from above or a combination of
     juices
2   bananas, sliced thick
2   cups crumbled macaroon cookies
1   cup Madeira wine, or 1 more cup fruit syrup
½   stick butter, melted
½   cup brown sugar

Preheat oven to 350°. Combine all ingredients in a three quart casserole. Cover and bake for about 1 hour. This is good with any meat. It's a nice change from the curried fruit I usually serve. Serves 8 to 10.

Hot Curried Fruit

1 1 pound can cling peach halves, drained
1 1 pound can pear halves, drained
1 1 pound can pineapple slices, drained
1 1 pound can apricot halves, drained
½ cup Sherry
½ cup brown sugar
1 teaspoon curry powder (or up to 2 teaspoons if you really like curry)
4 tablespoons butter or oleo
1 21 ounce can cherry pie filling

In an 8" x 10" baking dish, arrange the drained peaches, pears, pineapple and apricots. Pour cherry pie filling over the fruits. In a small bowl, combine brown sugar with curry powder. Sprinkle this over the fruits. Dot top with butter and sprinkle the Sherry over all. Bake, uncovered, at 325° for 45 minutes. Serve warm. Serves 6 or 8. Superb with turkey, chicken, pork or beef. A terrific winter fruit dish.

Layered Fruit Cup

✎ *The Hot Curried Fruit is to winter what Layered Fruit Cup is to summer.*

2 cups diced watermelon
1 cup diced cantaloupe
1 cup seedless grapes
1 cup blueberries
1 tablespoon finely shredded orange peel
¾ cup orange juice
2 tablespoons orange-flavored liqueur (such as Cointreau, Triple Sec, etc.)
2 tablespoons sugar

Layer fruits in six 8 ounce glasses. Stir remaining ingredients together in a small saucepan. Heat and stir **only** until sugar is dissolved — do not let it get too hot. When sugar is dissolved, remove from heat and cool. Pour over fruit in the glasses. Put plastic wrap over glass top and refrigerate at least one hour. Serves 6.

Sherried Peaches

- 1 1 pound, 13 ounce can cling peach halves, drained and save syrup
- ½ cup light brown sugar
- ¼ cup white sugar
- ¼ teaspoon ground ginger
- ¼ teaspoon ground cinnamon
- ½ cup Sherry
- 2 tablespoons lemon juice

In a saucepan, combine ½ cup peach syrup with the rest of ingredients, except the peach halves. Simmer syrup until sugar is dissolved. Put peach halves in a glass jar. Pour warm syrup over. Let cool, then cover and refrigerate. Will keep several days in the refrigerator. One recipe serves 6, but can double or more this recipe. Great for a gift!

Company Baked Apples

- 1 cup light raisins (or dark)
- 1½ cups white wine
- 8 cooking apples, cored
- ½ teaspoon grated lemon peel
- 8 tablespoons sugar
- 2 tablespoons butter

Soak raisins in wine for ½ hour. Drain and save wine. Stuff cored apples with the raisins. Sprinkle each apple with a little lemon peel and 1 tablespoon of sugar. Dot each with butter. Pour wine around apples — they should fit into a 9" x 13" baking dish that has been buttered. Bake at 400° for about 45 minutes, or until apples are tender, but not falling apart. Good warm or cold. Serves 8.

Fresh Fruit Dip

Combine an **8 ounce package of softened cream cheese, 2 tablespoons of orange juice concentrate** and a **7 to 9 ounce jar of marshmallow creme**. Dunk fresh strawberries, bananas, apple wedges, fresh pineapple chunks, etc., into this wonderful dip.

Cinnamon Candied Apples

Combine **1 cup sugar, 2 cups water** and **1 cup cinnamon red hot candies**. Bring to a boil and simmer until candies are melted. Peel and core **firm small apples**. Drop apples into the boiling syrup — keep syrup boiling, so just add 1 or 2 apples at a time. Cook until apples are just tender, but not mushy. Beautiful as a garnish on the meat tray, but also delicious.

Fried Apples

⅓ **cup sugar**
1 **teaspoon ground nutmeg**
½ **teaspoon ground cinnamon**
⅛ **teaspoon salt**
6 **large cooking apples**
5 **to 6 tablespoons butter**

Mix sugar, spices and salt. Wash, core and slice apples into ½" rings. Heat butter in a large fry pan or skillet. Add apple rings. Sprinkle half the sugar mixture over apples. Fry about 3 minutes. Turn. Sprinkle apples with rest of sugar mixture and continue to cook until apples are almost transparent. Do not cook until rings fall apart, however. Good apples to use are McIntosh, Rome Beauty, Jonathan, firm Red or Yellow Delicious. Fried apples are a great accompaniment to pork chops, pork roast, or fried chicken.

Spiced Oranges

Combine ¾ **cup sugar, 1 cup water, 1 cup dry red wine, 5 whole cloves, 2 cinnamon sticks**, and **4 lemon slices** in a heavy saucepan. Bring to a boil. Lower heat and simmer about 10 minutes. Pour over **6 navel oranges, peeled and sectioned** and refrigerate. A great pork or poultry garnish. A beautiful gift.

Baked Tomatoes with Fresh Herbs

🍃 *Serve these next to a broiled steak, grilled chicken or with just about anything. Only fresh herbs will do for this recipe.*

- ½ cup fresh parsley leaves, chopped fine (Italian flat leaf is best)
- 1 cup fresh basil leaves, chopped fine
- 3 cloves garlic, minced fine
- 3 large ripe tomatoes
  salt and pepper
- ¼ cup fine fresh bread crumbs
- ½ cup good olive oil

Combine parsley, basil and garlic in a small bowl. Set aside. Peel and core tomatoes. Slice each tomato into three slices. Put a little extra olive oil in a shallow baking dish and grease the dish thoroughly. Lay tomato slices in the dish in one layer. Sprinkle with salt and freshly grated pepper. Distribute the herb-garlic mixture over the tomato slices. Sprinkle the bread crumbs over them, then drizzle them with the olive oil. Bake in a 450° oven for 10 to 15 minutes, or until the tops are golden brown. Serves 4.

Broiled Tomatoes with Parmesan and Basil

- 3 large tomatoes, halved
- ½ cup grated Parmesan cheese
- 1 tablespoon fresh basil, chopped OR 1 teaspoon dried
- ½ teaspoon salt
  pepper
- 2 tablespoons butter, softened
  fresh chopped parsley

Do not peel tomatoes. The skin helps hold them all together. Put tomato halves on broiler pan. Sprinkle with the cheese. Combine the basil, salt and pepper and sprinkle over the cheese. Dot each half with some of the butter. Broil 6 to 8 minutes, not too close to source of heat. Let them get nice and browned, but watch carefully so they don't burn. Remove from broiler and sprinkle a little fresh chopped parsley on top. Serve immediately as a meat accompaniment.

Broiled Tomatoes and Cheese

❧ You probably think I'm pushing the broiled and baked tomatoes, but I believe tomatoes are too good to just always slice. I think you'll like these tomato slices with Mozzarella cheese.

2 or 3 large, ripe tomatoes, peeled and cored
    about 1 cup shredded Mozzarella cheese
2 tablespoons good olive oil
½ teaspoon dried oregano or 1½ teaspoons chopped fresh
1 small clove garlic, minced fine

Cut each tomato into 3 or 4 slices. Sprinkle each slice with some of the cheese. Put slices on rack in a broiler pan. Mix together the oil, oregano and garlic. Drizzle a little of this mixture over each slice. Broil 3 or 4 minutes or until cheese melts and is lightly browned. Delicious with grilled meats, seafood or pasta dishes. Serves 4.

Mix-In-Pan Macaroni and Cheese

❧ This goes together quickly because you don't cook the macaroni first. Wish I'd had this recipe a long time ago!

2 cups uncooked elbow macaroni
3½ cups milk
1 teaspoon Worcestershire sauce
½ teaspoon salt
2½ cups shredded Cheddar cheese
    paprika

In a well-greased 8" x 12" baking dish or deep casserole, stir together the uncooked macaroni, the milk, the Worcestershire sauce, the salt and 1½ cups of the cheese until well blended. Cover tightly with foil. Bake in a 350° oven for 50 minutes. Remove foil. Stir well. Cover with the other 1 cup cheese and sprinkle with paprika. Return to oven and bake 10 or 15 minutes longer, or until cheese is melted. Let stand a few minutes before serving so cheese can cool and set. Serves 6 to 8.

Potatoes with Cheese and Sour Cream

6 medium baking potatoes
2½ cups shredded sharp Cheddar cheese
¼ cup butter
1 cup sour cream, at room temperature
⅓ cup onion, chopped fine
salt and pepper to taste
paprika to sprinkle on top

Boil potatoes, with skins on, until tender. Drain. Cool slightly and peel. Shred potatoes into a large bowl. Preheat oven to 350°. Butter a 9" square baking dish. Heat 2 cups cheese and the butter in a heavy pan over low heat until barely melted, *stirring constantly*. Remove from heat. Stir in sour cream and onion, salt and pepper. Fold into the potatoes and pour into the prepared pan. Sprinkle remaining ½ cup cheese over the top. Sprinkle with paprika. Bake about 30 minutes, or until bubbly. Serves 6.

Potato Frills

These are fun to prepare and fun to eat. Fix one potato for each person.

Peel potato. Use a sharp vegetable peeler and peel ½" wide, paper thin strips from potatoes. Go round and round potato and try to make nice long strips. Drop the strips into a large bowl of water mixed with 1 teaspoon salt. In a large skillet over medium heat, heat 1" of salad oil to 400° (use your candy thermometer). Remove a handful of potato strips from the water and pat dry with paper towels. Carefully drop strips into the hot oil and fry until they are crisp and golden, about 2 minutes. With slotted spoon, remove potato strips to more paper towels to drain. Repeat with remaining potato strips. Sprinkle lightly with salt. You can serve these either warm or cold.

*A Thymely Footnote . . . If you want hummingbirds to come to your garden, plant a **pineapple sage**. It has lovely bright red, trumpet-shaped blooms on it that brings the birds. Rub the stems and you'll get a distinct pineapple aroma.*

Parmesan Potatoes

    6   large potatoes, peeled and cut into fourths
    ¼   cup flour
    ¼   cup grated Parmesan cheese
    ¾   teaspoon salt
        pepper
    ⅓   cup oleo

Mix flour, cheese, salt and pepper in a bag. Moisten potato quarters with water and shake a few at a time in the bag, coating each well with the cheese mixture. Melt oleo in a 9″ x 13″ pan. Put potatoes in a single layer in the pan, not touching each other. Bake at 375° for about 1 hour. Turn potatoes about half way through baking time. These get brown and crispy and are very good. A friend from the Farm Progress Show gave me this recipe. Serves 6 to 8.

Ham and Cheese Stuffed Potatoes

A great meal-in-one for lunch or for a light supper.

    4   large baking potatoes
        shortening to rub on potatoes
    6   tablespoons oleo or butter
    2   tablespoons grated onion
    ¼   teaspoon pepper
    2   eggs
    1½ cups shredded Cheddar cheese
    1   cup diced ham

Scrub potatoes, dry, then rub shortening over each one. Prick several places with a fork. Bake for about 1 hour or until done. Cut potatoes in half lengthwise. Carefully scoop out inside leaving a thin shell. In a large bowl, beat the potatoes for a minute or so. Add butter, onion, pepper and eggs. Beat until smooth and fluffy. Fold in 1 cup of the cheese and the 1 cup of ham. Re-fill the potato shells. Sprinkle rest of cheese on top. Bake at 375° for 15 minutes or until potatoes are hot. Serves 4.

New Little Potatoes with Lemon-Chive Butter

16   small red new potatoes
3   tablespoons butter
2   tablespoons chopped fresh chives, OR 1 tablespoon dried
1   tablespoon fresh lemon juice
    salt

Peel a thin strip around middle of each potato. In a fairly large saucepan over high heat, heat potatoes and enough water to cover to boiling. Reduce heat and cook, covered, about 15 minutes, or until potatoes are just tender. Drain potatoes and return to pan. Over low heat, melt butter. Add chives, lemon juice and salt to taste. Gently toss until potatoes are well coated. Serve these anytime in the Spring, but especially serve them with Spring lamb — worth wading through Winter for! Serves 4.

Sweet Potatoes with Coconut Topping

3   cups mashed sweet potatoes
¾   cup sugar
2   eggs, beaten
1   cup evaporated milk
¼   cup butter or oleo, melted
1   teaspoon vanilla
    Topping (recipe follows)

Mix sweet potatoes, sugar, eggs, milk, oleo and vanilla together. Pour into a well-greased two quart casserole. Cover with Topping. Bake at 375° for about 30 minutes.

Topping:

1   cup light brown sugar
⅓   cup oleo, melted
1   cup coconut
1   cup pecans, chopped

Combine ingredients and mix well to form crumbs. Sprinkle over the potatoes. Very rich and very delicious. Serves 6.

Stuffed Sweet Potatoes

Select **6 medium sweet potatoes**. Scrub. Bake at 425° for 40 minutes or until done. Cut slice from top of each. Scoop out inside, careful not to break shell. Mash potatoes. To mashed potatoes, add ¼ **cup soft oleo, 1 tablespoon brown sugar, 1 teaspoon salt**, enough **hot milk** to moisten. Beat until fluffy. fold in ⅓ **cup tiny marshmallows** and ¼ **cup chopped walnuts**. Put mixture back into potato shells. Top with a few more marshmallows. Bake in 350° oven 15 or 20 minutes or until hot and browned. (The walnuts are optional.) Serves 6.

Joan's Best in the West Baked Beans

ᏕᏍ *Excellent baked beans.*

10   slices bacon, diced
½   pound ground beef or sausage (I like the sausage)
½   cup onion, chopped
⅓   cup brown sugar
⅓   cup white sugar
¼   cup ketchup
¼   cup barbecue sauce
 2   tablespoons prepared mustard
 2   tablespoons molasses
½   teaspoon salt
½   teaspoon chili powder
½   teaspoon pepper
 1   16 ounce can kidney beans, drained
 1   32 ounce can pork and beans, drained

Brown meats. Drain off fat. Add onion and sauté until onion is tender. Add sugars and rest of seasonings. Mix well. Add the drained beans. Mix again. Pour into a three quart casserole and bake at 350° for about 1 hour. Serves 10 to 12.

*A Thymely Footnote . . . Coriander is a dual annual herb. The seeds are lemony flavored and are prized in baking and especially in the making of curry. The parsley-looking leaves (some people call it Chinese parsley) are used fresh. These leaves are called **cilantro**. The salsa you like probably has fresh cilantro in it.*

Easy Candied Sweet Potatoes

3 or 4 large sweet potatoes
1 cup brown sugar
  grated rind of 1 orange
½ cup water
4 tablespoons butter
  ground cinnamon

Boil whole potatoes until tender. Remove skin and slice potatoes into ½ inch slices. Put a layer of potatoes in a buttered baking dish. Sprinkle layer with some of the sugar and a little cinnamon. Dot with some of the butter. Continue layering until potatoes are gone. Sprinkle top layer of potatoes with rest of sugar, butter, cinnamon, and orange peel. Pour the ½ cup water over all and bake at 350° for about 30 minutes or until dish is well-candied. Serves 6. Can be made ahead of time and refrigerated. Very good!

Sweet Potato Soufflé

4 cups mashed sweet potatoes (use either fresh cooked or canned)
2 or 3 tablespoons Sherry
¼ teaspoon salt
½ cup sugar
½ cup chopped pecans
2 eggs, beaten
½ cup melted butter or oleo

Combine all ingredients in your mixer bowl and beat until smooth. Place in a greased 2 quart casserole and bake at 350° for about 40 minutes or until golden brown. A different and delicious sweet potato dish. Serves 6.

Pilaf

• *This is a favorite rice dish. Great with just about any meat. It's a nice change from potatoes.*

Melt **4 tablespoons butter or oleo** in a large skillet. Add **1½ cups uncooked medium or long grain rice** and cook, stirring constantly, until rice takes on a golden color. Add **3½ cups chicken broth, 2 tablespoons instant minced onion**, a pinch of **saffron***, and **salt** and **pepper** to taste. Mix thoroughly. Turn into a 2 or 2½ quart baking dish. Cover. Bake in a 425° oven for 20 to 30 minutes, or until liquid is absorbed and rice is tender. Serves 8.

***Saffron** gives this dish its distinctive color (yellow) and flavor. Saffron is very expensive because it is processed by hand. The stigma of certain crocuses are picked by hand and dried. It is indispensable in Spanish and Mediterranean cooking. You can order Saffron from Williams and Sonoma, San Francisco. Their address is in "Useful Addresses" on page 64.

Cheesy Cabbage

    4   cups shredded cabbage
    2   tablespoons butter or oleo, melted
   1½   tablespoons flour
    ½   teaspoon salt
    1   cup milk
    1   cup shredded Cheddar cheese
    2   cups soft bread crumbs
    ¼   cup butter or oleo

Boil cabbage for 4 or 5 minutes. Drain well. Combine 2 tablespoons melted butter, flour and salt in a saucepan. Cook over low heat, stirring constantly, until bubbly. Gradually add the milk. Cook, stirring constantly, until smooth and thickened. Alternate layers of cooked cabbage, cheese, and sauce in a greased 1½ quart baking dish. Combine bread crumbs and the ¼ cup melted butter. Sprinkle crumbs over casserole. Bake, uncovered, at 350° for 25 to 30 minutes. Do not brown. Serves 6. This is a delicious and different vegetable dish.

Wild Rice Casserole

Melt **2 or 3 tablespoons of butter or oleo** in a heavy pan or Dutch oven. Sauté **1 cup chopped celery,** ½ **cup chopped onion** and **12 slices of bacon, diced**. Cook and stir until bacon is cooked (no need to cook it crisp). Add **1 pound cleaned, sliced fresh mushrooms** and stir until mushrooms are cooked. Add ½ **to 1 teaspoon salt**, or to taste. Now add **2 cups wild rice** and **2 cups white rice** (not instant). Stir all together. Add **1 quart (or more) chicken broth** and **3 tablespoons soy sauce**. Stir. Mixture should be pretty liquid. Turn into a large baking dish and bake at 350° for 1 hour or more until liquid is all absorbed and rice is tender. Time of baking depends on size and shape of baking dish. You can prepare the dish a day or so in advance, **but** do not add the broth or soy sauce until you're ready to bake casserole. Be sure to use raw rice, not instant. Delicious with beef or pork. Serves 16. You may halve the recipe or make it all and put half in the freezer for a later date.

Company Cauliflower

Cook a **large head of cauliflower** (don't overcook). Drain and place head in a large greased casserole. Dot heavily with **butter**. Sprinkle liberally with grated **Cheddar cheese** and bits of cooked, drained **bacon**. Now sprinkle liberally with **buttered bread crumbs**, then a little chopped **chives** and chopped **parsley**. Bake in a hot oven — 425° — for about 5 minutes. Pretty to serve and delicious.

Pasta Primavera

⬥ This is one of the first pasta dishes I did for cooking classes. It's a big hit!

1   cup small broccoli flowerets
½   cup sliced fresh mushrooms
2   tablespoons butter or oleo
7   ounces fettucine, cooked and drained
2   cups chopped fresh tomatoes
½   cup grated Parmesan cheese
¼   teaspoon dried oregano, or 1 teaspoon chopped fresh
¼   teaspoon dried basil or 1 teaspoon chopped fresh
1   cup heavy (whipping) cream

Sauté broccoli and mushrooms in butter until tender-crisp (do not overcook). Put drained pasta back into cooking pot. Add the sautéed vegetables and all the other ingredients. Heat gently and thoroughly, tossing all the time to keep from burning or sticking. Serve immediately on warm plates. Sprinkle with more Parmesan, if desired. Remember to buy your Parmesan cheese in your supermarket deli. It's **so much** better than the shelf variety. Serves 4 to 6. Imagine this with a broiled steak!

Stir Fried Broccoli, Asparagus or Green Beans

⬥ If you make the Hot Stir Fry Oil on page 48, use some to stir fry green vegetables in. This really zips up the vegetable!

Clean **fresh broccoli, asparagus** or **green beans**. Separate into broccoli flowerets or 1½" asparagus pieces, or whole beans. Put **1 to 2 tablespoons Hot Stir Fry Oil** in a large skillet or wok. Place over high heat. Add chosen vegetable to the hot oil along with **2 tablespoons white wine vinegar, rice vinegar** or **herb vinegar**. Stir fry for 3 minutes, lifting and tossing all the time. Sprinkle with **salt and pepper**. Spicy and different.

Fresh Asparagus for a Crowd

For eight to ten servings:
- **2 pounds fresh asparagus, trimmed**
- **¼ cup butter, melted**
- **1 teaspoon salt (or less to taste)**
- **pepper**
- **1 tablespoon water**

Preheat oven to 350°. In a 9" x 13" glass baking dish, arrange asparagus evenly in layers. Drizzle the butter over the asparagus. Sprinkle with salt and pepper and the tablespoon of water. Cover pan tightly with foil and bake for 15 to 30 minutes, depending on thickness of asparagus. Do not overbake — just cook until tender.

Blender Hollandaise Sauce

This is easy in the blender. Have ingredients measured and ready to make at serving time. A friend of mine made a beautiful Hollandaise Sauce one time. Dinner was delayed for some reason, and the sauce got cold. She asked me to re-heat it. I did, but in the process I ruined it. I heated it too hot and it turned thin and watery. I've never forgotten that, so now I always make it like this. Serve this sauce over fresh cooked asparagus or broccoli or other green vegetable.

- **3 egg yolks**
- **2 tablespoons fresh lemon juice**
- **¼ teaspoon salt**
- **1 stick butter, melted**

Put egg yolks, lemon juice and salt in blender container. Cover and blend to mix. At medium speed, pour warm melted butter in a very thin stream into egg yolk mixture. Blend *only* until thick and fluffy.

*A Thymely Footnote . . . Your cat will love you if you plant some **catnip** (catmint) for it to romp in! It is a perennial mint. Besides your cat liking it, brew a cup of catnip tea for yourself. It's supposed to induce sleep.*

BREADS
AND
COFFEECAKES

Pineapple Zucchini Bread

❧ I helped judge a pineapple contest one summer. It was great fun and there were many wonderful pineapple recipes. Kathy Greenwood's bread was especially good.

3 eggs
1 cup oil
2 cups sugar
2 teaspoons vanilla
2 cups shredded, unpeeled zucchini
1 8¼ ounce can crushed pineapple, well drained
3 cups flour
2 teaspoons baking soda
2 teaspoons ground cinnamon
1 teaspoon salt
1 teaspoon ground nutmeg
¼ teaspoon baking powder
1 cup chopped dates
1 cup chopped pecans

Beat eggs, oil, sugar and vanilla until thick. Stir in remaining ingredients and mix well. Pour into two greased 9" x 5" loaf pans. Bake at 350° for about 1 hour. If using glass pans, bake at 325°. Cool loaves and wrap well. Keep in refrigerator, or loaves freeze well. Moist and delicious. Makes 2 loaves.

Pumpkin Bread

3⅓ cups flour
  2 teaspoons baking soda
  ½ teaspoon salt
  3 teaspoons ground
     cinnamon
  2 teaspoons ground
     nutmeg

4 eggs, beaten
1 cup vegetable oil
2 cups canned pumpkin
3 cups sugar
   nuts and raisins,
   optional

Sift first 5 ingredients together and set aside. Combine beaten eggs, oil, pumpkin and sugar. Add to dry ingredients. You can add ½ cup to 1 cup chopped nuts and ½ cup raisins, if desired. Mix well. Divide batter between 2 greased 9" x 5" loaf pans. Bake at 350° for 1 hour. Makes 2 loaves.

Pineapple Glazed Nut Loaf

This was another pineapple contest winner from the Warren County Fair Open Class. Thanks to Mary Alice Altman for this recipe.

In a large bowl, combine:
- **2 cups sugar**
- **3 cups flour**
- **2 teaspoons baking powder**
- **½ teaspoon salt**

Cut in: **2 sticks oleo**, softened, until mixture resembles coarse meal.

Add:
- **1 teaspoon vanilla**
- **2 eggs**
- **1 13 ounce can evaporated milk**
- **1 cup well drained crushed pineapple (save juice)**
- **¾ cup chopped nuts**

Mix well, but do not beat. Grease and flour two bread pans. Bake in a 350° oven for about 1 hour, or until a pick comes out clean.

For the glaze:
- **4 tablespoons pineapple juice**
- **2 tablespoons frozen orange juice concentrate**
- **3 tablespoons sugar**

Mix glaze ingredients together in a small saucepan. Bring to a boil and boil 3 to 4 minutes. Brush on loaves while they are still warm. Let loaves cool. Re-heat juice and brush loaves again. This is a very good quick bread. Makes 2 loaves.

A Thymely Footnote . . . Some scented basils to try in your garden are: lemon basil, cinnamon basil, licorice basil. Other aromatic and wonderful basils I grow are: sweet Genovese (fabulous), Spicy Globe (a little bush-type), Piccolo (the best pesto basil), and a fairly new lettuce-leaf type called Napoletano.

Pineapple-Orange Quick Bread ⊂▓MOTHER♡▓⊃

¾ cup brown sugar, packed
¼ cup oleo, softened
1 egg
2 cups flour
1 teaspoon baking soda
½ teaspoon salt
⅓ cup frozen orange juice concentrate, thawed
1 8¾ ounce can crushed pineapple, undrained
½ cup chopped pecans

Cream sugar and shortening. Add egg and beat well. Combine dry ingredients. Alternately add dry ingredients and orange concentrate to creamed mixture, stirring after each addition. Stir in pineapple and pecans. Put in a well-greased 8½" x 4½" x 2½" loaf pan. Bake in a 350° oven for 50 to 60 minutes or until it tests done. Makes 1 loaf.

Wonderful Orange Bread ⊂▓MOTHER♡▓⊃

🍃 *This is a very old recipe from Mother's collection.*

1 cup ground orange peel
½ teaspoon baking soda

Cover peel and soda with water and simmer for 15 minutes. Drain off water. Add **1 cup sugar** and **1 cup water** to peel. Boil until thick. Let cool and set aside. Cream **1 cup sugar, 2 eggs**, and **4 tablespoons melted butter**. Add alternately **3½ cups flour** and **3 teaspoons baking powder** (mixed together) with **1 cup milk**. Mix all well. Lastly, add ½ **cup chopped nuts** and the orange peel mixture. Pour into greased and floured loaf pans. Bake in a 325° oven for 45 minutes or until done. Makes 1 large or 2 smaller loaves.

A Thymely Footnote . . . Rue is a lovely blue-green perennial that is not for culinary use. Many people are violently allergic to it. In spite of this, it is called the "herb of grace".

Rhubarb Nut Bread

🍃 *I have made this with macadamia nuts, which was very good. But if they're not available, use pecans, walnuts or almonds.*

    1 **cup oil**
    3 **eggs**
    2 **cups brown sugar, packed**
    2 **teaspoons vanilla**
 2½ **cups fresh cooked rhubarb, measured after cooking and draining**
  ½ **cup chopped nuts**
    3 **cups flour**
    2 **teaspoons baking soda**
    2 **teaspoons ground cinnamon**
    1 **teaspoon salt**
  ½ **teaspoon baking powder**
  ½ **teaspoon ground nutmeg**
  ½ **teaspoon ground allspice**

Grease two 9" x 5" loaf pans. Combine first four ingredients. Beat with mixer until thick and foamy. Fold in well-drained rhubarb and chopped nuts. In another bowl, combine rest of ingredients. Gently combine flour mixture and rhubarb mixture. Mix until blended. Pour batter into loaf pans. Bake at 350° (325° for glass pans) for 45 minutes or until it tests done. Cool loaves in pans on their sides for 10 to 15 minutes. Then turn out of pans to cool. Cool thoroughly. Wrap well. Refrigerate or freeze. Wonderful! Makes 2 loaves.

Bread or Muffin Topper

For a nice crunchy topping, combine ½ **cup light brown sugar, 1 teaspoon ground cinnamon, ¼ cup flour** and **3 tablespoons melted butter or oleo**. Mix until crumbly. Sprinkle on top of batter before baking.

Date Black Walnut Bread

¾ cup finely chopped black walnuts
1 cup chopped dates
1½ teaspoons baking soda
½ teaspoon salt
¼ cup Crisco or oleo
¾ cup boiling water
2 eggs
½ teaspoon vanilla
1 cup sugar
1½ cups sifted flour

Combine nuts, dates, soda and salt in a large bowl. Add Crisco and boiling water. Let stand 15 minutes. Stir. In another bowl, beat eggs slightly. Add vanilla. Sift in sugar and flour and stir until dry ingredients are moistened. (This is a very stiff batter.) Add to the date mixture and mix until well blended. Grease 2 small or 1 large loaf pan. Pour batter into pans. Cover with foil. Bake in a 350° oven for 25 minutes. Remove foil and bake 10 minutes longer or until loaves test done. Cool 15 minutes, then remove from pans. Cool thoroughly. Can wrap well and freeze. Make at least one day before slicing. This is the best date-nut bread I ever ate!

Angel Biscuits

2½ cups flour
1 teaspoon baking powder
1 teaspoon salt
¼ cup sugar

½ cup oleo
¼ cup warm water
1 envelope dry yeast
1 cup buttermilk

Dissolve yeast in ¼ cup warm water and set aside. Mix dry ingredients in the order given. Cut in oleo as if you were making pie crust. Stir in the buttermilk and the yeast water. Blend thoroughly and refrigerate in a large covered bowl. Or you can make the biscuits now. To work the dough, turn it out onto a floured board and knead lightly. Let rise 30 to 45 minutes. Roll out dough ½" thick (no less) — even thicker for higher biscuits. Cut with a biscuit cutter. Put biscuits on a lightly greased baking sheet. Let raise for a few minutes. Bake at 450° for 10 to 12 minutes. **Wonderful with honey butter!** (Combine **⅔ cup soft butter** and **¼ cup honey**.)

Quick Hot and Crisp Herb Bread

1 loaf French bread
½ cup soft butter or oleo
½ teaspoon paprika
1½ teaspoons chopped fresh rosemary, or ½ teaspoon dried
¾ teaspoon chopped fresh thyme, or ¼ teaspoon dried
¾ teaspoon chopped fresh marjoram, or ¼ teaspoon dried
⅛ teaspoon salt

Preheat oven to 400°. Cut bread diagonally at about 1 inch intervals, but don't cut through to bottom. In a bowl, combine remainder of ingredients until well blended. Spread this mixture between bread slices. Wrap bread completely in foil. Bake 15 to 20 minutes or until hot all the way through. Fold foil back and continue to bake 4 or 5 minutes to crisp the crust. Remove loaf from foil and cut the rest of way through the crust. Serves 6 or 8.

Breakfast Bread

❧ *A hearty, fragrant, old-world tasting bread that is absolutely delicious toasted. Spread warm toasted slices with a little unsalted butter — nothing else.*

2 cups buttermilk
½ cup honey
¼ cup molasses
2 tablespoons baking soda
1 teaspoon salt
1½ cups whole wheat flour
½ cup wheat germ
1 cup white flour
¼ cup raisins, optional

Mix together the buttermilk, honey, molasses, baking soda and salt. In another bowl, combine the 2 flours and wheat germ. Add to the buttermilk mixture. Stir in the raisins and pour batter into a greased 9" x 5" x 3" loaf pan. Preheat oven to 400°. When you put pan in the oven, turn temperature down to 350°. Bake for 1 hour. Turn loaf out of pan and cool. Wrap and wait one day to slice and toast.

Apple Butter Bread

½   cup butter or oleo, softened
1   cup light brown sugar, packed
1   egg
¾   cup buttermilk
2   teaspoons baking soda
2   cups flour
1   teaspoon ground cinnamon
1   teaspoon ground nutmeg
1   teaspoon ground allspice
½   teaspoon ground cloves
1   cup apple butter
½   cup chopped pecans

Cream butter and sugar. Add egg and beat well. Combine the buttermilk and soda. Combine flour and spices. Add to the creamed mixture alternately with the buttermilk mixture, beginning and ending with flour. Stir in apple butter and nuts. Pour into a greased 9″ x 5″ x 3″ loaf pan. Bake at 350° for 1 hour, or until a wooden pick comes out clean. Cool in pan a few minutes, then remove from pan and cool. Wrap well and keep refrigerated. Very good. Makes 1 loaf.

Casserole Bread

   2   cups flour (all-purpose)
   ⅔   cup rye flour
   2   tablespoons dark brown sugar
   2   tablespoons oil
   1   teaspoon caraway seeds
   ¾   teaspoon salt
   1   package active dry yeast
   1   cup beer

Use the food processor — process 1 cup all-purpose flour, the rye flour, the sugar, oil, caraway seeds, salt and yeast in food processor about 5 seconds. Heat beer in small pan until very warm (120° to 130°). With motor running, add beer all at once through feed tube. Process about 30 seconds. With motor running again, add other cup of flour, ¼ cup at a time, through the feed tube. Process 5 to 10 seconds after each addition. Grease a one-and-a-half quart casserole. Pour batter in and smooth top. Brush with additional oil. Cover and let rise in a warm place until almost doubled, about 45 minutes. Bake in a 350° oven for 30 minutes or until a wooden pick comes out clean. After 10 minutes, remove bread from dish and cool. Makes 1 round loaf.

Cinnamon Toast Roll-Ups

These are good about anytime, but especially for a brunch, for the tea table, or with soups. Very easy.

   ¼   cup sugar
   2   teaspoons ground cinnamon
  12   slices of very fresh white bread, crusts removed
   ¼   cup butter, melted

Stir together the sugar and cinnamon. Put each slice of bread between sheets of waxed paper and roll the bread with a rolling pin to ¼" thick. Brush melted butter on both sides of the bread. Sprinkle about 1 teaspoon of the cinnamon-sugar on one side of each slice. Roll the bread tightly jelly-roll fashion (cinnamon-sugar on inside). Trim the ends on a diagonal to make a neat cut surface. Put the rolls, seam side down, on a baking sheet and bake them in a 350° oven for 15 minutes, or until they are lightly browned. Makes 12 roll-ups, but double or triple recipe for more.

Indiana State Fair Honey Wheat Batter Bread

4½ cups whole wheat flour
2 cups white flour
4 tablespoons honey
2 teaspoons salt
2 eggs
2 envelopes active dry yeast
2 tablespoons softened butter
2 cups warm water (120° to 130°)

Mix 1½ cups white flour, honey, salt and yeast in a large bowl. Add butter and warm water. Beat 2 minutes at medium speed. Add eggs and the other ½ cup white flour. Beat 2 minutes at high speed. Stir in whole wheat flour to make a soft dough. Cover, let rise until doubled. Stir down and turn into 2 well-greased 1½ quart casseroles. Cover and let rise until doubled again. Uncover and bake in a 375° oven for 35 to 45 minutes, or until done.

Old-Fashioned Homemade Bread

Pour **2 cups boiling water** over **1 cup dry rolled oats**. Let mixture stand for ½ hour or until oats are thoroughly softened. Add **2 envelopes active dry yeast** to ⅓ **cup lukewarm water** in a small bowl. To the oat mixture, add **1 tablespoon salt, ½ cup honey**, and **2 tablespoons melted butter**. Now stir in the yeast. Gradually add **4½ to 5 cups of flour**. Knead 5 to 8 minutes, adding flour as necessary, until the dough is smooth and elastic. Put dough in a large greased bowl, grease top of dough and cover bowl with a clean towel. Set bowl in a warm place. When dough has doubled in bulk, 1 hour or more, punch it down and divide it in half. Shape into 2 loaves and put each loaf in a greased 8" x 4" or 9" x 5" loaf pan. Warm oven to 325°. Mix a **few drops of water** into **an egg yolk** and use the mixture to brush all over tops of the loaves. Sprinkle **poppy seeds** on loaves and bake at 325° for 45 to 50 minutes. Delicious old-fashioned bread flavor.

Maybe-The-Best-Yeast Rolls

🍃 *Not only the best, but easy too!*

- ½ **cup butter or oleo, softened**
- ⅓ **cup sugar**
- 1½ **teaspoons salt**
- 2 **tablespoons instant potato flakes**
- 1 **cup hot water**
- 2 **envelopes active dry yeast***
- ½ **cup lukewarm water**
- 4½ **cups flour**
  melted butter or oleo

Combine butter, sugar, salt, potato flakes and hot water in a bowl. Stir and let cool to lukewarm. Sprinkle yeast on the ½ cup lukewarm water and stir to dissolve. Add yeast and 1 cup of flour to the potato mixture. Beat with an electric mixer at medium speed until smooth, about 2 minutes. Scrape bowl occasionally. Gradually add the rest of the flour to make a soft dough. Place dough in a large greased bowl — turn to grease the top. Cover and let rise in a warm place until doubled, about 1¼ hours. Turn dough out onto lightly floured surface and knead 6 or 8 turns. Divide dough into 24 smooth balls. Put balls in a large greased pan, or into 2 smaller pans. Brush tops carefully with melted butter. Let rise about 45 minutes. Bake at 375° for 20 minutes. Watch carefully — do not overbake. As soon as rolls come out of oven, brush tops again with melted butter. Makes 24 rolls.

*The quick rising yeasts are my favorites. Works very well in this recipe.

Toasted Herb Roll-Ups

- 1 **loaf thin sliced white bread (I like Pepperidge Farm for this recipe)**
- 2 **sticks unsalted butter, softened**
- 1 **tablespoon chopped fresh basil**
- 2 **tablespoons chopped fresh chives**

Add herbs to butter. Spread on bread slices, crusts removed. Roll slices starting at a corner. Place, seam side down, on a cookie sheet and bake in a 350° oven for about 30 minutes. Cool thoroughly and store in an airtight container. Wonderful with soups or salads.

Challah

🍂 *Challah is a traditional Jewish bread. The eggs make it a beautiful golden color.*

    5 to 5½ cups bread flour
    2 packages rapid-rise dry yeast
    1 teaspoon salt
    1 tablespoon sugar
    3 eggs
    2 tablespoons butter, softened
    1 cup very warm water (120°)

In a large bowl, combine 4 cups of flour, the yeast, salt and sugar. Separate 1 egg. Put the yolk in a small cup. Cover it and set it aside. Add the other 2 eggs and the egg white, the butter and warm water to the flour mixture. Beat with a wooden spoon until the mixture forms a smooth batter. Add 1 cup of the remaining flour and knead in flour as much as possible. Put the other ½ cup flour on board. Dump the bowl contents onto the flour and start kneading until a smooth ball forms. Will take about 5 minutes. Ball of dough must be smooth and elastic. Let dough rest on board, covered with a bowl, for about 20 minutes. Grease one large cookie sheet. Punch down dough and divide it into three equal pieces. Form each piece into a rope. Braid the three pieces together to make a large loaf. Put on the cookie sheet. Tuck ends under, if necessary, and shape to make a pretty loaf. Cover lightly with a towel and let rise for 30 to 40 minutes in a warm place free of drafts. Heat oven to 350°. To the reserved egg yolk, add 1 teaspoon of water. Beat with a fork and gently brush this egg wash all over the raised braid. Bake 30 to 35 minutes or until loaf is golden brown and sounds hollow when tapped. Brush with any leftover egg wash and return to oven for 5 minutes. Carefully remove braid to a rack to cool. Wrap well and serve the day it's made, if possible. This is a delicious golden bread. Makes 1 large loaf.

*A **Thymely Footnote** ... **Fennel** is a tender perennial, but in Indiana I treat it as an annual. It is anise (licorice) flavored and important in fish cookery. Florence fennel (finocchio) is smaller than fennel and its bulbous base is used widely in Italy as a vegetable. When fennel is growing, it looks like dill.*

Buttermilk Yeast Rolls

2 cups slightly warm buttermilk
2 envelopes active dry yeast
½ cup warm water
4½ cups flour
1 teaspoon baking soda
1¼ teaspoons salt
¼ cup sugar
½ cup butter or oleo

Heat buttermilk slightly over very low heat. Sprinkle yeast on warm water. Stir to dissolve. Add yeast to the buttermilk and stir well. Sift together the dry ingredients. Cut butter into flour mixture to resemble cornmeal. Add buttermilk-yeast mixture and beat for 10 minutes. Dough will be very soft. Cover dough with oiled waxed paper and refrigerate for at least 8 hours. You'll probably need to punch it down a time or two. Remove from refrigerator and punch down dough. Shape rolls to fit greased muffin tins. Cover muffin pans with oiled waxed paper and let rolls rise until doubled, up to 2 hours. Bake at 375° for 15 to 20 minutes. When rolls begin to brown, brush lightly with melted butter, then continue baking. Makes 2 dozen rolls.

Mozzarella Bread on the Outdoor Grill

1 long loaf Italian Bread
1 16 ounce package Mozzarella cheese, sliced
½ cup pimento-stuffed olives, chopped
olive oil
1 tablespoon fresh chopped oregano, or 1 teaspoon dried

Cut bread crosswise into 1" slices, but do not cut through crust. Fit a slice of Mozzarella and a few chopped olives between the slices. Brush a large sheet of heavy duty foil with olive oil. Brush a little olive oil over the outside of the loaf. Wrap the loaf tightly in the foil. Place over the charcoal grill (medium coals) and heat for 20 minutes or so. Fold foil back, sprinkle all over with the fresh oregano and serve. Gooey, but great with grilled meats or vegetables.

Sour Cream Cinnamon Rolls

I've made these dozens of times and they always turn out the same — just plain good! Quick to make too — only one dough rising.

1 **cup sour cream**
2 **tablespoons Crisco or oleo**
½ **cup sugar**
¼ **teaspoon baking soda**
1 **teaspoon salt**
1 **envelope active dry yeast**
¼ **cup lukewarm water**
1 **egg**
3 **cups sifted flour**
2 **tablespoons butter or oleo**
⅓ **cup brown sugar**
1 **teaspoon ground cinnamon**

Heat sour cream in a heavy saucepan until just lukewarm. Remove from heat and stir in shortening, sugar, baking soda and salt. Sprinkle yeast on lukewarm water and stir to dissolve. Add yeast and egg to sour cream mixture. Gradually mix in enough flour to make a soft dough. Turn out onto a floured surface and knead for 1 minute. Form into a ball and let rest for 5 minutes. Roll into a 9" x 13" rectangle. Spread dough with the softened butter. Sprinkle with brown sugar and cinnamon. Roll up like a jelly roll. With a sharp knife, slice into 12 equal slices. Place slices, touching, in a greased 9" x 11" x 2" pan. Let rise until doubled, 1 to 1½ hours. Bake in a 375° oven about 22 minutes. Cool to lukewarm. Drizzle with powdered sugar icing. Makes 12 rolls.

Italian Bread with Herbed Olive Oil

Slice a **large loaf of Italian bread** into 1½" slices. Make the Herbed Olive Oil on page 45. For each person at the table, pour a small amount of the oil into a shallow saucer. Pass the bread — each person dips the bread into the oil. No butter — no cholesterol! This is very "in" in California and the Southwest.

Crusty Pumpernickel Bread

❧ *This is a very dark, full-of-flavor bread that is very much like the loaves you might buy in a German or Austrian bakery. They call it "black bread."*

2 packages active dry yeast
1½ cups warm water
½ cup dark molasses
3 cups rye flour
⅓ cup cocoa
2 tablespoons caraway seeds
¼ cup oleo, softened
1 teaspoon salt
2 cups bread flour (may need a little more)
yellow cornmeal
additional caraway seeds (to sprinkle on top)

In a large bowl, dissolve yeast in warm water. Stir in molasses and let mixture set for 10 minutes, until it looks foamy. Add rye flour, cocoa, caraway seeds, soft oleo and salt to the yeast mixture. Beat with a wooden spoon until smooth. Stir in enough bread flour to make dough easy to handle. Turn dough out onto a lightly floured surface. Knead until smooth and elastic, 5 minutes. Put dough in a greased bowl, grease top of dough also. Cover with a clean towel and place in a warm location until doubled in volume, 1 hour or so. Punch down and let rise again — 20 to 30 minutes. Grease a large baking sheet. Sprinkle 2 or 3 tablespoons of corn meal all over sheet. Punch down the dough and shape into one large or two smaller loaves. Score top or tops of loaves with a sharp knife. Sprinkle a few caraway seeds over loaves. Let rise again for 40 minutes. Bake in a 375° oven for 30 to 35 minutes (depending on size of loaves). Loaves should sound hollow when tapped. Remove from pan and cool. Wrap very well. This is a wonderful bread to make on a cold winter morning. It isn't difficult or tricky, but there are three dough-rising periods, so it takes quite a while from start to finish. Makes 1 large loaf or 2 smaller ones.

A Thymely Footnote . . . *Another member of the mint family is* ***lemon balm.*** *It is a rapid spreader. It has a lemon flavor, but pales in flavor next to either lemon verbena or lemon thyme. I dry the leaves for potpourri — they stay green.*

Golden Granola Yeast Bread

3   to 3¼ cups flour
1   package active dry yeast
1   cup granola (put in a plastic bag and crush with a rolling pin)
¼   cup brown sugar, packed
1½   teaspoons salt
1   cup water
2   tablespoons oil
1   egg
    vegetable oil
    butter or oleo, softened

Heat oven to 375°. In a large mixer bowl, combine 1½ cups flour, yeast, granola, brown sugar and salt. Mix well. Add warm water (120° to 130°), 2 tablespoons oil and eggs. Blend at low speed until moistened. Beat about 3 minutes at medium speed. By hand, gradually stir in remainder of flour to make a firm dough. Knead until smooth and elastic on a floured surface for about 5 minutes. Place in a greased bowl. Turn to grease top. Cover. Let rise in a warm place until doubled, about 1 hour. Punch down dough. On a lightly floured surface, roll or pat to a 15" x 9" rectangle. Starting with shorter side, roll up tightly, pressing dough into roll with each turn. Press each end with side of hand to seal. Fold ends under loaf. Place seam side down in a greased 9" x 5" loaf pan. Brush loaf with vegetable oil. Cover and let rise until light and doubled, about 1 hour. Bake at 375° for 30 to 35 minutes, or until loaves are golden brown and sound hollow when tapped. Remove loaf from pan. Brush with softened butter. Cool. (If you use a glass pan, bake at 350°.) Makes 1 loaf.

A Thymely Footnote . . . Lavender is a beautiful perennial. There are 3 major varieties — all important to the gardener. English lavender has blue-green leaves and is the hardiest of the 3. It has gray-blue flowers and is very aromatic. French lavender has gray-green, fine-cut leaves and blue flowers. Spanish lavender has fairly dark green leaves and it has beautiful dark purple flowers. Late in summer, lavender is harvested in southern France and Spain — quite a sight!

Dilled Rye Bread

❧ Homemade rye bread is wonderful, but add dill, and it becomes something special.

½ cup lukewarm water
1 package active dry yeast
1 cup milk
1 cup boiling water
3 tablespoons salad oil
3 tablespoons light brown sugar
1 teaspoon salt
3 cups rye flour
3 cups bread flour
1 tablespoon dried dill weed
2 tablespoons dill seed

Dissolve yeast in water. Add milk, boiling water and oil, in that order. Sift together brown sugar, salt, flours and dill weed. Add to liquid mixture. Add a little more bread flour if dough is sticky. Knead for 5 to 8 minutes, keeping surface lightly floured so dough won't stick. Put dough in a large greased bowl. Grease top of dough and let rise 1½ hours. Punch down and shape into two round loaves. Heavily grease a large baking sheet. Sprinkle dill seeds in two circles on the greased sheet. Carefully put each ball of dough on a circle of seeds. Cover with towel. Let rise about 1 hour. Bake 40 minutes at 400°. Loaves should be crisp, lightly browned and sound hollow when tapped. Makes 2 round loaves.

Zelma's Quick Rolls

Dissolve **1 envelope active dry yeast** in **2 cups warm water**. Add **¼ cup sugar, ½ cup vegetable oil**, and **1 egg**. Beat lightly. Add **4 cups self-rising flour**. Cover and refrigerate for 24 hours. Do not knead or stir down. Spoon into greased muffin tins. Let rise 45 minutes in a warm place. Bake in a 425° oven for about 12 minutes. Unbaked dough will keep in the refrigerator for one week.

Potato Rolls 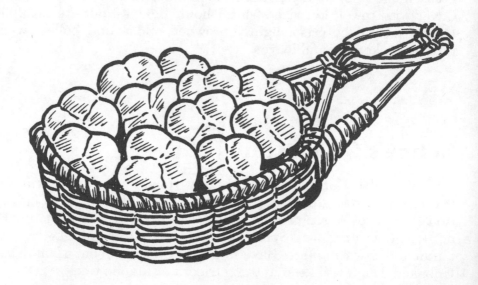 MOTHER

1½ cups milk
½ cup sugar
2 tablespoons salt
3 tablespoons oleo
2 packages active dry yeast
½ cup very warm water
1 egg
1 egg white
½ cup mashed potato
about 6½ cups sifted flour

Scald milk. Add sugar, salt and oleo. Cool to lukewarm. Sprinkle yeast into very warm water. Stir to dissolve. Add lukewarm milk mixture, egg and egg white, mashed potato and 3 cups sifted flour. Beat until smooth. Stir in rest of flour. Mix well. Cover. Let rise in warm place, free from draft, until doubled, about 45 minutes. Punch down, divide in half. Cut each half into eighteen pieces. Roll each piece into a rope about 6″ long. Tie each into a loose knot. Place in well-greased pans, rolls touching. Cover. Let rise in warm place until doubled, about 45 minutes. Bake at 375° for 25 minutes. Remove from pans. Brush tops with melted oleo or butter. Makes 4 or 5 dozen rolls, depending on size.

The Very Best Blueberry Muffins

4 eggs	2 teaspoons baking
1 cup melted butter	powder
2 cups sugar	½ teaspoon baking soda
2 cups sour cream	1 teaspoon salt
4 cups flour	2 cups fresh blueberries

Mix eggs, butter, sugar, and sour cream. Sift dry ingredients together, then add blueberries. Fold flour-blueberry mixture into egg mixture until blended. Spoon batter into greased muffin tins (or paper-lined tins) ½ full and bake at 375° for 25 minutes. Makes 2½ to 3 dozen fabulous muffins. (The sour cream is the secret.) Freeze any leftover baked muffins.

Refrigerator Gingerbread Muffins

1 cup sugar
1 cup oleo
1 cup dark molasses
4 eggs, beaten
3½ cups flour
1 teaspoon ground cinnamon
1 teaspoon ground ginger
1 teaspoon ground nutmeg
½ teaspoon salt
1 cup buttermilk
1 teaspoon baking soda
1 teaspoon hot water
1 teaspoon vanilla
1 cup raisins
1 cup chopped pecans

Cream shortening and sugar. Add molasses and stir. Add beaten eggs. Sift flour with spices and salt. Add dry ingredients and buttermilk alternately to the molasses and sugar mixture. Add baking soda that has been dissolved in 1 teaspoon hot water. Beat. Add vanilla. Stir in the raisins and nuts. Fill greased muffin tins (or paper-lined tins) ½ full. Bake at 375° for about 30 minutes. Use batter as needed and keep the rest stored, covered, in refrigerator for later use. Batter will keep for a week or more. Makes 2 to 2½ dozen muffins.

Frosty Date Muffins

1 cup flour
¼ cup sugar
3 teaspoons baking powder
½ teaspoon salt
1 cup quick oats, uncooked
⅔ cup chopped dates
3 tablespoons oleo, melted
1 egg, beaten
¾ cup milk
6 pitted dates

Combine flour, sugar, baking powder and salt in a large bowl. Stir in oats and dates. Add oleo, egg and milk. Stir only until dry ingredients are moistened. Fill greased muffin cups or paper-lined cups ⅔ full. Cut dates in half and place a half on top of batter in each muffin cup. Bake at 425° for 15 minutes. Makes 12 muffins.

Cranberry Muffins

2¼ cups flour
¼ cup sugar
¾ teaspoon baking soda
¼ teaspoon salt
1 egg, slightly beaten
¾ cup buttermilk
¼ cup vegetable oil
1 cup washed, dried, chopped raw cranberries
½ cup sugar

Combine flour, the ¼ cup sugar, baking soda and salt in a large bowl. Combine egg, buttermilk and oil in a small bowl and blend well. Add all at once to dry ingredients, stirring just to moisten. Combine cranberries with the ½ cup sugar and stir into the batter. Spoon into paper-lined muffin cups and fill ⅔ full. Bake in a 400° oven for about 20 minutes. Makes 12 muffins. Terrific with chicken salad or chicken casseroles.

Poppy Seed Muffins

3	cups flour
2¼	cups sugar
1½	teaspoons baking powder
1½	teaspoons salt
1½	cups vegetable oil
1½	cups milk
3	eggs
½	teaspoon almond extract
1½	tablespoons poppy seeds

Preheat oven to 350°. Grease two twelve cup muffin pans (or use paper liners). Combine first four ingredients in one bowl. Combine all other ingredients in another bowl. Add dry ingredients to the second bowl and whisk until batter is smooth. Whisk only until moistened. Fill muffin pans two-thirds full. Bake muffins until golden brown, about 30 minutes. These are very simple to make, but very good. The poppy seeds give them a little crunch. Makes 2 dozen.

Apple Muffins

3½	cups flour
3	cups peeled, finely chopped apples
2	cups sugar
1	teaspoon salt
1	teaspoon baking soda
1	teaspoon ground cinnamon
1½	cups vegetable oil
½	cup chopped nuts, toasted is best
1	teaspoon vanilla

Preheat oven to 350°. Grease and flour muffin pans (or use paper liners). Thoroughly combine flour, apples, sugar, salt, soda and cinnamon in a large bowl. Stir in oil, nuts and vanilla. Batter will be fairly stiff. Fill muffin cups about two-thirds full. Bake until a pick comes out clean, about 30 minutes. A good, moist muffin. Makes 2 dozen.

Squash Muffins

&amp#10;*❧ This is an Amish recipe.*

1½ cups light brown sugar, packed
½ cup molasses
1 cup soft butter
½ cup chopped pecans
2 eggs, beaten
2 cups cooked, mashed winter squash
2 teaspoons baking soda
½ teaspoon salt
3½ cups flour

Cook, drain and mash squash to the consistency of mashed potatoes. Cream sugar, molasses and butter. Add egg and squash and blend well. Mix flour with soda and salt. Blend into the squash batter. Fold in nuts. Fill paper-lined or greased muffin tins about half full. Bake at 375° for 20 minutes or until it tests done. Makes 2 dozen or more muffins. After muffins are cool, wrap well and freeze any left over ones.

Banana Bran Muffins

1 cup All-Bran cereal
1 cup milk
3 tablespoons oil
1 egg
1¼ cups flour
2 tablespoons sugar
1 tablespoon baking powder
¼ teaspoon salt
¾ cup mashed ripe banana
½ cup raisins

Preheat oven to 400°. Line muffin pans with paper cups. Stir cereal into milk in a large bowl. Let stand 2 minutes. Beat in oil and egg. Mix flour, sugar, baking powder and salt in another bowl. Stir into cereal mixture. Add banana and raisins and mix to combine, but don't overmix. Spoon batter into muffin cups — about two-thirds full. Bake about 30 minutes, or until a pick comes out clean. Best if served warm. Makes 12.

Cream Scones

Scones are traditionally served at tea time. Tea is becoming popular in the U.S. Many large city hotels are now serving tea in the late afternoon. The correct time to serve tea is four o'clock to six o'clock. Some places are serving tea as late as six o'clock and calling it "High Tea." An English friend tells me this is incorrect — by six o'clock, it should be called supper! At any rate, an afternoon tea is fun to do. Bring out your best linens, silver, and crystal. Light the candles and serve, among other things, these scones.

  2½ **cups flour**
   5 **teaspoons baking powder**
  2½ **tablespoons sugar**
  ¼ **teaspoon salt**
   6 **tablespoons cold butter, cut into small pieces**
  ¾ **cup heavy cream**
   2 **eggs, lightly beaten**
  ⅓ **cup currants or raisins (currants are better — they're smaller)**
     egg wash (mix 1 egg with ⅓ cup milk)

Sift together the flour, baking powder, 4 teaspoons of sugar and salt. Add butter and blend until mixture resembles corn meal. Stir in the cream, eggs and currants and mix until it just forms a dough. Pat out dough 1" thick on a floured surface. Cut with a 2" round cutter. Put scones on a buttered baking sheet. Brush the tops with the egg wash. Sprinkle rest of sugar on tops and bake in a 450° oven for about 15 minutes, or until tops are golden brown. May take 2 or 3 minutes more or 2 or 3 minutes less, depending on your oven. Makes 12 to 15.

Some of the best scones I ever had was in a little nondescript tea room in the heart of Devonshire Country, England. Reason they were so good? They were served with fresh-made strawberry jam and the famous clotted Devon cream!

Chocolate Chunk Coffee Cake

This is a moist, rich coffee cake. It would be perfect for a brunch.

The cake:
- 2¾ cups flour
- 2 teaspoons baking powder
- ½ teaspoon baking soda
- 1 cup butter, softened
- 1 cup sugar
- 3 large eggs
- 1½ teaspoons vanilla
- 1 cup sour cream

The filling:
- ¾ cup sugar
- 2 teaspoons ground cinnamon
- 12 ounces semisweet chocolate, coarsely chopped
- 1 cup walnuts, chopped

Preheat oven to 350°. Lightly grease bottom and sides of a 10″ tube pan. Lightly flour and tap out excess flour. Sift together the dry ingredients in a medium bowl. In a large bowl, beat the butter for 30 seconds with electric mixer. Gradually add sugar and beat for 1 to 2 minutes, or until light and fluffy. Add the eggs, one at a time, beating well after each addition. Beat in vanilla. Alternately add the dry ingredients with the sour cream. Put one-third of batter into the prepared pan. For the filling, combine all four ingredients. Put one-third of filling over batter. Put half of remaining batter over the filling and spread evenly. Cover batter with half the remaining filling. Scrape last of batter into the pan and spread it evenly. Cover with the last of the filling. Bake the coffee cake about 1 hour, or until it tests done. Cool the cake in the pan for about 15 minutes. Run a knife around the edge of the pan to loosen and invert onto your palm (very carefully!). Carefully re-invert cake onto serving platter. Cool. If desired, sprinkle a little powdered sugar on top or drizzle a little powdered sugar icing over top and let drip down sides of cake. Will serve 12 to 15.

Toffee Coffee Cake

1   cup brown sugar, packed
1   cup sugar
½   cup oleo or butter, softened
2   cups flour
1   teaspoon vanilla
1   teaspoon baking soda
1   cup buttermilk
1   egg
½   cup chopped nuts
6   small Heath bars, chopped (about 4 to 6 ounces*)

Mix first five ingredients together to form crumbs. Put aside ½ cup of these crumbs. To the rest of the crumbs, add the soda which has been dissolved in the buttermilk, and the egg. Beat well and pour into a greased and floured 9″ x 13″ pan. Sprinkle on top the ½ cup reserved crumbs, the nuts and the chopped Heath bars. (If bars are frozen first, they'll chop easier.) Bake at 350° for about 30 minutes, or until it tests done. A very good coffee cake. Serves 8 to 10.

*If you, the reader, live in or near Attica, Indiana, use the toffee from Wolf's Candy Store — the best I've ever eaten!

Rhubarb Coffee Cake

2½   cups flour
1   teaspoon baking powder
1   teaspoon salt
1½   cups light brown sugar, packed
1   egg, beaten
1   cup sour milk (add a tablespoon of vinegar to a cup of milk)
⅔   cup vegetable oil
1   teaspoon vanilla
1½   cups diced red rhubarb
1½   cups chopped pecans or walnuts

Sift dry ingredients. Add brown sugar. Combine egg, milk, oil and vanilla. Add to dry ingredients and blend well. Stir in rhubarb and nuts. Spread batter into a greased 9″ x 13″ pan. Combine ½ cup sugar, 1 teaspoon ground cinnamon and 1 tablespoon melted oleo or butter. Sprinkle over the batter and bake at 325° for about 1 hour. Serves 8 to 10.

Apple Coffee Cake

1 package active dry yeast	¼ cup butter
1 tablespoon sugar	½ cup sugar
1 cup milk, scalded and cooled	¼ teaspoon salt
4½ cups flour	2 eggs, beaten
	12 apples (6 for each pan)

Dissolve yeast and 1 tablespoon sugar in lukewarm milk. Add 1½ cups flour and beat until smooth. Cover and let rise in warm place, free from draft, until light, about 45 minutes. Cream butter. Add sugar and salt. Add to yeast mixture. Add well-beaten eggs and remaining flour. Knead lightly. Roll dough ½" thick and place in two well greased 9" x 9" pans, or one large jelly roll-type pan. Brush tops with **melted butter** and sprinkle each with ¼ **cup granulated sugar** (or ½ cup sugar if using one large pan). Peel and core the 12 apples. Cut each apple into eighths. Press apple slices into the dough, sharp edges downward and have slices close together. Mix **1½ teaspoons cinnamon with 1 cup sugar** and sprinkle over the apples in two pans. Cover and let rise in a warm place, about 45 minutes, or until doubled. Bake at 350° for about 35 minutes. During the first 10 minutes of baking time, cover pan or pans with heavy foil so the apples can cook thoroughly. After 10 minutes, remove the foil and continue baking 25 minutes or until cake is done. Cool cake and drizzle on a little powdered sugar icing, if desired. Serves 12 or more.

Coffee Cake Glaze

Drizzle this glaze on any coffee cake or sweet rolls that need a little dressing up or need an extra flavor boost.

2 tablespoons butter or oleo, softened
¾ cup confectioners' sugar
2 tablespoons fruit juice, liqueur (such as Kahlúa, Cointreau, etc.) brandy or rum

Beat all ingredients together until they are smooth. You may need to add a little more sugar or liquid to make it the right spreading or drizzling consistency. If you make the Apple Coffee Cake above, use some of your homemade Apple Brandy (on page 296) for the liquid.

Almond Puffs ⊂▤MOTHER♡▥⊃

∂◦ These are wonderful little sweet rolls. Very easy.

1   **package active dry yeast**
¼   **cup lukewarm water**
½   **cup milk**
¼   **cup Crisco**
1   **tablespoon sugar**
½   **teaspoon salt**
2   **to 2½ cups flour**
2   **eggs**
1   **cup almonds, blanched and chopped, divided**
4   **tablespoons sugar for topping**

Dissolve yeast in lukewarm water. Scald milk. Add Crisco, sugar and salt. Stir and cool to lukewarm. Add flour, beating thoroughly. Add dissolved yeast and eggs, one at a time, beating after each addition. Beat all together until quite smooth. Cover and let rise until doubled in bulk — 1 hour or more. Stir down and add ½ cup chopped almonds. Fill well-greased muffin pans one-half full. Combine other ½ cup almonds with 4 tablespoons sugar. Sprinkle almond-sugar mixture over tops of rolls. Cover and let rise until doubled in bulk — 30 minutes or so. Bake in a 375° oven for 15 to 20 minutes. Makes 2 dozen puffs.

Cheater Sweet Rolls

1   **loaf frozen bread dough, thawed (I like Rich's dough)**
¾   **stick butter or oleo, softened**
5   **teaspoons ground cinnamon**
½   **cup sugar**
½   **cup chopped pecans**

Roll out bread dough to about 7″ x 14″. Spread with softened butter. Sprinkle on cinnamon, sugar and nuts. Roll up dough into a log with spices in the center. Slice the log into twelve pieces. Put each piece in a well-greased muffin cup. Allow to rise in a warm place until doubled. Bake for about 20 minutes in a 325° oven. Makes 12 rolls.

Honey Nut Coffee Cake ⊂▭ MOTHER ♡ ▭⊃

2 packages active dry yeast
¼ cup lukewarm water
1 cup milk
¼ cup butter
½ cup sugar
1 teaspoon salt
2 eggs, beaten
5 cups bread flour

Dissolve yeast in lukewarm water. Scald milk. Add butter, sugar and salt. Stir to dissolve all. Cool. Add flour (about 3 cups) to make a thick batter. Add yeast and eggs and mix well. Add rest of flour to make a soft dough (may not need all 5 cups). Turn out on a lightly floured surface and knead for 4 or 5 minutes to make a satiny dough. Put dough into a greased bowl. Turn dough to grease top. Cover and let rise until doubled — 1 hour or more. When doubled, punch down. Shape dough into a long roll. Coil this roll into a large, round, greased pan, beginning the coil on the outside working toward the middle. Brush the Honey Nut Topping all over the top. Let rise until doubled in bulk and bake at 375° for 25 to 30 minutes. Serves 10 or 12.

Honey Nut Topping
Cream together **¼ cup soft butter, ⅔ cup confectioners' sugar, 1 egg white** and **2 tablespoons warmed honey**. Add **½ cup chopped nuts**.

Fruit-Streusel Coffee Cake Topping

1 21 ounce can fruit pie filling (cherry, blueberry, etc.)
1½ cups light brown sugar
½ cup butter or oleo, softened
1½ tablespoons flour
1 teaspoon ground cinnamon
1½ to 2 cups chopped pecans or walnuts

Spoon canned fruit filling over unbaked coffee cake batter. Combine rest of ingredients until crumbly. Sprinkle evenly over the fruit and bake according to your coffee cake directions.

CAKES

Maple Cake

This is a really good cake.

⅔ **cup Crisco**
2 **cups sifted flour (remove ¼ cup for nuts)**
1 **cup brown sugar, packed**
½ **teaspoon salt**
2 **teaspoons baking powder**
½ **cup plus 3 tablespoons maple syrup (real!)**
¼ **cup plus 2 tablespoons milk**
1 **teaspoon maple extract**
2 **eggs**
½ **cup chopped pecans**

Beat shortening and sugar together. Add 1¾ cups flour, salt and baking powder. Then add maple syrup, milk, extract and eggs. Beat until smooth. Mix nuts in the reserved ¼ cup of flour. Add nuts to mixture and stir until all traces of flour are gone. Pour into a greased 9″ x 13″ pan or 2 - 9″ cake pans. Bake at 350° for 30 minutes, or until done — depending on pan sizes. Watch closely. Frost with:

Maple Butter Cream

1¼ **cups sugar**
¾ **cup pure maple syrup**
¾ **cup water**
3 **eggs**
2 **cups butter, softened**
1 **teaspoon maple extract**

Cook the sugar, syrup and water together to 250° on a candy thermometer. Beat the eggs and gradually add the hot liquid, stirring continuously until cooled. Mix the butter and extract together and add to the cooled mixture. Stir until smooth. Ice the cake with this butter cream. Can sprinkle a few pecans on top, if desired. Very, very rich and good. Cake serves 10 to 12.

This recipe was given to me by a young farm wife in Vermont. She and her husband are in the business of making maple syrup — the best maple syrup I ever tasted, by the way. Their syrup won the blue ribbon for maple syrup at the Vermont State Fair. Can you think of a tougher fair to enter your maple syrup in?

Glazed Apple Cake

This is an excellent apple cake.

3½ cups peeled, diced tart apples
1½ cups oil
1½ cups sugar
½ cup brown sugar, packed
3 eggs
3 cups flour
3 teaspoons ground cinnamon
1 teaspoon baking soda
½ teaspoon ground nutmeg
½ teaspoon salt
1 cup chopped pecans or walnuts
2 teaspoons vanilla

Butter and flour a 10" tube pan. Shake out excess flour. Heat oven to 325°. Prepare apples and put in a large bowl of lightly salted water to keep them from browning. Combine oil and sugars in a large bowl and blend well. Beat in eggs, one at a time, beating well after each. Sift together dry ingredients and add to sugar mixture, blending well. Drain apples thoroughly. Fold apples, nuts and vanilla into the batter. Spread evenly into the prepared pan. Bake for 1¾ hours or until a pick inserted near the center comes out clean. Let cake cool in pan for 20 minutes. Turn cake out onto serving plate. Pour warm glaze over warm cake. Cake serves 10 to 12.

Glaze

3 tablespoons butter
3 tablespoons brown sugar
3 tablespoons sugar
3 tablespoons heavy cream
½ teaspoon vanilla

Combine all ingredients in a heavy pan. Bring to a boil over medium heat and boil for 1 minute. Spoon over the warm cake.

Apple-Nut Cake

4 **cups coarsely chopped apples**
2 **cups sugar**
2 **eggs**
½ **cup vegetable oil**
2 **teaspoons vanilla**
2 **cups flour**
2 **teaspoons baking soda**
2 **teaspoons ground cinnamon**
1 **teaspoon salt**
1 **cup chopped walnuts or pecans**

Peel apples and chop or dice. Add sugar to apples and stir well — set aside. Beat eggs slightly. Beat in oil and vanilla. Mix and sift flour, baking soda, cinnamon and salt. Stir into egg mixture alternately with apple-sugar mixture. Stir in nuts. Pour into a greased and floured 9" x 13" pan. Bake at 350° for 35 to 45 minutes — watch closely — or until done. Cool cake. Frost with **Lemon Butter Frosting**. Decorate with whole walnut or pecan halves. Cut into squares.

Lemon Butter Frosting: Combine **3 cups confectioners' sugar, 4 tablespoons soft butter, 2 tablespoons fresh lemon juice**, and **1 to 2 tablespoons water**. Beat to make a smooth frosting.

Autumn Pumpkin Cake

1 **18 ounce box yellow cake mix**
4 **eggs**
¾ **cup sugar**
½ **cup vegetable oil**
1 **cup canned pumpkin**
¼ **cup water**
1 **teaspoon ground cinnamon**
⅛ **teaspoon ground nutmeg**

Combine all ingredients and beat 5 minutes with an electric mixer. Pour into a greased and floured tube or Bundt pan. Bake at 350° for 35 to 45 minutes — check after 35 minutes. Especially good if frosted with a cream cheese icing. (See the one on page 220.) Best if baked, cooled, iced, then refrigerated for a day before cutting — but also good the first day it's baked!

Orange-Rum Cake

🍃 *Make this cake several days before serving. It is very moist and very good and great to have on hand for drop-in holiday visitors.*

    1   cup butter or oleo
    1   cup sugar
    2   eggs
        grated rind of 2 oranges (no white)
        grated rind of 1 lemon (no white)
   2½   cups flour
    2   teaspoons baking powder
    1   teaspoon baking soda
    ½   teaspoon salt
    1   cup buttermilk
    1   cup chopped pecans
        Orange-Rum Glaze

Beat butter until light and fluffy. Add sugar and beat well. Add eggs and grated rinds and beat until mixture is light. Combine dry ingredients and add to creamed mixture alternately with the buttermilk. Stir in pecans. Spoon mixture into a well-greased, lightly floured 10" tube pan. Bake at 350° for 1 hour or until cake tests done. Leave cake in pan and cool slightly. While cake is still warm, pour glaze over cake top. Cool cake. Cake should be covered tightly and left in the pan for several days before unmolding.

Orange-Rum Glaze
        juice of 2 oranges
        juice of 1 lemon
    1   cup sugar
    3   tablespoons dark rum

Mix all ingredients together in a saucepan. Bring to a boil, stirring often. Remove from heat and let cool only a few minutes. Pour warm glaze over warm cake.

Fresh Peach Cake ⊂▭⊐ MOTHER ♡ ⊂▭⊐

½   cup butter
1½ cups brown sugar, packed
1   egg
2   cups flour
1   teaspoon baking soda
    dash salt
1   cup buttermilk
4   peaches, peeled, diced
¼   cup sugar
1   teaspoon ground cinnamon

Cream butter with brown sugar until light and fluffy. Beat in egg. Sift flour with soda and salt. Add to creamed mixture alternately with buttermilk, beating until smooth after each addition. Gently fold in peaches. Pour batter into a greased 9 " x 13 " x 2 " pan. Sprinkle the ¼ cup sugar and 1 teaspoon cinnamon over top. Bake at 350° for 30 to 35 minutes, or until done. Wonderful served with whipped cream. Serves 10 or 12.

Pineapple-Pecan Upside Down Cake

This is quick because you start with a mix.

1   20 ounce can pineapple slices, drained and juice saved
5   tablespoons butter
½   cup light brown sugar
1   18¼ ounce white cake mix (I like Duncan Hines Deluxe)
1   cup pecans, chopped
3   eggs
⅓   cup oil
1¼ cups reserved pineapple juice (if not enough juice, add
    water to make 1¼ cups)

Grease 9 " x 13 " pan. Preheat oven to 350°. Melt butter and brown sugar together and spread over bottom of pan. Arrange pineapple slices over butter-sugar mixture. In a mixer bowl, combine cake mix, eggs, oil and juice. Mix until well blended. Add chopped pecans and blend all together. Pour into the prepared pan and bake 40 to 45 minutes, or until it tests done. Remove from oven and let stand in the pan for about 5 minutes. Invert onto a serving plate. Wonderful served with dollops of whipped cream. Serves 10 or 12.

Georgia Peach Pound Cake

A farm wife from Georgia gave me this recipe. It is truly delicious.

1   cup butter, softened
3   cups sugar
6   eggs, room temperature
1   teaspoon vanilla extract
1   teaspoon almond extract
3   cups flour
¼   teaspoon baking soda
½   teaspoon salt
½   cup sour cream
2   cups ripe peaches, peeled and chopped
     whipped cream (sweetened slightly)

Grease and flour a 10″ tube pan. Preheat oven to 350°. In a large bowl, cream butter and sugar until light and fluffy. Add eggs, one at a time, beating well after each. Stir in extracts. In a small bowl, combine dry ingredients and add to the creamed mixture. Fold in the sour cream and chopped peaches.

Pour batter into prepared pan. Bake for 1¼ to 1½ hours or until a wooden pick comes out clean. Will serve 12 to 15. For each serving, put a slice of cake on plate. Put a heaping spoonful of whipped cream on the cake. Add a dash of ground cinnamon on top of cream.

Spice-Coconut Cake

    1 cup oil
    1 cup brown sugar, packed
    1 cup sugar
    2 eggs
   2½ cups flour
    ½ teaspoon salt
    1 teaspoon baking soda
    1 teaspoon ground cinnamon
    1 teaspoon ground nutmeg
    1 cup buttermilk
    1 teaspoon vanilla
    1 cup flaked coconut
    1 cup pecans, chopped
       Cream Cheese Icing
    1 cup flaked coconut
       pecan halves

Combine oil and sugars. Beat well. Add eggs, one at a time, beating well after each addition. Combine flour, salt and spices. Add to creamed mixture alternately with buttermilk, beginning and ending with the flour mixture. Stir in the vanilla, 1 cup coconut and 1 cup chopped pecans.

Pour batter into 2 greased and floured 9″ round pans. Bake at 350° for 20 to 25 minutes or until a wooden pick comes out clean. Cool cakes in pans for 10 minutes. Remove from pans and cool. Spread Cream Cheese Icing between layers and on top and sides. Sprinkle top with the other cup of coconut. Gently press pecan halves into side of cake, all around. Cake serves 10 to 12.

Cream Cheese Icing

Use this on the Spice-Coconut Cake, or any other cake.

    1 8 ounce package cream cheese, softened
    ¼ cup butter or oleo, softened
    1 16 ounce package powdered sugar, sifted

Combine cream cheese and butter. Beat until light and fluffy. Add powdered sugar and beat until smooth. If necessary, add a tablespoon of milk or cream, if consistency is too thick.

Lemon Cake ⊂▭ MOTHER ♡▭⊃

    1 18½ ounce package yellow cake mix
    1 3 ounce package lemon gelatin
    ¾ cup oil
    4 eggs, beaten
    ½ cup water
    ¼ cup fresh lemon juice
       Lemon Glaze

Grease and flour a Bundt pan or a 9" x 13" pan. Preheat oven to 350°. Beat, with electric mixer, the first 6 ingredients together until smooth, 3 or 4 minutes. Pour batter into prepared pan. Bake 35 to 45 minutes, depending on pan size. Check for doneness and don't overbake. Cool cake in pan a few minutes, then turn out onto serving plate (or leave in 9" x 13" pan, if using that size).

Lemon Glaze
    1 cup powdered sugar, sifted
    3 tablespoons fresh lemon juice
    1 tablespoon grated lemon peel

Stir the powdered sugar, lemon juice and the peel together to form a smooth glaze. Pierce the still-warm cake all over with a sharp wooden skewer. Spoon the glaze over the top and let it drip down the sides also. Cakes serves 10 or 12.

Peanut Butter Frosting

    3 cups (or more) confectioners' sugar
    ½ cup peanut butter, smooth or chunky
    ¼ cup butter or oleo, softened
       milk to moisten

Combine all in mixer bowl and beat until smooth. Add more confectioners' sugar or milk to make a smooth icing. Delicious on angel food cake, chocolate, white or yellow cake.

Pumpkin Cake ⊂≡[MOTHER♡]⊃

& *This was Mother's favorite pumpkin cake.*

1¼ cups sugar
½   cup butter or oleo, softened
2   eggs
1   cup canned pumpkin
2   cups flour
3   teaspoons baking powder
½   teaspoon ground ginger
½   teaspoon salt
½   teaspoon baking soda
1   teaspoon ground nutmeg
1   teaspoon ground cinnamon
¾   cup milk
1   cup chopped nuts, if desired

Cream sugar and oleo. Add the eggs and pumpkin and mix well. Sift the dry ingredients together. Add the milk alternately with the dry ingredients. Mix well to form a smooth batter. Add the 1 cup of chopped nuts, if desired.

Preheat oven to 350°. Pour the batter into 2 greased and floured 9" layer pans or a 9" x 13" x 2" baking pan. Bake for 20 to 30 minutes, or more. Baking time depends on size of pans used. A brown sugar icing is wonderful on this cake. Serves 10 to 12.

Candied Fruit (Microwave)

If you need to age candied fruit or raisins in brandy or liqueur (to use in cookies, fruitcakes, breads, etc.), microwave ¼ **cup brandy** in a glass bowl for 30 seconds. Add **fruit** to the bowl and stir. Microwave on high for 2 minutes. Remove from oven and let cool for 10 to 15 minutes, or until all the liquid is absorbed. Fruits are ready to use. I have a great fruitcake recipe that calls for soaking the fruits in brandy overnight and then the next day, proceed with the cake directions. This is surely faster and more convenient.

The Best Chocolate Cake

A friend gave this recipe to me, assuring me it was the best chocolate cake she had ever eaten. After tasting it, I have no argument!

1½   cups flour
1½   teaspoons baking soda
¼   teaspoon salt
1   cup milk
¼   cup sour cream
2   teaspoons vanilla
½   cup butter, softened
2   cups sugar
3   eggs
5   1 ounce squares unsweetened chocolate, melted and
     cooled slightly

Preheat oven to 350°. Grease a 9″ x 13″ baking pan (not glass). Line bottom with waxed paper and grease paper. Set aside. Combine flour, soda and salt in a small bowl. In another bowl, combine milk, sour cream and vanilla. Set aside. In mixer bowl, cream butter. Gradually add sugar and beat until well mixed, 2 or 3 minutes. Add eggs, one at a time, beating well after each addition. Beat until light and fluffy. Gradually add chocolate and beat until smooth. Add flour mixture alternately with milk mixture, beginning and ending with flour. Mix until well blended. Pour evenly into prepared pan. Bake 45 to 50 minutes, or until a wooden pick comes out clean. Cool in the pan for 10 minutes. Invert cake and carefully peel off waxed paper. Carefully invert again and put cake on large serving platter or use a tray. Frost top and sides with this excellent frosting:

Frosting

5   1 ounce squares unsweetened chocolate
6   tablespoons butter, divided
2½   cups confectioners' sugar, sifted
½   cup warm milk
1   egg yolk
1   teaspoon vanilla

In a small, heavy saucepan, melt chocolate and 5 tablespoons butter over low heat. Put this mixture in a mixer bowl. Add sugar alternately with milk, beating well after each addition. Beat in egg yolk and vanilla. Beat in the other 1 tablespoon of butter. Frost top and sides of cake.

Will serve 15 or more, depending on size of servings, but experience tells me you'll be asked for seconds, along with the recipe!

Hot Water Chocolate Cake

      2 cups flour
     ½ cup cocoa
      2 teaspoons baking soda
     ½ teaspoon salt
     ½ cup butter
    1½ cups sugar
      2 eggs
     ½ cup milk
      1 teaspoon vanilla
      1 cup boiling water
         Chocolate Frosting

Sift first 4 ingredients together. Set aside. Cream butter and sugar in a bowl until light and fluffy. Add eggs, one at a time, beating well after each addition. Stir in milk and vanilla. Add dry ingredients to creamed mixture and mix well. Add boiling water and stir well. Pour into greased 9" x 13" x 2" pan or 2 - 8" cake pans. Line pan, or pans, with waxed paper. Bake in a 325° oven 30 minutes, more or less, depending on pans used. Always test for doneness. Cool layers a few minutes, then remove from pans.

Chocolate Frosting
      3 cups confectioners' sugar, sifted
     ⅓ cup butter, softened
      2 1 ounce squares unsweetened chocolate, melted and
         cooled
      3 to 4 tablespoons milk
      1 teaspoon vanilla

Combine all ingredients in a large bowl. Beat until smooth and creamy. Cake serves 10.

A Thymely Footnote . . . Caraway is grown mainly for its seed. German and Austrian bakeries couldn't exist without caraway seeds for their wonderful rye breads! Caraway is a biennial. It has leaves that look like carrot leaves. The first year, it produces foliage; the second year, it produces flowers, then seed heads.

Pecan Whiskey Cake

This is another great holiday cake.

1	cup butter, softened
2	cups sugar
6	eggs, beaten
3½	cups cake flour, sifted
4	teaspoons baking powder
⅔	teaspoon salt
2	teaspoons ground nutmeg
1	cup good whiskey (you can be the judge as to what's good!)
2	to 3 cups raisins (depends on you)
4	cups pecans, chopped coarsely
½	cup cake flour, sifted

Cream butter. Gradually add sugar and beat until fluffy. Add eggs and beat well. Dredge raisins and nuts in the ½ cup flour and set aside. Sift dry ingredients together. Add alternately with whiskey to the creamed mixture. Add raisins and nuts to batter and mix well. Butter, then line a 1 - piece angel food cake pan with waxed paper. Butter the waxed paper and pour batter into pan.

Bake at 350° for about 1 hour or until it tests done with a wooden pick. Serve cake with whipped cream, a whiskey sauce, or a hard sauce. Serves at least 12.

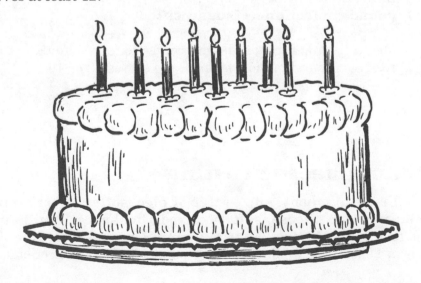

Mississippi Mud Cake

Rich, gooey and luscious!

- 2 sticks oleo
- 2 cups sugar
- 1½ cups flour
- ½ cup cocoa
- 1 cup pecans, chopped
  dash of salt
- 4 eggs, beaten
- 2 teaspoons vanilla
- 1 jar marshmallow cream (7 to 10 ounce size, or larger — size depends on how much marshmallow cream you want on the cake)

Melt oleo and put into a large bowl. Add all dry ingredients and pecans. Add the beaten eggs and vanilla. Mix well and put into a greased 9" x 13" pan and bake for 30 to 40 minutes at 350° — test for doneness after 30 minutes. As soon as cake comes out of oven, spread the jar of marshmallow cream over top. Let set a few minutes to cool, then ice with the following:

- ½ stick oleo
- ½ cup cocoa
- 6 tablespoons milk
- 1 pound confectioners' sugar, sifted

Melt oleo. Add cocoa, milk and confectioners' sugar. Beat well and spread over marshmallow layer. Cake serves 10 or 12.

Cream Cheese Frosting

Cream together ½ cup butter or oleo, softened, an 8 ounce package cream cheese, softened, and 1 teaspoon vanilla until light and fluffy. Gradually add a 1 pound box of sifted confectioners' sugar. Beat well. If too thick, add a little milk or cream.

Chocolate Cream Cake ⊏≣⎤MOTHER♡⊐

1 cup boiling water
2 squares (2 ounces) unsweetened chocolate
½ cup butter or oleo, softened
1 teaspoon vanilla
1¾ cups brown sugar, firmly packed
2 eggs
1¾ cups plus 2 tablespoons flour
1 teaspoon baking soda
¼ teaspoon salt
½ cup sour cream

Pour boiling water over chocolate in bowl. Let stand until cool and melted. Cream butter and vanilla. Add brown sugar and blend well. Add eggs, one at a time, beating well after each addition. Spoon unsifted flour into dry measuring cup. Level off and pour measured flour onto a square of waxed paper. Add soda and salt to flour and stir to blend. Stir blended dry ingredients into creamed mixture. Mix well. Blend in sour cream and chocolate mixture.

Pour into a greased, waxed paper-lined 9" x 5" x 3" aluminum loaf pan. Bake at 325° for 1 hour and 15 minutes, or until cake pulls away from sides of pan. Cool on rack for 10 minutes. Turn cake out of pan and remove waxed paper. Frost top and sides with a favorite frosting. Cut into 1" slices to serve. Cake serves 8 or 9.

Date-Pecan Fruitcake

&❧ *This is expensive to make (2 pounds of dates and 4 cups of pecan halves!), but if you feel like splurging on a fruitcake (and if you also don't like all those candied fruits and peels), this is the one to splurge on.*

1 **cup sugar**
1 **cup flour**
½ **teaspoon baking powder**
½ **teaspoon salt**
2 **pounds pitted dates, halved**
4 **cups pecan halves**
2 **cups candied red cherries**
4 **eggs, at room temperature**
1 **tablespoon vanilla**

Sift together the first 4 ingredients. Add the dates, pecans and cherries. Toss to coat fruit and nuts well. Beat eggs in another bowl until they are thick. Add vanilla and beat well. Pour over the fruit-flour mixture and mix well.

Butter a 10" tube pan. Line the bottom with a ring of waxed paper. Butter the waxed paper. Spoon batter into prepared pan and press it down so it's smooth on top. Bake in a 300° oven for 1¾ to 2 hours. Test with a wooden pick — it should come out clean. Let cool for 15 minutes, then carefully remove cake from pan. Peel off waxed paper and cool cake completely. If desired, soak cheesecloth in brandy, squeeze out and wrap cake in the cloth. Then wrap cake well in heavy foil and refrigerate for a week before cutting. After cutting, be sure to re-wrap well in foil and keep refrigerated.

This just gets better and better. Since there are no spices in this cake, the date and pecan flavors dominate. It's delicious!

Old-Fashioned Broiled Frosting

Combine ¾ **cup butter or oleo, 1½ cups brown sugar, 1½ tablespoons heavy cream**, and **1 teaspoon vanilla** in a heavy saucepan and heat gently until thickened, stirring constantly. Add a **3½ ounce can of coconut** and **1 cup chopped pecans**. Spread on baked, warm cake. Broil 4 or 5 inches from source of heat only until the mixture bubbles. It burns easily, so watch closely. This is a great change from a confectioners' sugar frosting.

Superb Apricot Fruitcake

     1 pound unsalted butter, softened
     2 cups sugar
    12 large eggs
  2½ pounds dried apricots, chopped
     1 pound golden raisins
    ½ pound candied orange peel
     2 pounds chopped pecans
    ½ cup light molasses
  2½ cups flour
     2 tablespoons ground allspice
     1 cup apricot preserves, heat, then strain
    ½ cup apricot brandy, or plain brandy

Preheat oven to 275°. Grease and flour two 9" x 5" bread pans. Line bottoms of pans with waxed paper. Grease waxed paper. Cream butter and sugar until fluffy. Beat in eggs, one at a time. Stir in fruits and molasses. Sift flour with allspice and stir into the batter a little at a time. Mix well. Spoon batter into prepared bread pans. Set pans in a large pan which has been filled with 2 inches of hot water. Keep water level at about 2 inches during baking time.

Bake at 275° for 3 hours, or until a wooden pick comes out clean. Cool a few minutes then remove cakes from pans. Remove paper from bottoms. Heat apricot preserves and brandy together for the glaze. Brush glaze all over cakes, tops and sides. Can decorate with pieces of apricot and pecan halves, if desired. Glaze again. Really fabulous!

Note that on my fruitcake recipes, I don't tell you how many servings the recipe makes. Some people want a sliver, some want a big piece, so it's impossible to give an exact number of servings.

Fluffy White Frosting

Combine **1 cup sugar,** ⅓ **cup water,** ¼ **teaspoon cream of tartar** and **a dash of salt** in a heavy saucepan. Bring to a boil, stirring until sugar dissolves. Very slowly, add the sugar syrup to **2 unbeaten egg whites** in mixer bowl. Beat constantly with electric mixer until stiff peaks form, about 7 minutes. Beat in **1 teaspoon vanilla**. Spread between cake layers and on top of cake.

Orange Fruit Cake

This is the best white fruitcake I know of.

  2 cups sugar
  1 cup butter
  4 eggs
  ½ cup buttermilk
  1 teaspoon baking soda
3½ cups flour
  2 tablespoons grated orange peel
  1 cup grated coconut
  1 cup golden raisins
  1 cup coarsely chopped dates
  1 cup coarsely chopped pecans

Preheat oven to 300°. Grease and flour a 10" tube pan, or 4 small (1 pound each) loaf pans. Line bottom of pan (or pans) with waxed paper. Grease paper. Cream sugar and butter. Add eggs, one at a time, and beat well after each addition. Combine soda and buttermilk. Add buttermilk alternately with flour. Mix well. Add orange peel, coconut, raisins, dates and pecans. Spoon into prepared pan. Bake the 1 pound loaf pans for 1 to 1¼ hours or until they test done. Tube pan will take 1¼ to 1½ hours, or more. If the cake appears to be browning too much on top, lay a piece of foil over the cake the last few minutes of baking. When done, remove cakes from the oven. Cool cakes slightly. Carefully turn cake (or cakes) out of pan and peel off waxed paper. Put cake back into pan and carefully poke holes all over top of the cake — I use a sharp wooden skewer. Drizzle the following glaze on the cake.

Glaze

Dissolve ⅓ **cup sugar** in **the juice of 1 orange**. Heat to a boil and simmer a minute or two. Remove from heat. Add **1 tablespoon grated orange peel**. Drizzle the glaze on — let soak in, and drizzle more on. Use as much of the glaze as the cake will absorb.

A Thymely Footnote . . . Santolina, Hyssop, and Germander are all small decorative perennial herbs. They are not culinary. They are all lovely if cultivated as low borders or hedges. Many knot gardens depend on 1 or all 3 of these plants for their edging.

Date Cake

🍂 *This is another cake I try to have ready for Christmas callers. This cake is very dark and moist, very rich, and I hate to use the same word, again, but it's also very delicious.*

¾ cup (1½ sticks) butter	1 cup walnuts, chopped
1½ cups packed dark brown sugar	2 eggs, beaten
	½ teaspoon salt
1 pound dates, pitted and coarsely chopped	1 cup boiling water
	1 teaspoon baking soda
1 cup flour	2 tablespoons dark rum

Preheat oven to 350°. Line bottom and sides of a 10" tube pan with parchment paper, or with brown grocery sack paper. Butter paper heavily. Cream the butter with the brown sugar in a large bowl until light and fluffy. Blend in dates, flour, walnuts, eggs and salt. Combine 1 cup boiling water with the baking soda in a small bowl. Stir to combine. Pour soda water into the batter, blending well. Transfer to prepared pan. Bake until tester inserted near the center comes out clean, about 1 hour. Immediately sprinkle the 2 tablespoons of rum over the top of cake. Let cake stand in pan until outside of pan feels cool. Then invert cake onto platter.

Frosting
Combine 1½ **cups confectioners' sugar**, ¾ **cup butter** (at room temperature), and **2½ to 3 tablespoons dark rum** together in a medium bowl. Blend well. You may need to add a few drops of water for the correct consistency. Spread frosting on top of cake. You can either refrigerate cake or leave cake out on the platter and cover it with a glass dome. Will serve 18 to 20 because it's so rich.

A Christmas Tea Menu

🍂 *I find that people love a Christmas Tea! Look for the starred items in the index.*

Hot Spiced Tea, Coffee, Pecan Whiskey Cake*, Orange Fruit Cake*, Date Cake*, English Trifle*, Fabulous Pecan Bars*, Little Lemon Tarts*, Chocolate Black Walnut Bon Bons*, Assorted Tea Sandwiches, Cinnamon Toast Roll-Ups*, Cream Scones* and Jam

Blueberry Cheesecake

1½ cups graham cracker crumbs
½ cup sugar
¼ cup butter or oleo, melted
4 eggs
1 teaspoon vanilla
2 8 ounce packages cream cheese, softened
1 cup sugar
2 cups rinsed fresh blueberries
2 tablespoons cornstarch
¼ cup water
½ cup sugar
1 teaspoon lemon juice

Mix graham cracker crumbs, ½ cup sugar and the melted butter. Pat on the bottom of an 8" x 10" pan. Combine the eggs, vanilla, cream cheese and 1 cup sugar. Beat until creamy. Pour into the crust and bake at 375° for 15 to 20 minutes or until cheese filling is set. Combine the 2 tablespoons of cornstarch with ¼ cup water. Mix cornstarch into the blueberries and put into a small saucepan. Cook gently until thickened. Add the ½ cup sugar and the lemon juice. Cook and stir another minute or two. Remove from heat and cool. When cool, spread over the cooled cheesecake. Serves 6 or 8.

No-Bake Cheesecake

3 cups graham cracker crumbs
½ cup butter or oleo, melted
1 3 ounce package lemon gelatin
1 cup boiling water
1 8 ounce package cream cheese, softened
1 cup sugar
3 tablespoons lemon juice (fresh, if possible)
1 13 ounce can Milnot, whipped

Combine the cracker crumbs and melted butter. Pack ⅔ of this mixture on the bottom and sides of a 9" x 13" pan or dish. Dissolve gelatin in boiling water. Chill until thickened slightly. Cream together cheese, sugar and lemon juice. Add to gelatin and mix very well. Fold in the stiffly whipped Milnot (see back of can). Pour filling into the crust. Sprinkle rest of crumbs over the top. Cover and chill several hours or overnight. Serves 12 or more.

Petite Cherry Cheesecakes

    2 8 ounce packages cream cheese, softened
    ¾ cup sugar
    2 eggs
    1 tablespoon lemon juice
    1 teaspoon vanilla
   24 vanilla wafers
    1 20 ounce can cherry pie filling

Beat cream cheese, sugar, eggs, lemon juice and vanilla until light and fluffy. Line small (not miniature) muffin pans with paper baking cups. Put a vanilla wafer in the bottom of each cup. Fill the cups ⅔ full with the cream cheese mixture. Bake in a 375° oven for 15 to 20 minutes or until set. Remove from oven and top each cake with about 1 tablespoon of cherry pie filling. Cover and chill. Makes 2 dozen. (Other good topping choices are blueberry pie filling, lemon filling, peach filling, etc.)

Date Cream Filling

This wonderful filling can go between chocolate cake layers, white or yellow cake layers, or other cakes of your choice.

    1 cup milk
    ½ cup dates, chopped
    1 tablespoon flour
    ¼ cup sugar
    1 egg, beaten
    ½ cup chopped walnuts or pecans
    1 teaspoon vanilla

Combine milk and dates in top of double boiler. Heat over medium heat. In a small bowl, combine the flour and sugar. Add egg and mix until smooth. Stir this (using a whisk) into the hot milk mixture. Cook over the simmering water, stirring constantly, until thickened. Cover and cool. Stir in nuts and vanilla.

The Best Cheesecake

❧ 40 Ounces of Cheese!

Crust

Combine **1 cup flour** and ¼ **cup sugar**. Cut in ½ **cup butter or oleo** until mixture is crumbly. Add **1 egg yolk, lightly beaten**. Blend thoroughly. Pat about ⅓ of dough on the bottom of a 9" springform pan (side removed). Bake at 400° for 6 minutes, or until golden. Cool. Butter sides of pan and attach to the bottom. Carefully pat remaining dough evenly on sides to a height of 1½ to 2 inches.

Cheese Filling

-   5 **8 ounce packages cream cheese, softened**
-   ¼ **teaspoon vanilla**
-   ¾ **teaspoon grated lemon peel**
-   1¾ **cups sugar**
-   3 **tablespoons flour**
-   ¼ **teaspoon salt**
-   5 **whole eggs**
-   2 **egg yolks**
-   ¼ **cup heavy (whipping) cream**

Beat cream cheese until fluffy. Add vanilla and lemon peel. Mix sugar, flour, and salt. Gradually blend into the cheese. Add eggs and yolks, one at a time, beating well after each. Gently stir in cream. Turn into the crust-lined pan. Bake in a very hot oven (500°) for 5 to 8 minutes, or until top edge of the crust is golden. Reduce oven heat to 200°. Bake for 1 more hour. Turn off oven. Crack oven door and leave cake in oven until oven is cool. **Very** carefully, remove cake from oven and place on a rack to finish cooling. (I find this helps keep the cake from cracking across the top.) Cool cake thoroughly in the pan before removing the sides. Add glaze, then refrigerate cake until ready to serve.

Strawberry Glaze

Crush **1 cup fresh, ripe strawberries**. Add **1 cup water** and cook 2 minutes. Sieve to remove some of the seeds and the pulp. Mix **1½ tablespoons cornstarch** with ½ **to** ¾ **cup sugar**. Stir into the hot berry mixture. Bring to a boil, stirring constantly. Cook and stir until thick and clear. Add a **few drops of red food coloring**, if needed. Cool to room temperature. Put additional **2 cups strawberries** on top of cheesecake. Pour glaze over the berries. Chill at least 2 hours.

Caramel Icing

🍂 *There are lots of caramel icings. This one is very easy and delicious.*

   4 tablespoons butter
   1 cup light brown sugar
      dash of salt
   ¼ cup light cream (half and half)
   1 teaspoon vanilla
   1½ cups or more confectioners' sugar, sifted

Combine first 4 ingredients in a heavy saucepan. Bring to a boil, reduce heat and cook 3 minutes, stirring constantly. Cool to lukewarm. Add vanilla and enough confectioners' sugar to thicken to spreading consistency. Good on apple cake, pumpkin cake, spice cake. Fabulous on a chocolate cake! (You may need to add a little more cream before adding the confectioners' sugar.)

Creamy Maple Frosting ⊂═[MOTHER ⊘]═⊃

   ½ cup pure maple syrup
   1 pound box confectioners' sugar, sifted
   ¼ cup butter, melted
   ¼ cup milk
      dash of salt

Heat maple syrup to boiling and cook gently for 3 minutes. Cool slightly. Set aside. Combine sugar, butter, milk and salt. Mix well. Slowly add hot syrup to sugar mixture and beat until light and thick. Makes enough frosting for two 9" cake layers or a 9" x 13" cake. *Wonderful* on apple cake, white or yellow cake. Divine on an angel food cake!

A Thymely Footnote . . . I don't have a lot of success growing herbs inside in the winter — the house is too hot and especially too dry. Some herbs that do work fairly well inside are **bay trees**, *a pot of* **parsley**, **Greek oregano, thyme, rosemary** *(if you keep it misted) and some* **scented geraniums**. *I don't have much luck at all with the annual herbs inside, such as* **basil**.

Decorator Icing

🍂 *Are you one of those people that just loves the fluffy icing on a wedding cake? If so, this recipe is for you.*

    1 cup Crisco
    4 cups (1 pound) confectioners' sugar, sifted
       about 2 tablespoons whipping cream
    1 teaspoon vanilla

Cream Crisco until it's light and fluffy. Add sugar, cream and vanilla. Beat at medium speed until all ingredients are well mixed. Blend another minute or so until creamy, but do *not* overbeat.

This makes 3 cups of stiff icing. Put in an airtight container and refrigerate if not using right away. When ready to use, bring icing to room temperature and add **1 to 2 teaspoons of cream per cup of icing** for desired spreading consistency.

Whipped Cream Frosting

🍂 *If you like to frost a cake with whipped cream, but don't want the cream to wilt and get soft and runny, add some plain gelatin to the cream. Here's how —*

For each cup of cream to be whipped, **mix 1 teaspoon unflavored gelatin into 2 tablespoons cold water**. Heat over low heat until the gelatin is melted. Let cool to room temperature. Then whip the cream. As it begins to mound, add the gelatin mixture slowly as you continue to beat. Continue beating cream until stiff enough to ice with. This is great on a cake that needs to set out on a buffet table for awhile.

*A **Thymely Footnote** . . . Herbs for a shady or partially shady garden are:* **chervil, sweet cicely, mints, sweet woodruff, violets** *and* **violas, parsley, basils** *(a little shade is okay),* **lovage, costmary, borage, angelica**.

Chocolate-Peanut Butter Frosting

    1 6 ounce package semisweet chocolate chips
    ½ cup butter or oleo, softened
    ½ cup confectioners' sugar, sifted
    1⅓ cups creamy peanut butter

Melt chocolate chips in top of double boiler over hot water. Set aside. Combine remaining ingredients in a small mixing bowl. Beat on medium speed until smooth. Add melted chocolate to peanut butter mixture. Beat until smooth. You may need to add a little more confectioners' sugar. Chill 15 minutes, or until it will spread easily. Enough for a 9" x 13" cake or 2 cake layers. Delicious on a chocolate cake.

Minute-Boil Fudge Frosting MOTHER♡

    2 ounces semisweet chocolate, cut fine
    1½ cups sugar
    7 tablespoons milk
    2 tablespoons soft shortening (Crisco, for example)
    2 tablespoons butter
    1 tablespoon corn syrup
    ¼ teaspoon salt

Place all ingredients in a pan. Bring slowly to a full rolling boil, stirring constantly. Boil briskly for 1 minute. (On a rainy or very humid day, boil for 1½ minutes.) Cool to lukewarm. Add **1 teaspoon vanilla** and beat until thick enough to spread. If too thick, add a little cream.

*A Thymely Footnote . . . It is told that certain herbs filled the manger Jesus was laid in. Those herbs were **rosemary** (symbol of fidelity and remembrance), **thyme, lady's bedstraw** (when dried, this smells like sweet mown hay) and **pennyroyal** (a fragrant mint).*

Honey Glaze

ᘒ *If you like honey, this is a good glaze for a pound cake, or a Bundt cake.*

Combine ½ **cup honey** and **1 cup confectioners' sugar** in a saucepan. Heat just to boiling over low heat. Drizzle on cake.

Chocolate Curls

ᘒ *Ever wonder how to make chocolate curls? These are nice to decorate the top of a cake or cheesecake with.*

  4 **ounces bittersweet or semisweet chocolate, finely chopped (can't use unsweetened)**
2½ **tablespoons unsalted butter**

Melt chocolate and butter in top of double boiler over barely simmering water, stirring until melted and smooth. Pour onto a large ungreased baking sheet. Refrigerate until firm. Use a narrow metal spatula and carefully scrape chocolate into long curls. Use a toothpick to carefully transfer the chocolate curls from the baking sheet to the top of the cake. Thanks to Nancy Clark for this tip.

Swiss Chocolate Glaze

ᘒ *Use this wonderful glaze on top of plain cake layers and especially on top of baked, cooled cheesecake.*

½ **cup whipping cream**
2 **ounces semisweet chocolate, chopped**
1 **teaspoon vanilla**

Scald cream in a small heavy saucepan over high heat. Add chocolate and vanilla and stir for 1 minute — stir vigorously and do **not** burn the chocolate. Remove from heat and stir until all the chocolate is melted and smooth. Cover glaze and refrigerate it for 10 to 15 minutes. Set cooled cake or cheesecake on serving platter. Pour glaze over cake and smooth top and sides with a flat spatula. Can double recipe if you need more glaze.

PIES

Jody's Pie Crust

🍃 *This recipe is in* Take A Little Thyme, *but it's so good and so essential and so fool-proof, I thought you'd like it in this book also. So, for your convenience —*

Mix in your mixer:
  3 cups flour
  1 teaspoon salt
  1 cup lard or 1¼ cups Crisco

Beat:
  1 egg

Add to the beaten egg:
  5 tablespoons cold water
  1 tablespoon vinegar

Add the egg-vinegar mixture to the flour mixture. Mix on low speed until ball of dough leaves sides of bowl. Do *not* overmix. Chill, or if in a hurry like I usually am, roll out on a well-floured board. Will make 3 - 9" single crusts.

Do this in seconds in a food processor. Follow same general directions — after flour, salt and Crisco is combined, add egg-vinegar-water through the feed tube with the motor running. Process only seconds until ball of dough forms along one side of work bowl. Very easy, very quick.

To keep the bottom crust of your fruit pies from getting soggy, you can follow this suggestion: "Paint" the bottom crust with a slightly beaten egg white, then let crust dry before filling it with fruit. Really helps.

Graham Cracker Crust

For a 9" crust, combine **1¼ cups graham cracker crumbs** and **3 tablespoons sugar**. Stir in **¼ to ⅓ cup melted butter or oleo** and blend well. Pack into a 9" pie pan and press firmly to bottom and up the sides. Chill one hour before filling, or bake in a 350° oven for 8 minutes. Then cool and fill.

Apple Cream Pie

🍎 *This is my family's favorite pie!*

    1 9" pie shell, unbaked
 1½ cups sugar
    4 tablespoons flour
    2 cups whipping cream
        dash of salt
    1 tablespoon butter
        ground nutmeg to sprinkle on top
    1 or 2 apples, cored, peeled and sliced thin

Combine sugar, flour, cream and salt. Mix well, but don't beat air into it — just combine well. Add sliced apples (my favorite is Rome Beauty, but you may use any kind). Stir apples into batter. Pour into the prepared crust. Dot with butter and sprinkle nutmeg on top. Bake at 325° for 1 hour and 10 to 15 minutes. After this amount of time, gently shake pie — if it's still liquid in the center, bake another 10 minutes or so. If it shakes like custard, it's done. You won't believe how good this is! Another time, leave out the apples for the best old-fashioned cream pie you ever tasted!

Martha Washington Pie ⊂▭MOTHER♡▭⊃

🍎 *This is from an old, old church cookbook that was my Grandmother's.*

Fill a pie tin with your favorite pastry. Pare and cut in small chunks good **tart apples**. Fill the crust. Mix ½ **cup sugar** and **2 tablespoons flour** and sprinkle over apples. Dissolve ¼ **cup sugar** in **1 cup boiling water**. Carefully pour over apples. Sprinkle **cinnamon** and **nutmeg** on top. Dot with **2 tablespoons butter**. Bake at 350° for about 1 hour, or until golden, bubbly and thickened. These are fine.

This is the description as it appears in the old book! I tried this easy-to-make apple pie and it is fine!

A Thymely Footnote . . . Mulch perennial herbs after the first freeze with straw. Plants should remain frozen during the dormant period. It's the freezing and thawing that damages our perennial herbs and flowers.

Peach-Raspberry Pie

1   9″ pie crust, unbaked (plus enough dough to cut into
     strips for a lattice crust on top)
6   cups ripe peaches, peeled and sliced
⅔   cup sugar (or 1 cup if you want pie sweeter)
2   teaspoons fresh lemon juice
2   tablespoons instant tapioca
1   cup fresh black raspberries
1   egg, beaten

Preheat oven to 450°. In a large bowl, combine peaches, sugar, lemon juice, tapioca and raspberries. Carefully stir together until all dry ingredients disappear. Spoon filling into crust. Cut lattice strips and lay over the filling. Crimp edges of dough. Beat the egg and brush egg all over the lattice strips. Sprinkle a little more sugar on the top. Bake pie 15 minutes. Reduce heat to 350° and bake another 45 minutes. Let pie cool before cutting.

Fresh Blueberry Pie

1   9″ pie crust, unbaked
4   cups blueberries, picked over and washed
1¼   cups sugar
2   tablespoons flour
2   tablespoons cornstarch
8   ounces cream cheese, softened
2   large eggs
1   teaspoon vanilla
½   cup heavy cream

In a bowl, combine the blueberries, 1 cup of sugar, flour and cornstarch. With a fork, mash a few blueberries to make juice. Now combine the blueberries with the sugar mixture until all the dry ingredients are dissolved. Pour mixture into the pie crust and bake in a 450° oven for 20 minutes.

In another bowl, beat together the cream cheese, the ¼ cup sugar, the 2 eggs, vanilla and the ½ cup cream until mixture is smooth. Pour this over the hot pie. Reduce heat to 350° and bake pie for another 45 minutes or so. Let pie cool and garnish with more whipped cream, if desired. This is a wonderful combination of flavors.

Fresh Purple Plum Pie

This could become a favorite August-September fruit pie. If you've never tried fresh plums in a pie, you're in for a treat.

½ cup sugar (or a little more)
¼ cup flour
1 tablespoon fresh lemon juice
¼ teaspoon ground cinnamon
  dash of salt
4 cups fresh, ripe purple plums, sliced and pitted (1½ to 2 pounds)
1 9″ pie shell, unbaked
½ cup sugar
½ cup flour
¼ teaspoon ground cinnamon
¼ teaspoon ground nutmeg
¼ cup butter

Combine the first 5 ingredients and add to the sliced plums. Toss to mix well. Put plum mixture into the pie shell. Mix remaining flour, sugar, cinnamon and nutmeg. Cut in butter until mixture is size of peas. Sprinkle this over the plums.

Cover edge of pie with foil to keep crust from over-browning. Bake at 425° for 25 minutes. Remove foil. Bake another 25 to 30 minutes. Cool.

Dutch Apple Pie ⊂▭MOTHER♡▭⊃

❧ *This is another one of Mother's wonderful apple pie recipes.*

	pastry for a 1 crust 9″ pie
3	or 4 tart cooking apples
1	cup sugar
3	tablespoons flour
⅛	teaspoon salt
½	teaspoon ground cinnamon
¼	teaspoon ground nutmeg
1	egg, slightly beaten
1	cup whipping cream
1¼	teaspoons vanilla
4	teaspoons butter
½	cup chopped walnuts, optional

Prepare the pastry shell, but do not bake. Set aside. Wash, core, peel and thinly slice apples. Put sliced apples into the pastry shell. Mix together the sugar, flour, salt and spices. Blend together the egg, cream and vanilla. Add sugar mixture gradually, mixing well. Pour over apples. Dot with butter. Sprinkle nuts on top.

Bake at 450° for 10 minutes. Reduce heat to 350° and bake 35 to 40 minutes longer, or until apples are tender and top is lightly browned. Drizzle a little powdered sugar icing over top. This is terrific!

Lemon Pie

1	9″ pie crust — baked to a pale golden brown (Remember to prick the crust before baking in a 425° oven for 15 to 20 minutes — watch closely.) Cool crust.
½	cup plus 1 tablespoon unsalted butter
1¼	cups sugar
4	large eggs
1	teaspoon grated lemon peel
⅔	cup fresh lemon juice

Beat the butter and sugar together until light and fluffy. Beat in eggs, one at a time. Stir in the rind and the lemon juice. Pour filling into the baked shell.

Bake at 350° for about 45 minutes, or until the center is firm. Let pie cool at room temperature, then chill several hours before serving it.

Spicy Pumpkin Molasses Pie

❧ Old timers almost always put some molasses in their pumpkin filling — makes it dark and rich.

3   eggs
1   9″ pie crust, unbaked
2   cups (16 ounce can) pumpkin
1   cup milk
½   cup sugar
½   cup molasses
2   teaspoons ground cinnamon
½   teaspoon ground nutmeg
½   teaspoon ground ginger
½   teaspoon salt
1   teaspoon vanilla

Heat oven to 400°. Put eggs in a large bowl. Remove a little egg white from bowl and brush over bottom of the pie crust. Add rest of ingredients to the egg bowl and stir until very smooth. Pour into the prepared crust and bake at 400° for 50 minutes to 1 hour.

Brown Sugar Pecan Pie ⊂▱MOTHER♡▱⊃

    pastry-lined pie plate
¼   cup butter or oleo
1   cup light brown sugar
1   cup white corn syrup
¼   teaspoon salt
3   eggs
1   teaspoon vanilla
1   cup pecans

Preheat oven to 450°. Cream together butter and sugar, syrup and salt. Add eggs, one at a time and beat until fluffy. Add vanilla and pecans. Turn into pastry-lined plate. Bake at 450° for 10 minutes. Reduce heat to 350° and bake until filling is set, about 40 to 50 minutes.

Alabama Pecan Pie

This is my old stand-by pecan pie recipe that was also lost for a while. I like it because the light corn syrup makes a pretty, almost clear filling.

1   **9" pie crust, unbaked**
1   **cup light corn syrup**
1   **tablespoon butter**
     dash of salt
3   **eggs**
½   **cup sugar**
1   **teaspoon vanilla**
1½ **cups chopped pecans**

Mix all together in one bowl. Don't, however, overmix this filling, just blend it all together. Put into an unbaked 9" pie crust. Bake 1 hour at 350°.

Another Old-Fashioned Cream Pie

This cream pie uses brown sugar.

1   **9" pie crust**
1   **cup dark brown sugar**
3   **tablespoons flour (heaping)**
¼   **teaspoon salt**
1½ **cups Half and Half OR whipping cream, warmed**
1   **teaspoon vanilla**
4   **tablespoons butter, softened**
     dash of ground nutmeg

Heat oven to 450°. Fit dough into pie pan. Prick with a fork and bake 5 minutes. Carefully prick crust again and bake another 3 or 4 minutes. Remove from oven and reduce heat to 375°.

Thoroughly mix sugar, flour and salt. Pour into the partially baked shell and spread evenly across the bottom. Warm cream, but *don't* boil. Add vanilla to it. Pour cream over the sugar. Dot with the butter and dash nutmeg over the top. Bake about 8 minutes at 375°. Reduce heat again to 325°. Bake about 40 minutes. Remove from oven and cool. Pie will have brown splotches on top.

Lemon Chess Pie

&● A good friend, Ellen Wright, gave this recipe to me many years ago. It's superb!

    1 unbaked 9" pie crust
    2 cups sugar
    1 tablespoon flour
    1 tablespoon cornmeal
    ¼ cup fresh lemon juice
    ¼ cup milk
    4 eggs
    ¼ cup melted butter or oleo

Put all ingredients together in a medium bowl, except the crust. Use a wire whisk and blend all together. Blend thoroughly, but don't overbeat. Pour into a 9" unbaked pie crust. Bake 8 minutes at 425°. Reduce heat to 350° and bake another 20 minutes.

Mom's Cream Pie Filling

    1   baked and cooled 9" pie crust
    ¾   cup sugar
    ⅓   cup flour
    2   cups milk
    3   egg yolks, slightly beaten
        pinch of salt
    1½ tablespoons butter or oleo
    1   teaspoon vanilla

Mix sugar and flour thoroughly. Add milk gradually, using a wire whisk. Add slightly beaten egg yolks and the salt. Cook and stir until thickened. Remove from heat. Add butter and vanilla. Cover top of filling with plastic wrap to keep a skin from forming. Cool filling thoroughly. Pour filling into a baked, cooled pie crust. Top with a meringue or whipped cream.

Lemon Filling: Omit vanilla and add ¼ cup fresh lemon juice.

Coconut Filling: Add 1 cup shredded coconut to the filling.

Chocolate Filling: Stir 2 to 4 tablespoons cocoa (amount depends on how much you like chocolate) into the dry ingredients.

Butterscotch Pie

❧ This makes enough filling for 2 pies. If you've never had a really good butterscotch pie, don't deprive yourself any longer. This is truly superb! Read through recipe before you begin.

> 2 **baked, cooled 9" pie crusts**
> 1 **1 pound box light brown sugar**
> 1 **stick oleo**
> 1 **cup water**
> 5 **egg yolks (save the whites)**
> ½ **cup flour**
> 4 **cups milk**
> 1 **tablespoon vanilla**

Cook brown sugar, oleo and water together in a large heavy skillet to a thick syrup. This will take a few minutes at a low to medium boil. Remove from heat and set aside. Put the 5 egg yolks in a large bowl. Very gradually, add 2 tablespoons flour to make a smooth paste. Now add a little of the milk to thin the paste. Gradually add the rest of the flour until the ½ cup is gone. Now add the rest of the milk, very gradually, whisking all the time to incorporate it smoothly. (This seems a bit confusing, but these steps are necessary to insure a smooth mixture.) Using the whisk, start adding the egg-milk mixture into the hot syrup, adding only a small amount at a time until the hot syrup has cooled down. Finish adding the egg-milk mixture. Bring mixture to a boil, stirring constantly. Reduce heat a little and let boil for a full minute. Remove from heat and add the vanilla. Cool filling, covered. Make a **meringue** of **5 egg whites, ½ teaspoon cream of tartar** and ½ **cup sugar**. Beat whites until foamy with the cream of tartar. Add sugar gradually until stiff peaks form. Make sure no sugar granules remain. Pour cooled filling into the baked, cooled crusts. Divide meringue between the pies, sealing well to edges. Bake at 350° for 10 to 12 minutes or until meringue is nicely browned. Cool pies at room temperature.

Brown Sugar Pumpkin Pie

&. *Of all the pumpkin pies, we think this one is best.*

1½ cups canned pumpkin
1 cup packed brown sugar
2 teaspoons pumpkin pie spice (Spice Islands is best.)
3 eggs
1 cup half and half cream
1 unbaked 9" pie crust

Combine all ingredients, except pie crust, in a large mixer bowl. Mix thoroughly. Pour filling into the crust. Bake at 425° for 15 minutes. Reduce heat to 350° and bake another 30 to 40 minutes, or until a knife inserted near center comes out clean. Cool. If crust browns too much, make a ring of aluminum foil and lay over crust the last 15 minutes of baking time. Serve with whipped cream, seasoned with a little powdered sugar and a little ground cinnamon.

Grated Apple Pie

&. *This will probably be the easiest apple pie you'll ever make.*

2 cups grated apples (heaping cups)
1 cup sugar
1 teaspoon ground cinnamon
2 tablespoons flour
⅔ to 1 cup evaporated milk
2 tablespoons butter or oleo
1 unbaked 9" pie crust

Mix the apples, sugar, cinnamon, flour and evaporated milk together. Spoon into the unbaked pie crust. Dot with 2 tablespoons butter. Bake in a 350° oven for 45 minutes to 1 hour. Serve with a scoop of ice cream on top for a delicious dessert. Serves 6.

Peaches and Cream Pie

1 9" unbaked pie crust
6 or 8 fresh peaches, peeled and sliced
4 tablespoons flour
1 cup sugar
1 teaspoon vanilla
1 cup heavy or whipping cream
½ teaspoon ground cinnamon

Heat oven to 450°. Put peach slices into the pie crust. Mix flour and sugar together and sprinkle over the peaches. Mix the cream and vanilla together and carefully pour over the peach mixture. Sprinkle with cinnamon. Bake for 10 minutes. Reduce heat to 350° and bake for another 50 minutes. Serve with whipped cream or ice cream to 6 lucky people.

Anne Byers' Grasshopper Pie

Combine **18 crushed Oreo cookies** and **2 tablespoons of melted butter, or oleo**. Pat into a 9" pie pan — on bottom and up sides as much as possible. Put **24 large marshmallows** and ⅔ **cup milk** in the top of a double boiler and heat over simmering water until marshmallows are melted. Cool. Stir in ¼ **cup Crème de Menthe** and **2 tablespoons Crème de Cacao**. Cover and chill until partially thickened. Whip **2 cups of heavy cream**. Fold 1 cup into the pie filling. Turn filling into the crumb crust. Spread the other cup of whipped cream on top. You can crush 2 or 3 more Oreos and sprinkle crumbs on top of whipped cream. Chill pie thoroughly. Serves 6 or 8.

A Thymely Footnote . . . Preserve certain flowers and herbs in a glycerine-water solution. Combine 4 ounces glycerine with 8 ounces water in a small plastic pail or bucket. Cut baby's breath or Sweet Annie (artemesia annua), or experiment with other plants. Plunge the stems into the glycerine-water solution. Let them set in this solution 4 or 5 days. Remove from the solution and tie 5 or 6 stems together. Hang bunches upside down for a week. These are now ready to use in dried arrangements — will not break and shatter when touched or handled! Glycerine is available through your druggist.

Old-Fashioned Custard Pie ⊂🔲MOTHER♡⊃

4   eggs, slightly beaten
½   cup sugar
¼   teaspoon salt
1   teaspoon vanilla
2½ cups milk, scalded
1   9″ pie crust, unbaked

Preheat oven to 475°. Thoroughly mix eggs, sugar, salt and vanilla. Slowly stir in hot milk. Pour into an unbaked pie crust.* Sprinkle a little ground nutmeg over the top. Bake in a hot oven — 475° — for 5 minutes. Reduce heat to 425° amd bake another 10 minutes or until a knife comes out clean. Cool. Serve cool, or even chilled.

*Brush a little egg white over the crust before adding the prepared filling. This will help keep the crust from getting soggy.

Chocolate Peanut Butter Pie

🍃 *If you like peanut butter cups, you'll love this!*

4   eggs
1   cup butter, softened
6   ounces semisweet chocolate, melted and cooled
2   cups confectioners' sugar, sifted
¾   cup smooth peanut butter
1   cup heavy cream
1   10″ pie shell, baked
    Chocolate Curls (see index)

Beat the eggs with ¾ cup of the butter, the chocolate and sugar for 4 or 5 minutes (preferably in your heavy-duty mixer). Mixture must be smooth and thick. In another bowl, beat peanut butter with the other ¼ cup butter. While beating, slowly add about ⅓ cup of the cream, to make the peanut butter mixture spreadable. Pour chocolate mixture into the pie shell. Drop peanut butter mixture onto chocolate in teaspoonfuls. Swirl the peanut butter into the chocolate, using a table knife. Beat rest of heavy cream and spread over pie. Garnish with Chocolate Curls.

Cover very carefully and refrigerate until ready to serve. I don't need to tell you how rich this is, or how full of calories this is, so I would definitely serve smallish pieces and let them ask for more (they will!). Should serve 8 to 10, and hope, there isn't any left over — it's addictive.

Ice Cream And Toffee Pie

This is a wonderful pie to prepare the day before you need it. It's rich, so it should serve 8.

1   9″ chocolate pie crust, baked
1   pint coffee ice cream, softened
6   to 8 ounces almond toffee candy
¾   cup hot fudge ice cream topping
1   quart butter pecan ice cream, softened
    whipped cream

Spoon coffee ice cream into pie crust. Spread evenly over crust. Cover and freeze until firm. Put candy in a plastic bag and crush with a rolling pin or hammer. Take pie from freezer, spread fudge topping over the coffee ice cream. Sprinkle with 1 cup of the crushed candy. Spread butter pecan ice cream over top. Cover and freeze again until firm. To serve, cut into wedges, put a dollop of real whipped cream on top and sprinkle a little of the reserved candy on each serving.

Ice Cream Crunch Pie

Another good frozen pie — will serve 12.

2   cups flour
1   cup walnuts or pecans, chopped
1   cup butter, softened
½   cup light brown sugar, packed
1   18 ounce jar hot fudge topping (or about 2 cups of
    homemade)
½   gallon vanilla ice cream, softened

Preheat oven to 375°. Using an electric mixer, blend first 4 ingredients at low speed until just crumbly, 3 to 4 minutes. Put this mixture into a jelly roll pan or large cookie sheet with sides and bake until light brown, stirring occasionally, 15 to 20 minutes. Cool slightly.

Sprinkle half of these crumbs in a 9″ x 13″ pan. Drizzle half the hot fudge topping over the crumbs. Spoon all of ice cream into pan. Drizzle with rest of hot fudge. Sprinkle with rest of crumbs. Cover well and freeze until firm, at least 2 hours. Refrigerate for a few minutes before cutting to serve.

COOKIES

Chocolate Chip Melt-Aways

❧ What did we ever do before chocolate chips?

    1 cup butter or oleo, softened
    1 cup vegetable oil
    1 cup sugar
    1 cup confectioners' sugar, sifted
    2 eggs
    4 cups flour
    1 teaspoon baking soda
    1 teaspoon cream of tartar
    1 teaspoon salt
    1 teaspoon vanilla
    1 12 ounce package semisweet chocolate chips
       additional sugar

Combine first 5 ingredients in a large mixing bowl. Beat until smooth. Combine flour, soda, cream of tartar and salt. Add to butter mixture. Beat until smooth. Stir in vanilla and chocolate chips. Shape mixture into 1" balls. Roll in granulated sugar. Put 2" apart on ungreased cookie sheets and bake at 375° for 10 to 12 minutes. Cool. Makes 7 to 8 dozen. Can wrap well and freeze.

Butterscotch Ice Box Cookies

Combine in a large bowl, **2 sticks butter, softened, 2 sticks oleo, softened, 1½ cups granulated sugar, 1½ cups light brown sugar, 3 eggs, 6 cups flour, 1 teaspoon baking soda, 1 teaspoon vanilla** and **1½ cups finely chopped pecans**. Mix well with electric mixer. Divide dough into halves or fourths and make into smooth rolls. Wrap each roll in plastic wrap and chill (or freeze if wrapped very well). Remove 1 roll at a time and slice into ¼" thick rounds. Put slices on a greased cookie sheet and bake at 350° for 8 to 12 minutes — watch closely, don't overbake. Makes about 100 old-fashioned and good cookies.

Deluxe Pecan-Chocolate Chip Cookies

This is a new (to me) Nestle's cookie recipe. If you haven't got it, you should have it.

2¾ cups flour
1¼ teaspoons baking soda
1 teaspoon salt
1½ cups butter, softened
1½ cups brown sugar, packed
2 eggs

1 teaspoon vanilla
2 cups pecans, chopped
1 24 ounce package (4 cups) Nestle's Toll House Semi Sweet Morsels

Preheat oven to 375°. In a bowl, combine flour, soda and salt. Set aside. In another bowl, combine butter and brown sugar and beat until creamy. Add eggs and vanilla. Beat until light and fluffy. Gradually blend in flour mixture. Stir in chocolate bits and pecans. Drop by well-rounded tablespoonfuls onto ungreased cookie sheet. Bake for 10 to 12 minutes. Allow cookies to stand 2 or 3 minutes, then remove them from cookie sheet. I always put my cookies out on brown paper grocery bags to absorb some of the grease. Makes 3 to 4 dozen large cookies, or 4 to 6 dozen small cookies.

Pineapple Drop Cookies

1 cup packed light brown sugar
¼ cup Crisco
¼ cup butter, or oleo, softened
1 egg
1 teaspoon vanilla
¾ cup drained, crushed pineapple

2 cups flour
1 teaspoon baking powder
½ teaspoon baking soda
½ teaspoon salt
1 cup chopped nuts

Cream together sugar, Crisco and butter. Add egg and vanilla and mix well. Add drained pineapple. Stir in the dry ingredients, then the nuts. Drop by teaspoonfuls onto ungreased cookie sheets. Bake at 375° for 10 to 12 minutes, or until lightly browned. Frost, if desired, with **1 cup confectioners' sugar** mixed with about **3 tablespoons pineapple juice**. Makes about 4 dozen cookies.

Sugar Cookies ⊂▌MOTHER♡▐⊃

This is an unusual sugar cookie. It's very good and crisp. Watch closely when baking, they burn easily.

1 **cup butter**
1 **cup oil**
1 **cup sugar**
1 **cup powdered sugar**
2 **eggs**
1 **teaspoon vanilla**
1 **teaspoon baking soda**
1 **teaspoon cream of tartar**
4 **cups flour**

Mix all ingredients. You may need to add a little more flour if dough sticks to hands. (Add a tablespoon at a time until dough is of proper consistency.) Form dough into balls and put on cookie sheet. Flatten with bottom of a glass dipped in sugar. Bake at 375°. Check after 6 minutes. If not done, continue baking until pale golden brown and firm to touch. Makes 6 to 8 dozen cookies.

Mince Meat Drop Cookies ⊂▌MOTHER♡▐⊃

3½ **cups flour, sifted**
1 **teaspoon baking soda**
1 **teaspoon salt**
1 **cup nuts, chopped**
1 **cup shortening**
2 **cups light brown sugar**
2 **eggs**
½ **cup cold coffee**
2 **cups mince meat, drained and saved**

Sift together 3 times the measured flour, soda and salt. Add nuts. Cream together shortening and sugar. Beat in eggs, one at a time. Add flour mixture alternately with coffee and any juice drained from the mince meat. Stir in mince meat. Mix well. Drop by teaspoonfuls on buttered baking sheet. Bake at 375° for 15 minutes. Makes about 5 dozen.

Mother's Fruitcake Cookies ⊂▤ MOTHER♡ ▷⊃

After much searching, this recipe has been found. It is very good.

4 cups flour, sifted
1 teaspoon baking soda
1 teaspoon salt
1 cup vegetable shortening, such as Crisco
2 cups brown sugar, packed
2 eggs
⅔ cup buttermilk
1 cup pecans, chopped
2 cups dates, chopped
1 cup candied cherries, quartered
1 cup candied fruits and peel
  cherries for top

Sift and measure flour. Sift flour with soda and salt. Cream shortening. Add sugar and eggs. Beat until light and fluffy. Add buttermilk and flour mixture. Add nuts and fruit. Chill dough several hours or overnight. Drop by teaspoonfuls about 2" apart onto a lightly greased baking sheet. Top each with ½ of a candied cherry. Bake at 375° for 8 to 10 minutes. Makes about 8 dozen.

Great Cookies

1 cup oleo, softened
1 cup peanut butter
1 cup sugar
1 cup packed brown
  sugar

2 eggs
2 cups flour
1 teaspoon baking soda
1 6 ounce package
  chocolate bits

Use electric mixer and beat oleo and peanut butter (smooth or chunky) until blended. Gradually add sugars and beat until fluffy. Add eggs, one at a time, and beat until smooth. Sift flour with soda. Beat into butter-sugar mixture, at low speed, until well blended. Stir in chocolate bits. You could add ½ to 1 cup chopped nuts, if desired. Drop by tablespoonfuls onto ungreased cookie sheets. Slightly flatten each with the back of a spoon. Bake in a 325° oven for 12 to 15 minutes. Cool. These freeze well. Makes 6 dozen 2" cookies.

Sugar Babies

1   cup butter, softened
1½ cups light brown sugar, packed
1   egg
1   teaspoon vanilla
2   cups unbleached flour (or regular will do)
1   teaspoon baking soda
1   teaspoon ground cinnamon
1   teaspoon ground ginger
1   teaspoon salt
1   12 ounce package (2 cups) semisweet chocolate chips
1   cup walnuts or pecans, chopped
1   cup confectioners' sugar

In electric mixer bowl, cream butter. Add brown sugar, egg and vanilla; beat well. Combine flour, baking soda, cinnamon, ginger and salt. Blend into the butter mixture. Fold in chocolate chips and nuts. Refrigerate 1 hour or overnight, if desired. Preheat oven to 375°. Lightly grease baking sheets. Roll small pieces of dough between your palms to make 1" rounds. Roll these balls in confectioners' sugar. Arrange balls on the baking sheet and put them about 2" apart. Bake 10 minutes or until done. Makes 5 dozen or more cookies. Freezes well.

Soft Molasses Drops

¾   cup butter, or oleo, softened
1½ cups light brown sugar
3   eggs
1   teaspoon vanilla
2   tablespoons molasses
1   teaspoon baking soda
3   cups flour
1   cup raisins

Cream butter and sugar together until light and fluffy. Add eggs and vanilla. Beat well. Combine molasses and baking soda. Add to creamed mixture. Gradually stir in flour. Stir in raisins. Drop by teaspoonfuls onto a greased baking sheet. Bake at 350° for 8 minutes or until done. Makes 5 or 6 dozen cookies.

Granola Cookies

🍃 *There is a wonderful recipe for Homemade Granola in* Take A Little Thyme, *or buy your favorite at the grocery. These are good cookies.*

- 1 **cup oleo, softened**
- 1 **cup light brown sugar, packed**
- 1 **egg**
- 1 **teaspoon vanilla**
- 1½ **cups unbleached flour**
- 1 **teaspoon baking soda**
- ½ **teaspoon salt**
- 1⅔ **cups granola**
- ⅔ **cup raisins**
- ½ **to 1 cup walnuts or pecans, chopped**

Cream together oleo and sugar. Beat in egg and vanilla. Add flour, baking soda and salt. Mix well and stir in rest of ingredients to make a stiff dough. Drop by spoonfuls on lightly greased cookie sheet and bake in a 375° oven for 10 to 12 minutes. Makes about 4 dozen cookies.

Pecan Tarts

🍂 *These are a little tedious, but are delicious and pretty on the cookie tray. Makes 3 or 4 dozen tarts.*

For the pastry:
- 1 **cup butter, softened**
- 2 **3 ounce packages cream cheese, softened**
- 2½ **cups flour**
- ½ **teaspoon salt**

For the filling:
- 1½ **cups pecans, finely chopped**
- ½ **cup white corn syrup**
- 1 **cup light brown sugar**
- 2 **eggs, slightly beaten**
- 2 **tablespoons butter, melted**
- ½ **teaspoon vanilla**
- ¼ **teaspoon salt**

Pastry: To the softened butter and cheese, add the flour and salt, a little at a time, to make a smooth dough. Gather dough into a ball. Wrap and refrigerate for at least an hour. Press spoonfuls of dough into tiny, 2" or less, muffin pans. Put about 1 teaspoon of chopped pecans into each dough-filled pan.

Filling: Use a hand beater or wooden spoon and gradually add sugar and syrup to eggs. Add butter, vanilla and salt. Pour this filling over the pecans in the tart pans. Fill pans ¾ full. Bake at 350° for 20 minutes.

Little Lemon Tarts

Use the same pastry (above in Pecan Tarts) to line tiny muffin pans. Prick the shells with fork tines and bake in a 400° oven for 10 minutes, or until nicely browned. Open a **21 ounce can prepared lemon pie filling, or buy or make lemon curd**. Fill cooled tart shells with the lemon filling. Put a **dab of whipped cream** on top of each. Lovely on the tea table.

Christmas Cookies ⊂▯MOTHER♡▭⊃

&❧ *Makes lots of cookies (100 or more). Great to have these in the freezer.*

1 cup butter or oleo, softened
1 cup white sugar
1 cup light brown sugar
2 tablespoons molasses
2 tablespoons honey
2 teaspoons lemon extract
1 teaspoon orange extract
2 eggs
3 cups flour
1 teaspoon baking soda
2 teaspoons baking powder
1 teaspoon ground cinnamon
1 teaspoon ground ginger
1 teaspoon salt
1 cup rolled oats
½ cup buttermilk
8 ounces dates, chopped
1 cup raisins
1 cup candied fruits, chopped
1 cup coconut
1 cup walnuts, chopped

Cream butter and sugars until light and fluffy. Add molasses, honey, extracts and eggs. Beat well. Add dry ingredients and oats alternately with buttermilk, beating until smooth after each addition. Stir in remaining ingredients. Drop from a teaspoon onto greased cookie sheets. Bake at 375° for 12 to 15 minutes, or until a golden brown. Do not overbake.

Speaking of Christmas:

Dried Apple Hearts

Slice unpeeled **Red Delicious apples** from top to bottom into ¼" thick slices. Combine **2 cups bottled lemon juice** and **1 tablespoon of salt**. Soak the apple slices in lemon mixture for 3 to 4 minutes. Remove slices and put them on a cake rack in a 175° oven. Leave door ajar and dry apples 6 hours or until slices begin to curl. Wonderful added to Christmas potpourri (page 39); hang them on the tree; glue them on a wreath, etc.

Sour Cream Sugar Cookies

❧ *Soft, puffy and wonderful. Mother gave this recipe to me years ago and we make them every Christmas.*

1 cup butter	1 teaspoon baking
1 cup sugar	powder
1 egg	1 teaspoon ground
½ cup sour cream	nutmeg
2½ cups flour	¼ teaspoon baking soda

Cream butter. Add sugar and beat until light and fluffy. Beat in egg. Blend in sour cream. Sift dry ingredients together and gradually add to creamed mixture. Dough will be very soft. Put dough in an airtight plastic bag and chill dough thoroughly. When ready to bake, work with about one fourth of the dough at a time. Keep rest refrigerated. On a floured surface, roll dough to ⅛" to ¼" thickness. Cut in desired shapes. Bake at 350° for 7 to 10 minutes. Watch closely. Frost and decorate cookies as desired or according to the season. Makes 2 to 2½ dozen medium size cookies.

Williamsburg Ginger Cookies

❧ *These are the cookies served from the cookhouse in the back of the Wyeth House at Colonial Williamsburg. Several 4-H mothers have called or written to tell me their daughters won a blue ribbon with this cookie — that's nice.*

3 sticks oleo	2 teaspoons ground
½ cup molasses*	cinnamon
2 cups sugar	1 teaspoon ground cloves
2 eggs	1 teaspoon ground
4 cups flour	ginger
4 teaspoons baking soda	sugar

Melt oleo. Add molasses, sugar and eggs. Beat well. Sift together flour, soda, cinnamon, cloves and ginger. Add to molasses mixture. Mix well. Wrap and refrigerate several hours or overnight. Roll into small balls. Roll balls in sugar. Bake at 350° for 8 to 10 minutes. Watch closely — do not overbake.

*I like Brer Rabbit gold label molasses.

Fabulous Lemon Bars

🍋 *They really are! Especially good in the summer.*

1 cup butter, softened	½ teaspoon baking
½ cup confectioners'	powder
sugar	⅓ cup fresh lemon juice
2 cups flour	(must be fresh)
4 large eggs	1 cup pecans, chopped
2 cups granulated sugar	fairly fine
1 tablespoon flour	

Cream the butter and confectioners' sugar. Gradually stir in the 2 cups flour until blended. Pat dough over the bottom of an ungreased 9" x 13" baking pan. Bake in a preheated 325° oven for 15 minutes (reduce heat to 300° if using a glass pan). Remove from oven. At once, beat the eggs slightly. Add the granulated sugar, the 1 tablespoon flour, the baking powder, lemon juice and nuts. Stir — **do not beat** — until well-mixed. Pour this over the still warm crust. Return to the oven and bake until golden brown on top — about 45 minutes, but watch closely and don't overbake. Loosen edges with a knife. Cool a few minutes. Carefully cut into squares or bars while still warm. Freezes beautifully.

Raspberry Brownies

🍋 *This great brownie recipe came from Pam Byers in Virginia.*

3 3 ounce squares	2 tablespoons Chambord
unsweetened chocolate	(raspberry liqueur)
½ cup butter or oleo	1 cup flour
3 eggs	1½ cups pecans, chopped
1½ cups sugar	⅓ cup black raspberry
1½ teaspoons vanilla	jam (seedless if
¼ teaspoon salt	available)

Melt chocolate and butter over warm water. Cool. Blend together eggs, sugar, vanilla, salt and Chambord. Stir into the chocolate mixture. Add flour and mix well. Add pecans. Pour into a well-greased 8" square pan. Bake at 325° for about 40 minutes. Spoon the jam over the hot brownies, spreading carefully. Cool. You may spread with a thin chocolate frosting or glaze, if desired.

Holiday Cupcake Cookies

2 cups flour, sifted
1 teaspoon baking soda
½ teaspoon salt
1 teaspoon ground cinnamon
½ teaspoon ground allspice
½ cup butter or oleo, softened
1 cup brown sugar, packed
2 eggs, beaten
1 cup dates, cut fine
1 cup pecans, coarsely chopped
½ cup red candied cherries, chopped
½ cup candied pineapple, chopped
⅔ cup milk
1⅓ tablespoons cider vinegar

Sift flour once, measure. Add baking soda, salt and spices. Sift again. Set aside. Cream butter and brown sugar together until fluffy. Add eggs, beat again. Add the fruit and nuts. Combine vinegar and milk and add alternately with the sifted flour-spice mixture, beating well after each addition. Bake in paper-lined tiny muffin tins in a 375° oven for 20 to 25 minutes. Makes about 3 dozen tiny cupcakes. Glaze the tops with a little warmed white corn syrup. Beautiful on your holiday cookie tray or makes a great gift.

Delicious Brownies

1 cup butter, softened
2 cups sugar
4 eggs
2 teaspoons vanilla
1 cup flour
1 cup chopped walnuts or pecans
4 1 ounce squares unsweetened chocolate, melted

Cream butter with sugar. Beat in eggs. Blend in melted chocolate and vanilla. Stir in flour, then nuts. Pour into a greased 9" x 13" pan. Bake at 350° for 30 minutes, or until done. Makes about 2 dozen nice-sized brownies. I use Chocolate Frosting from page 220 to ice the top. I never use a glass baking dish for these brownies — the edges get too hard.

Turtle Cookies

❧ I get lots of good recipes from church carry-in dinners. This is one of them from Joyce Houser.

2 cups flour
1 cup light brown sugar
½ cup butter
1 cup pecans, chopped
⅔ cup butter
½ cup light brown sugar
1 package milk chocolate chips (Depending on how thick of a chocolate topping you want, use a 6 ounce or 12 ounce package of chocolate chips — or somewhere in between.)

Mix flour, brown sugar and butter in a food processor. Spread into an ungreased 9″ x 13″ pan. Top with the chopped pecans. Put the ⅔ cup butter and ½ cup brown sugar in a saucepan and bring to a boil. Boil for 30 seconds. Pour this over the pecans.

Bake at 350° for about 20 minutes, or until crust is light brown and bubbly. Remove from oven and immediately spread the chocolate chips over the top. Cool completely before cutting.

Date Bars

1½ cups pitted dates
1½ cups orange juice
2½ cups flour
½ teaspoon salt
1½ cups light brown sugar, packed
3 sticks butter or oleo, softened
1 cup flaked coconut
1 cup pecans or walnuts, chopped
1½ cups old-fashioned rolled oats

Simmer the dates and orange juice together for about 30 minutes, stirring often. Mixture needs to cook until thickened. In a bowl, combine the flour, salt and brown sugar. Mix in the butter. Stir in coconut, nuts and oats. Press half of the mixture into bottom of a 9″ x 13″ pan. Press as flat as you can. Spread the date mixture over the dough to within ½″ of the edge. Top it with rest of dough and flatten lightly. Bake in a 350° oven for 45 minutes. Let cookies cool in the pan, then cut into bars.

Turtle Brownies

This is another good recipe making the rounds. I kept losing it, so decided to include it so I could always find it.

1   14 to 15 ounce package light caramels (I like Kraft)
1   cup evaporated milk
1   package German or Swiss chocolate cake mix (18¼ ounce size)
1   stick butter or oleo, melted
1   12 ounce package milk chocolate bits
1   cup pecans, toasted and chopped

Unwrap caramels and melt slowly in a saucepan with ½ cup evaporated milk. While they are melting, mix together the cake mix, butter and ½ cup evaporated milk.

Grease a 12″ x 18″ jelly roll pan and spread half the cake mixture in pan. Bake 6 minutes at 350°. Spread melted caramels over this, then sprinkle on the chocolate bits and the pecans. Drop rest of cake batter onto the top by spoonfuls. Return to the oven and bake another 20 minutes.

Black Walnut Refrigerator Cookies

½   cup butter
2   cups brown sugar
2   eggs
3¾ cups flour
1   teaspoon baking soda
1   teaspoon cream of tartar
4   tablespoons milk
⅔   cup black walnuts, chopped
1   teaspoon vanilla

Cream butter 2 or 3 minutes in mixer bowl. Gradually add sugar. Add eggs, one at a time. Beat another couple of minutes, scraping sides and bottom of bowl once or twice. Add vanilla and milk. Combine nuts and sifted dry ingredients. Add dry ingredients and mix on low until well blended, a minute or two.

Shape dough into 3 rolls about 1½″ in diameter. Wrap rolls in foil and put in refrigerator for several hours. Slice ¼″ thick. Put slices on an ungreased cookie sheet. Bake at 400° for 8 to 10 minutes. Makes 5 to 6 dozen cookies.

Fabulous Pecan Bars

Crust:
  ½ **cup cold butter**
  1½ **cups flour**
  ¼ **cup ice water**

Filling:
  1½ **cups light brown sugar, packed**
  1 **cup butter**
  ½ **cup honey**
  ⅓ **cup sugar**
  1 **pound pecans, chopped**
  ¼ **cup whipping cream**

Use a pastry blender to cut butter into the flour. Mixture should resemble cornmeal. Add water and toss with a fork. Gather dough into a ball. Wrap in plastic wrap and refrigerate for 1 or 2 hours. Butter and flour a 9" x 13" pan. Roll dough out to about an 11" x 15" rectangle. Fit dough into the prepared pan and let it come up about 1" on all sides. Pierce dough with a fork. Chill while making the filling. Preheat oven to 400°. Combine brown sugar, butter, honey and sugar and bring to a boil in a heavy saucepan over medium heat, stirring constantly. Boil until thick and dark, 3 or 4 minutes. You must stir constantly. Remove from heat. Stir in pecans and whipping cream. Pour over dough in pan. Bake at 400° for about 25 minutes. Cool in pan. Cut into strips. Makes 5 or 6 dozen strips, depending on how large you cut them. Almost better than pecan pie!

Mound Bars

Combine ½ **cup butter or oleo, 2 cups graham cracker crumbs** and ¼ **cup confectioners' sugar**. Press into a 9" x 13" pan. Bake for 10 minutes in a 350° oven. Mix **2 cups coconut** and a **14 ounce can sweetened condensed milk**. Spread over baked crust and bake for another 15 minutes. Remove from oven. Lay **6 or 8 unwrapped Hershey Chocolate bars** on top and spread as the chocolate melts. Cool before cutting. Tastes like a Mound candy bar!

Chocolate Glazed Marshmallow Brownies

- 1   stick butter, softened
- 1¼ cups sugar
- 1½ cups flour
- 4   eggs, beaten slightly
- ½   cup milk
- 4   ounces unsweetened chocolate, melted and cooled
- 2   teaspoons vanilla
- ½   teaspoon salt
- 2   cups nuts, chopped
- 16 large marshmallows, cut in half, crosswise
      Chocolate Glaze

Butter a 9″ x 13″ baking pan. Cream the ½ cup butter with sugar in a bowl. Blend in flour, eggs, milk, chocolate, vanilla and salt. Stir in nuts. Pour into prepared pan. Bake 15 minutes (or more) in a 350° oven until it tests done in the center.

While brownies are baking, cut marshmallows in half, rinse them under cold water and pat dry on paper towels. Arrange the marshmallow halves on top of the hot brownies. Pour glaze over the brownies. Cut each brownie with a marshmallow on top (so if you use 32 halves, you'll cut 32 brownie squares).

Chocolate Glaze For Brownies

- 4   ounces unsweetened chocolate, coarsely chopped
- 1   stick butter
- 1   cup sugar
- ½   cup milk
- 2   teaspoons vanilla

Melt chocolate with butter in a heavy saucepan over low heat. Stir constantly. Mix in sugar, milk and vanilla. Increase heat and boil 1 minute, stirring all the time. Remove from heat and whisk until glaze forms a ribbon of chocolate, about 5 or 6 minutes. Pour over the **Marshmallow Brownies**.

Toffee Brownies

2 **cups light brown sugar**
2 **cups flour**
½ **cup oleo**

Mix together until crumbly. Set aside 1 cup of these crumbs. Mix remainder of crumbs with:

1 **egg**
1 **cup milk**
½ **teaspoon salt**
1 **teaspoon baking soda**

Beat until smooth and spread in a greased 9″ x 13″ x 2″ pan. To the reserved 1 cup of crumbs, add:

½ **cup nuts, chopped**
5 **Heath toffee bars, finely chopped (about 4 or 5 ounces)**

Sprinkle this mixture over the batter in the pan. Bake at 350° for about 25 minutes, or until done.

Pumpkin Bars

🍂 *This is one of our favorite Christmas cookies. When Ann and I wrote* Take A Little Thyme, *this recipe was inadvertently left out. I'm glad I found it again. (You can add finely chopped pecans or walnuts to batter, if desired.)*

> 1   **cup salad oil**
> 1½   **cups sugar**
> 2   **cups canned pumpkin (1 - 15 or 16 ounce can)**
> 4   **eggs**
> 2   **cups flour**
> 2   **teaspoons ground cinnamon**
> ½   **teaspoon salt**
> 1   **teaspoon baking soda**
> 2   **teaspoons baking powder**

Mix all together in one bowl. Grease a jelly roll pan and spread batter into the prepared pan. Bake at 350° for 25 to 30 minutes. Do not overbake. Cool and frost with Cream Cheese Frosting on page 220.

Apricot Nut Squares

> 1   **cup butter or oleo**
> 2   **cups flour**
> ½   **teaspoon baking powder**
> 1   **8 ounce package cream cheese, softened**
> 1   **8 ounce jar (1 cup) apricot jam**
> 1   **cup ground pecans**

Mix butter, flour, baking powder and cream cheese together. Form into a ball and chill thoroughly. Make filling by mixing jam and nuts together. Use ¼ dough at a time. Roll out and cut into 2" squares. Put about 1 teaspoon apricot filling on square and top with another square of dough. Seal edges with a fork. Bake at 375° for 15 to 20 minutes. Sprinkle with confectioners' sugar. Makes about 2½ dozen cookies.

Doan's Dream Bars MOTHER♡

You probably already have this, but if you don't —

½ cup butter
½ teaspoon salt
½ cup brown sugar
1 cup flour, sifted

Mix well and pat into ungreased 9″ x 13″ pan. Bake 15 minutes at 350°.

Blend the following and spread over above baked layer:

1 cup brown sugar
1 teaspoon vanilla
2 eggs, well beaten
2 tablespoons flour
½ teaspoon baking powder
⅛ teaspoon salt
1 cup nuts, chopped
1½ cups coconut

Bake 15 to 20 minutes in 350° oven. Cut while warm.

This recipe was lost for a long time. When I found it among Mother's recipes, I was so happy that I'm putting it here so I don't lose it again! Mother just called these **Dream Bars**. I call them **Doan's Dream Bars** because he is a great fan of this cookie!

Fruit Slices ⊂▭MOTHER♡⊃

1 cup butter, softened
1 cup confectioners' sugar
1 egg, slightly beaten
1 teaspoon vanilla
2 cups flour
1 cup pecan halves
2 cups maraschino cherries, well drained and cut in half
1 cup mixed candied fruit, chopped
¼ cup flour

Cream butter and sugar. Add egg and vanilla. Add flour and mix well. Stir in the pecan halves, cherries and candied fruits that have been dredged in the ¼ cup flour. Divide dough into thirds. Shape into rolls about 12" long each. Wrap rolls in foil and chill several hours. Cut into ¼" slices and put on an ungreased cookie sheet. Bake at 325° for 13 to 15 minutes, or until delicately browned. Makes 5 or 6 dozen.

Filled Date Bars

Mix together **2 cups flour, 2 cups quick oatmeal, ¼ teaspoon salt, 1 teaspoon baking soda** and **1 cup brown sugar**. Cut in **¾ cup butter or oleo** until mixture is crumbly. Pat half of this dough in the bottom of a 9" x 13" pan. Now combine in a medium saucepan, an **8 ounce package dates**, pitted and chopped, **1 cup sugar, 1 cup water** and **½ cup or more chopped nuts**. Heat and stir until sugar has dissolved, dates are soft, and the mixture is thick. Spread all of filling over the dough in the pan. Cover with rest of dry mixture and pat down to make a smooth top. Bake in a 325° oven for 30 to 40 minutes — watch closely. Cut into bars while still warm. Sprinkle with confectioners' sugar. Makes 24 bars.

DESSERTS

English Trifle

❧ Bring this beautiful dessert out for a wonderful Christmas or holiday dinner. You'll need a deep, round, crystal or glass dish for serving this in.

Make custard of:
- 1 **cup sugar**
- 1 **tablespoon cornstarch**
- ½ **teaspoon salt**
- 1 **quart milk**
- 8 **egg yolks**
- 2 **teaspoons vanilla**
- 1 **tablespoon sherry**

In a heavy saucepan, combine sugar, cornstarch and salt. Gradually add milk and stir until mixture is smooth. Cook over medium heat, stirring constantly, until mixture comes to a boil and thickens. Boil for 1 minute. Remove from heat. In a bowl, beat the egg yolks slightly. Gradually add a little hot mixture to the yolks and beat well. Stir this yolk mixture into rest of the hot mixture. Cook over medium heat, stirring all the time, until it boils. As soon as it comes to a boil, remove from heat and stir in the vanilla and sherry.

Strain the custard into a bowl while it's still hot. Cover (seal thoroughly) with plastic wrap and refrigerate until it's well chilled. Make this the day before you need it and assemble the trifle the day you want to serve it.

The remainder of the ingredients are:

- 2 **8″ sponge cake layers (use a simple sponge cake recipe and bake in 2 - 8″ round pans)**
- **about ¾ cup good quality sherry**
- **about ½ cup red raspberry preserves**
- ½ **cup slivered almonds, toasted**
- 1 **cup heavy cream, whipped**
- **red candied cherries, for decoration**
- **a few toasted almonds, for decoration**

Several hours before serving, split cake layers in half horizontally, making 4 layers. Sprinkle each layer with sherry. Spread the ½ cup red raspberry jam on 3 of the cake layers. Now put 1 sponge layer, jam side up, in the bottom of the trifle bowl. Sprinkle some of the ½ cup almonds on the layer. Spread about 1 cup of prepared custard on top. Do this with 2 more layers. Put the plain layer on top. Put rest of custard on this layer. Cover top completely with whipped cream.

Decorate top with a few red candied cherries and sprinkle a few more almonds on top. Cover with plastic wrap and refrigerate several hours. Will serve 8 or 10. The sponge cake can be made the day before also, cooled and wrapped. Do not sprinkle sherry on until time to assemble the trifle.

An English trifle bowl is always clear glass, 4″ to 6″, or more, deep, 9″ or 10″ across and on a low pedestal base. This is really beautiful to serve and relatively easy.

Annie's Apple Rolls

This is an old-fashioned and good recipe.

> 4   **medium apples**
> 1½ **cups sugar**
> 2   **cups water**

Peel, core and slice apples fine. Heat sugar and water in baking pan over low heat until sugar is dissolved and the syrup is hot. Make **Rich Biscuit Dough** (recipe follows). Roll out dough to ½″ thick. Spread with apples and roll up to form a long roll. Cut into pieces 1½″ to 2″ thick. Place with cut side down into hot syrup. Put **dabs of butter** on top of each roll and sprinkle rolls with **ground cinnamon** and **sugar**. Bake in a 350° oven for 20 to 30 minutes, or until crust is golden brown. Makes 8 to 10 rolls.

Rich Biscuit Dough

> 2   **cups flour**
> ½   **teaspoon salt**
> 4   **teaspoons baking powder**
> 2   **tablespoons sugar**
> 3   **tablespoons oleo or Crisco**
> ¾   **cup milk**

Combine dry ingredients. Cut shortening in to resemble coarse meal. Add milk and form a soft dough.

Figgy Pudding With Brandy Sauce

❧ *This good holiday recipe came from California where figs are plentiful.*

> 1 **pound dried figs, chopped fine**
> ½ **cup butter**
> 1 **cup flour**
> 1 **cup milk**
> 2 **cups fresh bread crumbs**
> 1 **cup sugar**
> 2 **eggs, well beaten**
> ½ **teaspoon salt**

Cream the butter until light. Stir in the chopped figs and set aside. Put flour in a bowl and gradually stir in the milk to make a smooth paste. Stir in the bread crumbs and let stand for 30 minutes. Add the sugar, eggs and salt and stir well. Stir in the butter and figs.

Butter a large tin pudding mold. Fill ⅔ full. (If you have more batter, butter another small mold and fill it ⅔ full also.) Put mold lid on, or cover tightly with heavy foil. Put a rack in a deep kettle. Set mold on rack and add boiling water until it comes half-way up on the mold. Cover kettle with its lid. Adjust heat so the water boils throughout the steaming. Check often and add water, if necessary, to keep water level up. The large pudding will need to steam for about 3 hours. Small ones, of course, would take less time. The pudding is done when it feels firm to the touch and when a pick comes out of the center clean.

After steaming, turn out of mold and cool completely. Wrap pudding tightly in plastic wrap, return it to the mold and store in the refrigerator. (This can all be done several weeks before holiday time and is actually better if done so.) To serve, remove the plastic wrap, butter the mold again, return pudding to mold. Cover and steam it again, this time only long enough to heat pudding through until it's hot. Serve with **Brandy Sauce**, or a custard sauce. Entire recipe serves 10 to 12.

A Thymely Footnote . . . If you're in Washington, D.C. with a half day that isn't planned, go to the National Herb Garden for a stroll. There are many beautiful herb gardens and the administration is very knowledgeable and helpful. Just about every herb imaginable is growing there.

Brandy Sauce For Figgy Pudding

3   tablespoons butter
2   tablespoons flour
1   cup boiling water
½   cup brown sugar
    brandy

Melt butter in a saucepan. Add the flour and stir over medium heat for a couple of minutes. Add the boiling water and brown sugar. Stir constantly until thick and smooth. Remove from heat and thin to desired consistency with brandy.

Old-Fashioned Peach Cobbler

Filling:
8   fresh peaches, peeled, pitted, sliced
½   cup water
1½ cups sugar
2   tablespoons self-rising flour
    dash of salt
½   cup butter or oleo, melted

Pastry:
1   cup self-rising flour
½   teaspoon salt
⅓   cup Crisco
4   tablespoons milk, or more

For the filling, cook peaches in water until tender. Mix flour, salt and sugar and add to the peaches. Mix well. Add the melted butter.

For the pastry, blend flour, salt and Crisco to resemble coarse meal. Add milk. Roll on floured surface. Pour peaches into a 9" x 13" pan. Cut the dough in wide (1" or so) strips for a lattice top. Lay strips longways and crossways just to edges of pan. Sprinkle strips with a little more sugar. Bake at 350° for about 40 minutes, or until golden brown and bubbly. Serves 8. You could use blueberries, raspberries, cherries, apples, etc., for the fruit. Delicious.

Apricot Tart From Normandy

❧ *Another time, substitute Calvados (the fiery apple brandy of Norman-dy), or regular apple brandy for the Cognac. As I've said before, the food of Normandy is superb.*

1   **egg**
½   **cup sugar**
¼   **cup flour**
¾   **cup heavy cream**
¼   **cup Cognac, or apricot nectar, or orange juice**
    fresh, ripe apricots, peeled, halved, pitted
1   **9″ tart shell (or pie crust) which has been partially baked**

In a bowl, beat egg and sugar until thick. Add flour. Beat until smooth. Add cream and Cognac and blend well. Fill the shell with apricot halves, cut side down (will take 8 or 10). Pour custard over the fruit and bake in a 375° oven for 30 to 40 minutes, or until custard is set and tart is golden. Serve warm or chilled. Serves 6.

Cognac, by the way, is not a product of Normandy. It's made in a little town called Cognac in southwest France, near Bordeaux.

Almond Creme

❧ *Almond creme is a marvelous light dessert for after a heavy meal. Serve this in a pretty goblet with a little fresh fruit on top, a dollop of whipped cream and a sprinkling of toasted, sliced almonds.*

1   **envelope unflavored gelatin**
¼   **cup water**
1½   **cups whipping cream**
½   **cup sugar**
2   **eggs**
½   **teaspoon almond extract**

In a small pan, sprinkle gelatin over water and let stand about 1 minute. Stir over low heat until gelatin is completely dissolved. Cool slightly. In blender or food processor, process cream, sugar, eggs and extract for 2 minutes. With motor running, gradually add gelatin mixture and process until blended.

Pour into dessert dishes or goblets. Cover each well with plastic wrap and refrigerate until serving time. At serving time, add the garnishes, if desired. Serves 4.

Delicious Bread Pudding

- 1   stick butter, room temperature
- 5   white bread slices (regular, not thin sliced)
- ½   cup light brown sugar, packed
- ½   cup raisins
- 1   tablespoon grated orange peel, no white
- 4   cups Half and Half cream
- 5   eggs
- ¼   cup brandy, to drizzle on top
- 1   cup whipping cream, whipped

Use all the butter and butter the slices of bread on 1 side. Cut each slice into 2 triangles. Arrange triangles, butter side up, in a 9″ x 13″ pan. Overlap triangles, if necessary. Sprinkle the ½ cup brown sugar over bread. Sprinkle with raisins and orange peel. Beat Half and Half cream and eggs to blend well. Pour over the bread.

Bake in a 300° oven for 45 to 50 minutes, or until firm. Drizzle the ¼ cup brandy over top of hot, baked pudding. Serve warm and pass whipped cream to put on top. Serves 8 to 10.

Brandy Sauce

- 1   cup sugar
- ⅓   cup butter, softened
- 2   eggs, beaten
- 1   cup heavy cream
- 1   teaspoon vanilla
- 4   tablespoons brandy

Cream sugar and butter. Add eggs and cream and mix well. Cook over low heat in a heavy saucepan until slightly thickened. Do *not* boil. Add the vanilla and brandy. Stir well.

You can make the sauce ahead of time and heat over hot water (use double boiler) just before serving. Serve this sauce on steamed puddings, fruitcake slices, bread pudding, etc.

Creme Brulee

&. *This is a fabulous baked custard!*

4 cups heavy cream
2 teaspoons vanilla
9 egg yolks
1 cup plus 2 tablespoons sugar
dash of salt
about ½ cup light brown sugar, packed

In a heavy saucepan, heat the cream until it is hot, but do *not* scald. Add the vanilla. In mixer bowl, beat the egg yolks and the sugar until mixture is thick and pale. Beat in the cream mixture and the salt. Mix until well combined.

Divide the custard into ¾ cup to 1 cup size baking dishes (about 12). Set the individual dishes in a large baking pan. Add enough hot water to reach halfway up the sides of the dishes.

Bake in a 325° oven for about 40 minutes, or until a knife inserted in the center comes out clean. Remove the dishes from the pan and set them on a heavy towel to cool. Force the brown sugar through a sieve and distribute evenly over the custard tops.

Set the cups on a large baking sheet. Put sheet under a pre-heated broiler about 6″ from the source of heat and broil for 1 or 2 minutes, or until sugar is melted and browned, but not black. Chill for at least 1 hour, covered, before serving.

Blueberry Crisp

4 cups fresh blueberries, washed and drained on paper towels to dry
⅓ cup sugar
2 teaspoons fresh lemon juice
4 tablespoons butter
⅓ cup light brown sugar
⅓ cup flour
¾ cup quick oats

Grease a deep baking dish. Put berries in dish. Sprinkle them with granulated sugar and lemon juice. Cream butter and brown sugar. Add flour and quick oats. Mix until crumbly. Spread this mixture over the berries. Bake for 40 to 45 minutes in a 375° oven. Best served warm. Serves 6.

Orange Cups

navel oranges
orange sherbet
Grand Marnier, or other orange-flavored liqueur, OR
orange juice
fresh mint sprigs
coconut, optional

Halve half as many oranges as guests (3 oranges, if 6 guests, for example). Scoop out orange pulp and save for fruit salad. Leave rind intact. Put a scoop of orange sherbet in the orange cup (make nice round balls). Cover each orange with plastic wrap and freeze. When ready to serve, remove oranges from freezer 15 to 20 minutes before dessert time. Pour about 1 tablespoon of liqueur **or** orange juice carefully over the sherbet. Sprinkle with a little coconut, if desired, and decorate with a mint sprig. Put the orange cup in a pretty dessert dish or sherbet dish and serve. Women love these for a luncheon dessert.

Ice Cream Snowballs

Use an ice cream scoop and shape **vanilla ice cream** into 2½" to 3" balls. Lay them on a waxed paper-lined baking sheet and freeze for at least an hour. On another baking sheet, spread **2 cups of canned, sweetened coconut**. Toast in a 350° oven for 10 minutes, stirring occasionally. Toast until golden. Let cool.

Roll the ice cream balls in the toasted coconut until they are well coated. Return them to freezer on the same paper-lined baking sheet. Freeze for 30 minutes. If not going to use right away, carefully wrap the frozen balls and freeze for later use.

To serve, put 1 or 2 balls in a pretty dessert dish. Pour **hot chocolate sauce** over and serve. Extremely easy and tastes like you spent a lot of time on them. Wonderful to have these in the freezer for unexpected company.

Bailey's Irish Cream Turtle Torte

🍀 *A wonderful frozen ice cream pie.*

1½ cups shortbread cookie crumbs (I like Keebler's Pecan
    Sandies)
¼ cup light brown sugar, packed
¼ teaspoon ground nutmeg
¼ cup butter, melted
1 quart butter pecan ice cream
¾ cup Bailey's Irish Cream Liqueur
1 12 ounce jar caramel ice cream topping
1 cup coarsely chopped pecans, toasted
1 quart chocolate ice cream
1 12 ounce jar fudge ice cream topping

Lightly butter sides of a 10" springform pan. Line the sides
with strips of waxed paper, then butter the bottom and paper-lined
sides. In a bowl, combine the cookie crumbs, sugar and nutmeg. Stir
in melted butter. Pat evenly on bottom of pan and refrigerate. Spoon
slightly softened butter pecan ice cream into a bowl and swirl in ½ cup
of the Irish Cream. (Do not overmix.) Pack this into the chilled crust.
Pour caramel topping into a small bowl and stir in 2 tablespoons of the
Irish Cream. Drizzle over the butter pecan layer, then sprinkle with
¾ cup of pecans. Freeze 1 hour.

Spread slightly softened chocolate ice cream on top of frozen
first layer. Pour fudge topping into another small bowl and stir in the
remaining 2 tablespoons of Irish Cream. Spoon this over chocolate ice
cream. Cover with foil and freeze until firm, 6 hours or overnight. To
serve, remove sides of pan. Carefully peel off waxed paper. Place
bottom of springform pan on serving plate. Garnish top with remaining ¼ cup pecans. Let torte stand for 10 minutes before slicing. If
desired, serve with a dollop of whipped cream atop each serving.
Serves 14 to 16.

Easy Thanksgiving Dessert

Make a caramel sauce (or buy a good one). Add chopped pecans
and heat sauce gently in a heavy saucepan. Serve this sauce over
scoops of pumpkin ice cream. Really easy, really good.

Raspberry Parfaits

Combine **1 quart softened vanilla ice cream** and ¼ **cup raspberry-flavored liqueur** (such as Chambord). Re-freeze ice cream for several hours. Scoop half the ice cream into 6 parfait glasses. Top each serving with **6 or 8 raspberries** (thaw and drain if using frozen berries). Top each serving with **1 tablespoon raspberry liqueur** and a **sprinkle of coconut**. Scoop the **rest of ice cream** into the glasses and top each with **more berries, 1 tablespoon of liqueur** and another **sprinkle of coconut**.

Either serve immediately or cover each glass with plastic wrap and freeze until serving time. At serving time, put glasses in refrigerator 15 or 20 minutes to soften a little. Serves 6.

Chicago Hot Fudge Sauce

    1   cup butter or oleo
    2   1 ounce squares semisweet chocolate
 1½   cups sugar
  ½   cup cocoa
    1   cup whipping cream
    2   teaspoons vanilla

Melt butter and chocolate in a heavy pan. Add sugar, cocoa and cream. Stir constantly and bring to a rolling boil. Remove from heat. Add vanilla and stir well. Cool, covered. Refrigerate. When ready to serve, heat, being very careful not to burn sauce. Makes 1½ to 2 cups.

Holiday Ice Cream

Slightly soften a **quart of vanilla ice cream**. Stir in **8 ounces of best quality mixed candied fruit** (no bitter peels or rinds), **8 ounces of chopped nuts, 4 tablespoons of Sherry**, and **1 tablespoon of brandy**. Mix thoroughly. Wrap well and put back in freezer until serving time. Put scoops of ice cream into your prettiest glass dessert dishes. Serve with Christmas or sugar cookies for an easy, beautiful and delicious dessert. Reminds me of Nesselrode Pie, only easier. Serves 6 or 8.

N.E.W. Ice Cream ⊂⊨MOTHER♡⊐

&. *This is the ice cream the N.E.W. Class (my parents' Sunday School Class at State Line Methodist Church) used to make for their ice cream socials. As a child, I thought this was the best ice cream I'd ever tasted! It probably was!*

 5   **eggs**
 5   **cups sugar**
 4   **heaping tablespoons cake flour**
1½   **teaspoons vanilla**
 ½   **gallon heavy cream**
     milk

Beat eggs slightly. Stir in sugar and flour (use a whisk to incorporate the flour). Scald **3 pints milk**. Pour slowly over egg mixture, whisking vigorously. Cook this mixture in the top of a double boiler over simmering water until it thickens and coats a spoon. Cover and cool thoroughly.

When ready to freeze, add ½ gallon heavy cream (I'm afraid this needs to be whipping cream!). Put all this in your freezer container and finish filling container to within 3″ of top with **milk**. Freeze according to ice cream freezer instructions. Makes 2 gallons.

Joan's Vanilla Ice Cream

&. *This ice cream is creamy and wonderful.*

 7   **eggs**
1⅓   **cups sugar**
 1   **quart Half and Half cream**
 1   **can sweetened condensed milk**
     dash of salt
 1   **tablespoon vanilla**
     milk

Beat the eggs until light. Slowly add sugar and beat well. Put cream, condensed milk and salt together in a heavy saucepan. Heat, stirring constantly, until warm and well mixed. Do not boil. Remove from heat and add vanilla. Slowly add milk mixture to egg mixture. Mix well. Pour mixture into your freezer container. Add milk to fill line on can, then freeze ice cream according to ice cream freezer directions. Serves 10 or 12.

Fruit Sauce For Ice Cream

  1 **tablespoon cornstarch**
  ¼ **cup sugar**
  ¼ **teaspoon ground ginger**
1½ **cups pineapple juice**
  1 **tablespoon fresh lemon juice**
  1 **teaspoon vanilla**

Combine cornstarch, sugar and ginger in a saucepan. Gradually stir in pineapple juice. Bring to a boil over medium heat, stirring constantly. Boil for 2 minutes, stirring. Remove from heat and stir in lemon juice and vanilla. Cool, then refrigerate, covered, until ready to serve. When ready to serve, stir in one or a combination of the following fresh fruits: sliced fresh peaches, fresh blueberries, fresh raspberries, fresh chunks of pineapple. Serve this fruit sauce over ice cream. Makes about 1½ cups.

Raspberry Sauce

🍂 *Serve this wonderful sauce over baked custard, ice cream or pound cake slices. Fabulous over a cold lemon mousse.*

1 **10 ounce package frozen, sweetened raspberries, thawed and drained**
6 **tablespoons seedless raspberry jam (Smucker's has a great one!)**
2 **tablespoons raspberry liqueur (such as Chambord or Framboise)**

Combine raspberries and jam in a heavy saucepan. Bring to a boil and boil 1 minute, stirring often. (If you use the jam with seeds, strain mixture at this point to remove the seeds.) Cool a few minutes. Add liqueur. Refrigerate and serve chilled.

*A **Thymely Footnote** . . . **Chamomile** is a perennial medicinal herb. Both **Roman Chamomile** and **German Chamomile** smell like apples. They both have small daisy-like flowers. They both make a good tea.*

Marshmallow Sauce
For Ice Cream Sundaes

4 cups tiny marshmallows (8 ounces)
6 tablespoons milk, divided
6 tablespoons sugar
1 tablespoon light corn syrup
1 teaspoon vanilla

Melt marshmallows with 2 tablespoons milk in a saucepan. Stir constantly. Remove from heat. Bring 4 tablespoons milk, sugar and corn syrup to a boil in another saucepan, stirring occasionally. Simmer about 5 minutes. Slowly pour syrup over the marshmallow mixture using an electric mixer to blend. Beat well. Add vanilla.

Serve warm or at room temperature over ice cream. Store in refrigerator, but heat over low heat to serve. The best sundae, when I was growing up, was vanilla ice cream with chocolate sauce and marshmallow sauce over all. We called it a "Black and White." It was wonderful.

Mom's Apple Dumplings ⊏═〘MOTHER♡〙═⊐

🍂 *This is an old family recipe.*

Make a dough of **2 cups flour, 2 teaspoons baking powder, ¼ cup butter** and **1 cup milk**. Roll out and cut into 6 squares, making each square big enough to wrap an apple in. Pare and core **6 medium-sized tart apples**. Wrap each apple in dough and place in a baking pan. Combine **2 cups hot water, 1 tablespoon butter, 1 cup brown sugar** and **1 teaspoon ground cinnamon**. Pour over dumplings. Bake in a 350° oven for 45 minutes to 1 hour or until bubbly and browned. These are delicious! Serves 6.

*A **Thymely Footnote** . . . Some of the most beautiful containers of herbs I have ever seen were at the National Arboretum in Washington, D.C. I'll never forget the fantastic tub of brilliant blue-flowered **Russian sage** and the glorious hanging baskets of **thyme**.*

Apple John ⊂▭ MOTHER ♡ ▭

🍎 *I don't know where this recipe got its name, but it's a good old-fashioned apple dessert served with a hot butter sauce.*

6   tart apples, peeled, cored, chopped
⅓   cup sugar (½ cup if apples are very tart)
¾   teaspoon ground cinnamon
½   teaspoon ground nutmeg
⅛   teaspoon salt
2   cups flour
3   teaspoons baking powder
¾   teaspoon salt
½   cup butter
⅔   cup milk

Butter an 8" x 12" baking dish. Prepare the apples and put in bottom of dish. Mix sugar, spices and salt and sprinkle over apples. Sift flour with baking powder and salt. Cut in butter with a pastry blender until it resembles coarse meal. Add milk, mixing until a soft dough forms. Knead lightly on floured board for about 20 seconds. Roll and fit over apples. Brush with milk. Bake in a 425° oven for 25 to 30 minutes. Serve warm with warm **Butter Sauce**. Serves 6 to 8.

Butter Sauce
1   cup sugar
2   tablespoons flour
¼   teaspoon ground nutmeg
    dash of salt
2   cups boiling water
2   tablespoons butter

Mix sugar, nutmeg, flour and salt in saucepan. Add boiling water, stirring constantly until blended. Add butter and boil gently for 5 minutes.

A Thymely Footnote ... Saffron is an exotic and expensive herb. The saffron is the gathered stigma of fall blooming crocus flowers. It takes 40,000 flowers to make 1 pound of saffron. It is indispensable for Mediterranean cooking.

Rhubarb Crisp ⊂▢MOTHER♡▷

Topping:
- 1   cup flour
- ½   cup rolled oats (quick or regular)
- 1   cup light brown sugar
- ½   cup butter, melted

Filling:
- 4   cups rhubarb, cut into ½″ pieces
- 1   cup sugar
- ¼   cup flour
- ½   teaspoon ground cinnamon
- ½   cup water

Combine flour, oats and sugar. Mix well. Stir in melted butter to make crumbs. Set aside. Combine rhubarb, sugar, flour, cinnamon and water. Mix well. Put rhubarb mixture into greased 9″ x 9″ pan. Sprinkle with the crumb topping. Bake at 325° for 30 to 45 minutes or until golden and bubbly. Serves 6 to 8.

Yellowstone Park Gingerbread ⊂▢MOTHER♡▷

🍃 *This recipe came from my Grandmother Clem and it supposedly came from that famous park lodge.*

- 2   eggs
- ½   cup molasses
- ¾   cup sugar
- 1   teaspoon baking soda
- 1   cup sour cream
- 1½ cups flour
- 1   teaspoon ground ginger
- 2   teaspoons ground cinnamon
- ½   teaspoon salt

Beat eggs. Add molasses and sugar. Put baking soda in sour cream and mix. Add sour cream mixture to sugar-egg mixture. Sift dry ingredients together and add to mixture. Beat well. Pour into a 9″ x 9″ pan. Bake for 30 minutes in a 350° oven. Serves 6.

Cheesecake Pie

  2 **cups graham cracker crumbs**
 ½ **cup butter, melted**
  1 **pound cream cheese, softened**
  1 **cup sugar**
  4 **large eggs**
  1 **teaspoon vanilla**
 ½ **cup sour cream**

Combine crumbs and butter and press into a 10" glass pie plate. Chill for a half hour. Cream the cheese in mixer bowl. Beat in sugar gradually and beat until mixture is fluffy. Add eggs, one at a time, and beat well after each. Add vanilla and sour cream. Mix well. Pour into cooled crust and bake at 350° for 25 minutes or until filling is set. Let cool.

For topping: Combine ½ **cup sour cream, 2 teaspoons sugar** and **2 teaspoons vanilla**. Spread over the pie. Return to oven and bake at 450° for 5 minutes. Let cool. Chill several hours before serving. Serves 6 to 8.

Fruit Cobbler

  1 **stick butter or oleo**
  1 **cup sugar**
  1 **cup flour**
  3 **teaspoons baking powder**
     dash of salt
  1 **cup milk**

Melt butter in a 9" x 13" pan. Make a batter of sugar, flour, baking powder, salt and milk. Pour batter over melted butter. **Do not stir**. Top batter with **3 cups fresh peach slices or apples or blueberries or cherries or other fresh fruits, sliced and sweetened to taste — usually ½ to 1 cup sugar**. Do not stir fruit into batter. Bake at 350° for 1 hour. Very easy — very good.

Chocolate And Peanut Butter Cheesecakes

¾ cup chocolate covered graham crackers, made into
crumbs (use your blender or food processor)
1 8 ounce package cream cheese, softened
1 3 ounce package cream cheese, softened
½ cup sugar
1 teaspoon vanilla
½ cup milk
2 eggs
½ cup chocolate bits, melted and cooled
⅓ cup peanut butter

Line muffin tins with paper liners. Put about 1 tablespoon of crumbs in bottom of each cup. Set aside. In small bowl, beat cream cheese until smooth. Add sugar and vanilla and beat until fluffy. Beat in milk. Add eggs and beat until blended. Do not over mix. Divide mixture in half. Gradually stir half the cheese mixture into the melted chocolate. Gradually stir rest of cheese mixture into the peanut butter.

Put 2 tablespoons of peanut butter mixture in each muffin cup and spread evenly. Spoon 2 tablespoons of chocolate mixture over the peanut butter mixture. Spread evenly. Bake at 325° for 20 to 25 minutes or until set. Cool, then refrigerate, covered. Remove paper liners. Serves 12.

Coconut Cream Cheesecake

🍃 *I have a weakness for cheesecake, I fear. Here is yet another wonderful one.*

For the crust:
- ⅔ cup flour
- 1 tablespoon sugar
- 5 tablespoons cold butter, cut into small pieces

Mix flour and sugar in a large bowl. Use a pastry blender and cut in butter until mixture resembles coarse meal. Gather into a ball. Wrap in plastic wrap and refrigerate for 15 to 20 minutes.

Preheat oven to 325°. Press dough into bottom of a 10″ springform pan. Bake 15 to 20 minutes, or until golden brown. Cool slightly. Reduce oven to 300°.

For the filling:
- 3 8 ounce packages cream cheese, room temperature
- 1½ cups sugar
- 4 eggs, room temperature
- 2 egg yolks, room temperature
- 2 cups canned coconut
- 1 cup whipping cream
- 1 teaspoon fresh lemon juice
- 1 teaspoon vanilla extract
- ½ teaspoon almond extract

Use electric mixer. Beat cheese and sugar until smooth. Beat in eggs and yolks, one at a time. Stir in coconut, whipping cream, lemon juice and extracts. Pour filling into baked and cooled crust. Bake until edges of filling are firm, about 1 hour and 10 to 15 minutes.

Carefully remove cheesecake from oven and put pan on a rack. Let cake cool completely before attempting to remove the springform sides. (If cake, or any cheesecake, cools *too* rapidly, the top is likely to crack, so don't disturb it or set it in a cool draft while it's cooling.) Remove springform. Cover cheesecake with plastic wrap. Refrigerate 3 or 4 hours before serving. Sprinkle a little toasted coconut on top, if desired. Will serve 12 or more.

White Chocolate Cheesecake

✎ *This recipe won a cooking-with-chocolate contest. It is superb. By the way, did you know that white chocolate is not chocolate at all? It does not have any of the properties of the cocoa bean, so it is not truly chocolate. Whatever it is, it's wonderful in this cake.*

Make a graham cracker crust of **1½ cups graham cracker crumbs, 6 tablespoons melted butter** and **1 tablespoon sugar**. Press crumbs into bottom and on sides of a 9" or 10" springform pan. Refrigerate 2 or more hours.

For the filling:
  2 pounds cream cheese, room temperature
  ½ cup unsalted butter, room temperature
  4 eggs, room temperature
  10 ounces white chocolate, melted
  5 teaspoons vanilla
    dash of salt

Preheat oven to 300°. Beat cream cheese and butter until smooth. Add eggs, one at a time, beating well after each addition. Add white chocolate, vanilla and salt and beat 1 minute. Pour into prepared crust and bake for 45 minutes. Turn off oven and let bake another 15 minutes. Crack oven door and let cake set in oven until it is cool enough to handle. Remove from oven and let cool completely. Remove pan sides. Cover with plastic wrap and refrigerate. This method of baking and cooling will prevent the cake from cracking across the top. Decorate the top of the cake with white and dark **Chocolate Curls** on page 232. Serves 12 or more.

Mom's Easy Baked Custard

Beat **3 eggs** slightly. Add **1½ cups sugar** and **1 teaspoon vanilla**. In a heavy small saucepan, scald **2½ cups milk** (when little bubbles start to float across the top, remove from heat.) Add scalded milk slowly to egg mixture whisking all the time. Pour into a lightly greased 1½ quart baking dish. Set dish in a pan of hot water. Bake in a 350° oven about 40 minutes, or until a knife inserted near the center comes out clean.

CANNING
AND
PRESERVING

Red Hot Spiced Peaches

꙰ Easy and pretty —

> 1 **29 ounce can cling peach halves**
> 1 **cup water**
> 1 **cup sugar**
> ½ **cup vinegar**
> ½ **cup cinnamon red hots**

Drain peaches, but save liquid. Add rest of ingredients to the liquid. Boil gently until the red hots have dissolved. Simmer for 5 minutes. Add peach halves and simmer another 5 minutes. Pour into a clean jar and store in the refrigerator. The longer peaches are stored in the refrigerator, the redder they'll get. Make at least 24 hours before serving.

Apple-Thyme Jelly

Remove blossom and stem ends from **5 pounds of tart apples**. Do *not* peel or core apples. Cut apples into small chunks. Add **5 cups water** and **1 cup fresh thyme**. Cover and simmer for 10 minutes, stirring occasionally. Uncover and crush apples and thyme with a potato masher. Then simmer 5 minutes longer. Strain apple-thyme mixture through several layers of damp cheesecloth. Add water, if necessary, to make 7 cups of juice.

Pour juice into a large kettle. Add **1 box Sure-Jell**, stir and bring to a full rolling boil. Immediately add **9 cups of sugar**. Stir and bring to a full rolling boil and boil hard 1 minute, stirring constantly. Remove from heat. Skim foam. Ladle into hot sterilized glasses or jars, leaving about ¾" head space. Place a rinsed and dried **sprig of thyme** into each glass. Seal with hot paraffin, then with hot lids.

Next time you make orange marmalade, add a 2" sprig of rosemary to the hot marmalade in each jar, then process.

A Thymely Footnote . . . An **herbal Advent wreath** *is a beautiful Christmas decoration. Make the wreath with* **rosemary, sage, lavender, rue, thyme, costmary**.

Rhubarb Marmalade ▱ MOTHER ♡ ▱

From one of Mother's very old cookbooks.

1 **15 to 20 ounce can crushed pineapple, drained**
   rind of 1 orange, chopped
6 **cups rhubarb, chopped**
7 **cups sugar**
½ **cup chopped nuts**

Combine the pineapple, orange rind and rhubarb in a large saucepan. Cook this mixture for 5 minutes, stirring to keep mixture from sticking. Now add the sugar. Cook, stirring occasionally, for 30 minutes. Add the nuts. Follow canning directions or refrigerate (after marmalade cools) if you plan to use it soon.

Quick Rhubarb Jam

Cook together **5 cups cut rhubarb, a 9 ounce can crushed pineapple, undrained**, and **4 cups sugar** until mixture comes to a boil. Then boil hard for 15 minutes. Add a **3 ounce box strawberry gelatin** and stir until dissolved. Can or freeze.

Bluebarb Jam

3 **cups finely chopped rhubarb**
3 **cups crushed blueberries**
7 **cups sugar**
1 **bottle liquid fruit pectin**

Combine fruits. Add sugar and mix well. Place over high heat in a large heavy saucepan. Bring to a full rolling boil and boil hard 1 minute, stirring constantly. Remove from heat. Add pectin. Stir and skim. Can in hot sterilized jars or cool thoroughly and refrigerate or freeze. Makes about 8 half pints. This is a delicious combination.

Peach Conserve

4   cups prepared peaches (peeled, pitted, chopped)
¼   cup lemon juice
1   tablespoon grated lemon rind
½   cup raisins
7   cups sugar
1   cup finely chopped nuts
½   bottle Certo

Combine fruit, juice, lemon rind, raisins and sugar. Bring to a boil. Boil hard 1½ minutes. Remove from heat. Add nuts and Certo. Stir. Skim, if necessary. Seal and process in hot water bath. An excellent conserve.

Inez's Pear Conserve MOTHER

5   pounds almost-ripe pears, chopped (remove stems, seeds and cores from pears, then chop)
5   pounds sugar
1   pound raisins
    rind of 3 oranges, chopped
    juice of 3 oranges
    juice of 2 lemons
½   pound chopped walnuts

Combine chopped pears (unpeeled) and the sugar. Let set, covered, overnight. Next day, add the raisins, rind and fruit juices. Bring to a boil. Reduce heat and simmer until conserve is quite thick (at least 1 hour). Add the walnuts a few minutes before removing from heat. Cool. Refrigerate or can in hot water bath. Delicious with meats and chicken. Wonderful way to preserve an oversupply of pears. This is a *very* old recipe from Missouri.

*A Thymely Footnote . . . Artemesia Annua, or **Sweet Annie**, can cause violent allergic reactions to some people. If you have a history of allergies, handle this plant with caution.*

Blueberry-Apple Conserve

    4 cups peeled, cored, chopped tart apples
    4 cups blueberries, washed and stemmed
    6 cups sugar
    ½ cup raisins
    ¼ cup lemon juice
    ½ cup chopped pecans, optional

Mix all ingredients, except the nuts, in a heavy saucepan and slowly bring mixture to a boil. Stir often. Cook quickly until thick, stirring often. Add nuts, if desired. Pour into hot sterilized half-pint canning jars. Adjust caps. Store in a cool, dark place. I usually put mine in the freezer. Makes about 6 pints.

I like all kinds of preserves, jellies and jams, but if I have a favorite, it's the conserves. They're chunky, beautiful and I love the combination of fruits in them.

Pear and Cranberry Conserve

    4   cups peeled, cored, chopped pears
    4   cups cranberries
    2   oranges, cut up and any seeds removed
    4½ pounds sugar

Use a food chopper or food processor and grind pears, cranberries and oranges together, but don't grind fine — keep it rather coarse. Put fruit mixture in a saucepan and bring to a boil. Reduce heat and simmer for 30 minutes. Add the sugar. Bring back to a boil and simmer until thick, 20 to 30 minutes more. Store in tightly covered jars and refrigerate if planning to use soon. Otherwise, put in jars and cover with paraffin and store in a cool, dark place. Will make 4 or 5 cups of good conserve. It's very pretty also — makes a nice gift from your kitchen.

*A Thymely Footnote ... Decorate your herb garden with a **sundial**, an **armillary sphere**, or a **bee skep**. They are available from your nursery or garden supply shop.*

Cornichons

🍂 *Cornichons are small pickles that originated in France. They are crisp and sour. The little pickles are good with lots of foods, and they're always served with meat pâtés. Here is a good way to use some of your homemade tarragon vinegar.*

For each quart (use 4 half-pint jars):
- 3½ to 4 **cups tiny cucumbers (each about 1½″ long)**
- 3 **tablespoons pickling salt**
- 4 **cups water**
- 4 **garlic cloves, peeled**
- 4 **sprigs fresh tarragon (one sprig for each jar)**
- 3 to 3½ **cups tarragon vinegar**

Clean cucumbers in cold water. Remove the stems and blossoms, if they're still on the cucumbers. Combine salt and water in a large, glass bowl. Add the tiny cucumbers and let them stand overnight at cool room temperature. Drain the next morning.

Sterilize the half-pint canning jars, lids and rings. Put 1 garlic clove and 1 sprig of tarragon in each drained, hot jar. Pack cucumbers into jars. In a small, non-aluminum pan, heat vinegar to boiling. Cover cucumbers with the boiling vinegar. Seal. Turn sealed jar upside down for 1 minute. Turn right side up and let jars cool thoroughly. Let cornichons cure for 3 to 4 weeks before using.

Old-Fashioned Stuffed Peppers ⌐[MOTHER]=

4 to 6 nice, fresh green peppers*
  brine
1 quart chopped, fresh cabbage
1 tablespoon salt
1 tablespoon whole cloves
1 teaspoon caraway seeds
1 tablespoon mustard seeds
1 cup sugar
  vinegar

Remove the stem ends of the peppers. Cut top off peppers to make caps or lids. Carefully remove the seeds and midribs and lay the peppers in brine made of ½ **cup salt** to **2 quarts of cold water**. Cover peppers, including the caps, completely with the brine. Cover and refrigerate for 24 hours. The next day, chop the cabbage fine and add the salt, cloves, mustard seeds, caraway seeds and sugar. Drain the peppers and stuff them with the cabbage mixture. Replace the caps and tie them on with white kitchen string. Pack the stuffed peppers in a stone jar and cover them completely with cold vinegar. Put lid on stone jar or weight down with heavy plate. Peppers will be pickled and ready to eat in 2 or 3 weeks.

This recipe was passed down from Grandmother Clem and possibly from her mother. So many people have asked me if I have or know of a recipe for old-fashioned stuffed peppers. I'm glad I found this among Mother's recipes.

*By fresh green peppers, I mean fresh from the garden. Store-bought peppers may be wax coated, and therefore, will not pickle in the brine as successfully.

Corn for Freezer

Cut **corn** off of cob to make **6 quarts**. Mix corn, ¾ **cup sugar** and **1 tablespoon salt** together in a large kettle and barely cover with water. Bring to a simmer, then cook for 4 minutes, stirring constantly. Cool thoroughly and package for freezer. This tastes like fresh corn and is wonderful on a cold winter day. This was Mother's recipe.

Grandma's Mince Meat ⊂≡[MOTHER♡]⊃

⠠ *From a very old Methodist cookbook —*

4   pounds meat, well-cooked (use chuck and simmer until tender)
8   pounds apples, chopped
2   pounds suet, chopped fine
2   pounds raisins
2   pounds currants
4   pounds brown sugar
2   tablespoons ground cinnamon
1   tablespoon ground allspice
1   tablespoon ground nutmeg
2   quarts boiled cider
½   pint molasses
   salt to taste

Mix meat, apples, suet, raisins and currants together. Chop all fine. Add other ingredients and cook over moderate heat until apples are tender. Can or refrigerate. Or make into pies and freeze.

If you love old-fashioned mince meat pies, this is fun to make and sure beats store-bought! It is truly delicious.

Mom's Pickled Beets ⊂≡[MOTHER♡]⊃

1   gallon beets (Cook, covered in water, until just tender. Cool enough to slip off skins—leave little beets whole, or slice larger ones.)
2   cups sugar
1   cinnamon stick
1   tablespoon whole allspice
3½   cups vinegar
1½   cups water

Mix all ingredients together, except beets, in large kettle and simmer until sugar is dissolved.

Add beets or beet slices to sugar-vinegar mixture. Bring just to a boil. Can in hot, sterilized jars. Process in hot water bath according to canning instructions. These are wonderful!

Holiday Liqueur

ê *Actually better than the cranberry liqueur you buy — a beautiful clear red liqueur. Decant into a crystal decanter for Holiday serving.*

Make a simple syrup of **4 cups sugar** and **2 cups water**. Boil 3 to 4 minutes to dissolve sugar. Take 1 cup of the syrup and put into a half gallon glass jar. Add **2 cups coarsely chopped fresh cranberries, 2 peeled and chopped Granny Smith apples, 1 cup unflavored brandy, 1 cup vodka, 1 teaspoon vanilla, 6 whole cloves** and **1 stick cinnamon**. Cap jar tightly and steep 3 weeks. Strain through a coffee filter into a bottle. Cork the bottle. Store in a dark, cool place for 3 more weeks. Makes about 3 cups per batch.

Raspberry Liqueur

ê *This is another beautiful and delicious liqueur. Nice to have year around.*

- **1 fifth (bottle) unflavored brandy**
- **1 quart fresh or frozen red raspberries**
- **1 cup water**
- **1 cup sugar**
- **¼ of a lemon peel (Use 1 whole lemon and pare off ¼ of its peel)**

Mix all above. Put in a tightly sealed jar. Let stand in a cool, dark place for 8 days. Remove lemon peel and discard it. Continue to let stand until raspberries lose most of their color. Remove the berries and strain liquid through a coffee filter into a pretty corked bottle or a decanter. Makes about 1 quart per batch. Great for a gift, but keep or make some for yourself!

Apple Brandy

4 cups coarsely chopped Granny Smith apples
1 cup sugar
4 sticks cinnamon, broken up
2 cups unflavored brandy

In a large glass jar, combine all the ingredients. Stir to dissolve sugar. Turn jar upside down every day for 4 or 5 days and shake to help dissolve sugar. Store in a cool, dark place 4 to 6 weeks. Strain through several layers of cheesecloth, then strain through a coffee filter into a bottle with a cork. Makes about 3 cups. This is wonderful for a gift or to have at Holiday time for a little after-dinner drink. Very smooth. All these liqueurs should be started the middle of November for Christmas gift giving.

Christmas Jam

3 cups fresh cranberries, washed and drained
1 20 ounce can crushed pineapple, undrained
1 cup peeled and chopped apple
3 cups sugar
1½ cups water
2 teaspoons grated lemon peel
2 tablespoons fresh lemon juice

Combine all in a large heavy saucepan. Cook, uncovered, over medium heat to 220° on candy thermometer. This will take up to 1 hour — perhaps a little longer, perhaps not as long. Watch thermometer closely. Cool thoroughly, then refrigerate, or remove from heat and can in hot sterilized jars. Wonderful on toast or English muffins. A great gift. Makes 4 or 5 pints.

MENUS

 # MENUS

Lots of people call me or ask me to help them plan a menu for Aunt Gertrude's birthday party or Johnny's graduation reception. They always apologize for "bothering" me, but I find it great fun and a challenge. So don't apologize! I have put together some menus on the following pages, using the recipes from this book as much as possible. But obviously, you should use these ideas as a guideline and substitute your own favorites along the way.

Look up the starred '*' items in the Index for page numbers.

*Ham-Noodle Casserole
*Cinnamon Candied Apples
Fresh Green Vegetables
*Banana Bran Muffins
Fresh Fruit and Cheese

*Mother's Ham Patties
*Cheesy Cabbage
Green Salad with *Buttermilk Ranch Style
Salad Dressing
*Wonderful Orange Bread
*Ice Cream and Toffee Pie

*Scalloped Chicken
*Favorite Cranberry Salad
Frozen Peas
*Pineapple Zucchini Bread
*Pumpkin Cake

*Herb Rubbed Roast Pork
*Fried Apples
Green Vegetables
*Ice Cream Snow Balls
*Sugar Babies

*Baked Steak
*Potatoes with Cheese and Sour Cream
Green Salad
*Maple Wheat Bread with Maple Butter
*Martha Washington Pie

Grilled Hamburgers
*Mix-in-Pan Macaroni & Cheese
Green Salad
*Spice-Coconut Cake

Fried Chicken
*The Real Waldorf Salad
Fresh Green Vegetable
*Poppy Seed Muffins
Chocolate Ice Cream with *Marshmallow Sauce

*Glazed Cranberry Chicken Breast
White Rice
Fresh or Frozen Buttered Broccoli
*Maple Walnut Muffins
*Mom's Apple Dumplings

*Quick Pasta Dinner
Green Salad with *Herbed Salad Dressing
Crusty Italian or French Bread
*Lemon Chess Pie

*Chicken Breasts with Tarragon-Wine Sauce
Buttered Noodles
Green Vegetable
*Fragrant Herb Bread
*Cherries Jubilee

*Chicken en Phyllo with Amaretto-Tarragon Sauce
Green Salad with Orange, Grapefruit and Avocado
Slices with Celery Seed Dressing
*Coconut Cream Cheesecake

*Pasta with Italian Sausages in Diablo Sauce
Green Salad with *Bleu Cheese Dressing
Crusty Italian or French Bread
*Raspberry Parfaits
*Sugar Cookies

*Vegetable-Herb Lasagna
Broiled or Grilled Chicken or Steak
Bread Sticks
*Old-Fashioned Peach Cobbler

*Pasta with Fresh Herbs
*Mediterranean Salad
*Dilled Rye Bread
*White Chocolate Cheesecake

*Chicken Normandy
Green Vegetable
*Potato Rolls
*Annie's Apple Rolls OR
*Mom's Apple Dumplings

*Chicken Wild Rice Casserole
Green Vegetable
*Fresh Peaches with Apricot Glaze
*Spicy Pumpkin Molasses Pie

*Thyme-Lime Chicken
*Wild Rice Casserole
*Fruit Salad in Orange Cups
*Challah
*Lemon Cake

*Chicken Cashew
White Rice with Parsley
*Peach-Raspberry Pie

*Oriental Chicken with Peaches
White Rice
Chinese Pea Pods
*Orange Cups
*Turtle Cookies

*Roast Pork with Cinnamon Apple Brandy
*Sweet Potatoes with Coconut Topping
Broccoli or Green Beans
*Easy Hot Cross Buns
*Yellowstone Park Gingerbread with Whipped Cream

*Old-Fashioned Cider Baked Ham
Escalloped Potatoes with Cheese
*The Real Waldorf Salad
Fresh Green Vegetable
*Doan's Dream Bars

*Baked Ham with Mandarin Oranges and Amaretto
*Stuffed Sweet Potatoes
Fresh or Frozen Asparagus
*Casserole Bread
*Almond Creme
*Sugar Cookies

*Broiled Lamb Chops with Thyme
*Broiled Tomatoes with Cheese
Asparagus or Broccoli
*Rhubarb-Nut Bread
*Apple Cream Pie

*Grilled Lamb Chops
Green Salad with *Buttermilk Ranch-Style Salad
Dressing
*Crusty Pumpernickel Bread
*Georgia Peach Pound Cake with Cinnamon-
Flavored Whipped Cream

*Sirloin Tips (with Mushrooms and Onions)
*Baked Tomatoes with Fresh Herbs
*Budapest Salad
*Golden Granola Yeast Bread
Ice Cream with *Fruit Sauce

*Veal Parmesan
*Fresh Herbed Tomato Salad
Side Dish of Pasta Dressed with a Little Butter
and Parmesan Cheese
Bread Sticks or Crusty Bread
*Ice Cream Crunch Pie

*Taco Burgers
*Potato Frills
Fresh Orange, Grapefruit and Banana Salad
*Mississippi Mud Cake

Barbecue Sandwiches
*Parmesan Potatoes
*Dilled Cucumbers and Onions
*Mother's Chocolate Cream Cake

*Seafood Fettucini
Green Salad with *Roquefort Dressing
Crusty Italian or French Bread
*Fresh Peach Cake with Whipped Cream

*Marinade for Shrimp
*Zucchini Provencal
*Fragrant Herb Bread
*Fresh Blueberry Pie

*Fettucini with Salmon
Fresh Green Beans
*Walnut and Roquefort Salad
*Maple Cake OR
White Chocolate Cheesecake

*Easy Scampi
*Marinated Antipasto
Side Dish of Pasta Dressed with a Little Herbed
Tomato Sauce and Parmesan Cheese
*The Best Chocolate Cake

*Wild Rice with Shrimp and Mushrooms
Green Salad with *Herbed Salad Dressing
*Hot Fruit Casserole
*Crusty Pumpernickel Bread
*Pineapple-Pecan Upside Down Cake

*Linguini with Scallops and Herbs
*Tomato, Onion, Mozarella and Basil Salad
Crusty Bread or Bread Sticks
*Joan's Vanilla Ice Cream with Your Favorite
Sauce

*Outdoor Grilled and Herbed Shrimp
*New Little Potatoes with Lemon-Chive Butter
*Fresh Tomatoes with Herbs
*Bailey's Irish Cream Turtle Torte

*Broiled Salmon with Herbed Lemon Butter
*Marinated Green Beans
Baked Potatoes
*Fabulous Pecan Bars OR
*Alabama Pecan Pie

*Paella
Green Salad with *Herbed Cream Cheese
Dressing
Crusty Italian or French Bread
*White Sangria OR
Red Sangria
*Lemon Pie OR any Lemon Dessert

INDEX

A

A Blend of Fine Spices 57
Alabama Pecan Pie...................................240
All-Purpose Marinade 153
Almond Creme 272
Almond Puffs 205
Amaretto-Tarragon Sauce For Chicken
   In Phyllo 73
Angel Biscuits 184
Anne Byers' Grasshopper Pie 244
Annie's Apple Rolls...................................269
Another Old-Fashioned Cream Pie 240
APPETIZERS
   Boursin 94
   Cheesy Triangles.................................93
   Chicken and Chicken Liver Paté 98
   Easy Swiss-Bacon Squares 92
   Herbed Cheese Spread.........................95
   Herbed Chevre (Goat Cheese) 99
   Herbed Olives......................................57
   Party Cheese Ball 93
   Roasted Pecans 96
   Roquefort Spread 95
   Salmon-Cheese Ball 94
   Salmon Dip...97
   Smoked Salmon Dip.............................96
   Stanley Griggs' Mushrooms 92
   Taco Dip 97
Apple Brandy 296
Apple Butter Bread 186
Apple Coffee Cake 204
Apple Cream Pie 235
Apple John 281
Apple Muffins 199
Apple-Nut Cake 210
Apple Strudel..70
Apple-Thyme Jelly 288
Apricot Glaze for Ham or
   Ham Loaves 155
Apricot Nut Squares.................................264
Apricot Tart From Normandy 272
Autumn Pumpkin Cake 210

B

Bailey's Irish Cream Turtle Torte 276
Baked Ham with Mandarin Oranges
   and Amaretto.......................................155
Baked Steak 160
Baked Tomatoes with Fresh Herbs 168
Baklava 74
Banana Bran Muffins 200

BAR COOKIES
   Apricot Nut Squares 264
   Black Walnut Refrigerator
      Cookies 260
   Chocolate Glazed Marshmallow
      Brownies...262
   Date Bars 259
   Delicious Brownies.............................258
   Doan's Dream Bars 265
   Fabulous Lemon Bars 257
   Fabulous Pecan Bars 261
   Filled Date Bars 266
   Fruit Slices 266
   Mound Bars 261
   Pumpkin Bars 264
   Raspberry Brownies 257
   Toffee Brownies 263
   Turtle Brownies 260
   Turtle Cookies 259
Barbecue Sauce, Colorado-Style 162
Basic Flower and Herb Potpourri 26
Basic Oil and Vinegar 128
Basil Mayonnaise with Lemon 126
BEEF
   Baked Steak 160
   Barbecue Sauce, Colorado-Style 162
   Hamburger Cheese Bake 160
   Herbed Standing Beef Ribs 159
   Sirloin Tips 158
   Spaghetti Bake 153
   Taco Burgers 162
   Veal Parmesan 161
   Vivian's Marinade 159
Beef Vegetable Soup 110
Best Barbecued Chicken 149
Best Cheesecake 228
Best Chocolate Cake 217
BEVERAGES
   Apple Brandy 296
   Champagne Framboise 104
   Champagne-Orange Cocktail 103
   Champagne-Strawberry Cooler 104
   Champagne Wedding Punch 102
   Christmas Cran-Raspberry-Peach
      Drink 100
   Easiest-Of-All Fruit Punches 102
   Fruit Tea 100
   Herbed Tomato Juice 101
   Holiday Liqueur 295
   Luau Refresher 101
   May Wine 105
   May Wine Punch 105
   Minted Iced Tea 100

Raspberry Liqueur 295
Spiced Apple Cider 104
Spiced Sun Tea 99
White Sangria 103
Black Walnut Refrigerator Cookies 260
Blender Hollandaise Sauce 178
Bleu Cheese Dressing 126
Blueberry Crisp 274
Blueberry-Apple Conserve 291
Blueberry Cheesecake 226
Bluebarb Jam 289
Bouquet Garnis 32
Boursin 94
Brandy Sauce 273
Brandy Sauce for Figgy Pudding 271
Bread or Muffin Topper 183
Breakfast Bread 185
Brie In Phyllo 71
Broiled Lamb Chops with Thyme 156
Broiled Salmon with Herbed Lemon
    Butter 134
Broiled Tomatoes and Cheese 169
Broiled Tomatoes with Parmesan
    and Basil 168
Brown Sugar Pecan Pie 239
Brown Sugar Pumpkin Pie 243
Brownies
    Chocolate Glazed Marshmallow
        Brownies 262
    Delicious Brownies 258
    Raspberry Brownies 257
    Toffee Brownies 263
    Turtle Brownies 260
Budapest Salad 117
Butter
    The Best Fresh Herb Butter
        I Know Of! 36
    Fine Herbes Butter 35
    Herb Butter I 33
    Herb Butter II 34
    Herb Butter III 34
    Parsley Butter 35
Butter Sauce 281
Buttermilk Ranch-Style Salad
    Dressing 122
Buttermilk Yeast Rolls 191
Butterscotch Ice Box Cookies 248
Butterscotch Pie 242

C

Cajun Seasonings 56
CAKES
    Apple-Nut Cake 210
Autumn Pumpkin Cake 210
Best Cheesecake 228
Best Chocolate Cake 217
Blueberry Cheesecake 226
Candied Fruit (Microwave) 216
Caramel Icing 229
Chocolate Cream Cake 221
Chocolate Curls 232
Chocolate-Peanut Butter Frosting 231
Cream Cheese Frosting 220
Creamy Maple Frosting 229
Date Cake 225
Date Cream Filling 227
Date-Pecan Fruitcake 222
Decorator Icing 230
Fluffy White Frosting 223
Fresh Peach Cake 212
Georgia Peach Pound Cake 213
Glazed Apple Cake 209
Honey Glaze 232
Hot Water Chocolate Cake 218
Lemon Cake 215
Maple Cake 208
Minute-Boil Fudge Frosting 231
Mississippi Mud Cake 220
No Bake Cheesecake 226
Old-Fashioned Broiled Frosting 222
Orange Fruit Cake 224
Orange Rum Cake 211
Peanut Butter Frosting 215
Pecan Whiskey Cake 219
Petite Cherry Cheesecakes 227
Pineapple-Pecan Upside Down
    Cake 212
Pumpkin Cake 216
Spice-Coconut Cake 214
Superb Apricot Fruitcake 223
Swiss Chocolate Glaze 232
Whipped Cream Frosting 230
Canadian Cheese Soup 108
Candied Fruit (Microwave) 216
CANDIES
    Chocolate Black Walnut Fudge 106
    Double Fudge 106
CANNING AND PRESERVING
    Apply Brandy 296
    Apple-Thyme Jelly 288
    Bluebarb Jam 289
    Blueberry-Apple Conserve 291
    Christmas Jam 296
    Corn for Freezer 293
    Cornichons 292
    Grandma's Mince Meat 294

Holiday Liqueur 295
Inez's Pear Conserve 290
Mom's Pickled Beets 294
Old-Fashioned Stuffed Peppers 293
Peach Conserve 290
Pear and Cranberry Conserve 291
Quick Rhubarb Jam 289
Raspberry Liqueur 295
Red Hot Spiced Peaches 288
Rhubarb Marmalade 289
Caramel Icing 229
Casserole Bread 187
Challah 190
Champagne Framboise 104
Champagne Sauce 143
Champagne-Orange Cocktail 103
Champagne-Strawberry Cooler 104
Champagne Wedding Punch 102
Cheater Sweet Rolls 205
Cheese
    Boursin 94
    Cheesy Triangles 93
    Herbed Cheese Spread 95
    Herbed Chevre (Goat Cheese) 99
    Party Cheese Ball 93
    Roquefort Spread 95
    Salmon-Cheese Ball 94
Cheesecakes
    Cheesecake Pie 283
    Chocolate and Peanut Butter
        Cheesecakes 284
    Best Cheesecake 228
    Blueberry Cheesecake 226
    Coconut Cream Cheesecake 285
    Mom's Easy Baked Custard 286
    No Bake Cheesecake 226
    Petite Cherry Cheesecakes 227
    White Chocolate Cheesecake 286
Cheesy Cabbage 175
Cheesy Triangles 93
Cherries Jubilee 86
Chicago Hot Fudge Sauce 277
CHICKEN
    Best Barbecued Chicken 149
    Chicken Breasts With Tarragon
        Wine Sauce 67
    Chicken Cashew 144
    Chicken and Chicken Liver Paté 98
    Chicken In Phyllo 72
    Chicken Normandy 141
    Chicken Soup 110
    Chicken Wild Rice Casserole 142
    Country Style Chicken Kiev 146

Creamy Chicken Soup 108
Glazed Cranberry Chicken Breasts 68
Mom's Chicken Noodle Casserole 147
Mom's Noodles 146
Oriental Chicken with Peaches 145
Raspberry Vinegar Sauced Chicken
    Breasts 148
Scalloped Chicken 140
Sour Cream Baked Chicken
    Breasts 148
Sue Rigg's Lemon-Basil Chicken
    in Pita Bread 147
Thyme-Lime Chicken 143
Chicken Breasts With Tarragon
    Wine Sauce 67
Chicken Cashew 144
Chicken and Chicken Liver Paté 98
Chicken In Phyllo 72
Chicken Normandy 141
Chicken Soup 110
Chicken Wild Rice Casserole 142
Chocolate Black Walnut Bon Bons 85
Chocolate Black Walnut Fudge 106
Chocolate Chip Melt-Aways 248
Chocolate Chunk Coffee Cake 202
Chocolate Cream Cake 221
Chocolate Curls 232
Chocolate Glazed Marshmallow
    Brownies 262
Chocolate Peanut Butter Pie 245
Chocolate and Peanut Butter
    Cheesecakes 284
Chocolate-Peanut Butter Frosting 231
Christmas Cookies 255
Christmas Cran-Raspberry-Peach
    Drink 100
Christmas Jam 296
Christmas Potpourri 39
Christmas Tea Menu 225
Cinnamon Candied Apples 167
Cinnamon Toast Roll-Ups 187
Clouté 52
Coconut Cream Cheesecake 285
COFFEE CAKES
    Almond Puffs 205
    Apple Coffee Cake 204
    Cheater Sweet Rolls 205
    Chocolate Chunk Coffee Cake 202
    Coffee Cake Glaze 204
    Fruit-Streusel Coffee Cake
        Topping 206
    Honey Nut Coffee Cake 206
    Rhubarb Coffee Cake 203

Toffee Coffee Cake 203
Coffee Cake Glaze 204
Conserves
    Blueberry-Apple Conserve 291
    Inez's Pear Conserve 290
    Peach Conserve 290
    Pear and Cranberry Conserve 291
COOKIES
    Apricot Nut Squares 264
    Black Walnut Refrigerator
        Cookies 260
    Butterscotch Ice Box Cookies 248
    Chocolate Black Walnut
        Bon Bons 85
    Chocolate Chip Melt-Aways 248
    Chocolate Glazed Marshmallow
        Brownies 262
    Christmas Cookies 255
    Date Bars 259
    Delicious Brownies 258
    Deluxe Pecan-Chocolate Chip
        Cookies 249
    Doan's Dream Bars 265
    Fabulous Lemon Bars 257
    Fabulous Pecan Bars 261
    Filled Date Bars 266
    Fruit Slices 266
    Granola Cookies 253
    Great Cookies 251
    Holiday Cupcake Cookies 258
    Little Lemon Tarts 254
    Mince Meat Drop Cookies 250
    Mother's Fruitcake Cookies 251
    Mound Bars 261
    Pecan Tarts 254
    Pineapple Drop Cookies 249
    Pumpkin Bars 264
    Raspberry Brownies 257
    Soft Molasses Drops 252
    Sour Cream Sugar Cookies 256
    Sugar Babies 252
    Sugar Cookies 250
    Toffee Brownies 263
    Turtle Brownies 260
    Turtle Cookies 259
    Williamsburg Ginger Cookies 256
COOKING CLASS FAVORITES
    Amaretto-Tarragon Sauce For
        Chicken In Phyllo 73
    Apple Strudel 70
    Baklava 74
    Brie In Phyllo 71
    Cherries Jubilee 86

Chicken Breasts With Tarragon
    Wine Sauce 67
Chicken In Phyllo 72
Chocolate Black Walnut Bon Bons 85
Cranberry Conserve 68
Easy Hot Cross Buns 82
English Date Pudding 88
Fragrant Herb Bread 69
Fresh Herbed Tomato Sauce 89
Fruit-Flower-Herb Topiary 79
Glazed Cranberry Chicken Breasts 68
Herbed Mayonnaise 87
Homemade Mayonnaise 87
Maple Walnut Or Pecan Muffins 84
Maple Wheat Bread With Maple
    Butter 83
Pasta Dough 76
Pasta With Fresh Herbs 81
Pasta With Italian Sausages
    In Diablo Sauce 78
Peach Glaze For Ham 86
Quick Pasta Dinner 77
Vegetable-Herb Lasagna 80
Zucchini Provencal 89
Company Baked Apples 166
Company Cauliflower 176
Corn for Freezer 293
Cornichons 292
Country Style Chicken Kiev 146
Crab Louis 136
Cranberry Conserve 68
Cranberry Muffins 198
Cream Cheese Frosting 220
Cream Scones 201
Creamy Chicken Soup 108
Creamy Maple Frosting 229
Creme Brulee 274
Crusty Pumpernickel Bread 193

D

Date Bars 259
Date Black Walnut Bread 184
Date Cake 225
Date Cream Filling 227
Date-Pecan Fruitcake 222
Day Later Turkey 149
Decorator Icing 230
Delicious Bread Pudding 273
Delicious Brownies 258
Deluxe Pecan-Chocolate Chip Cookies ... 249
DESSERTS
    Almond Creme 272

Annie's Apple Rolls 269
Apple John 281
Apricot Tart From Normandy 272
Bailey's Irish Cream Turtle Torte 276
Blueberry Crisp 274
Brandy Sauce 273
Brandy Sauce for Figgy Pudding 271
Butter Sauce 281
Cheesecake Pie 283
Cherries Jubilee 86
Chicago Hot Fudge Sauce 277
Chocolate and Peanut Butter
    Cheesecakes 284
Coconut Cream Cheesecake 285
Creme Brulee 274
Delicious Bread Pudding 273
Easy Thanksgiving Dessert 276
English Trifle 268
Figgy Pudding With Brandy
    Sauce 270
Fruit Cobbler 283
Fruit Sauce For Ice Cream 279
Holiday Ice Cream 277
Ice Cream Snowballs 275
Joan's Vanilla Ice Cream 278
Marshmallow Sauce For Ice Cream
    Sundaes 280
Mom's Apple Dumplings 280
Mom's Easy Baked Custard 286
N.E.W. Ice Cream 278
Old-Fashioned Peach Cobbler 271
Orange Cups 275
Raspberry Parfaits 277
Raspberry Sauce 279
Rhubarb Crisp 282
Rich Biscuit Dough 269
White Chocolate Cheesecake 286
Yellowstone Park Gingerbread 282
Diablo Sauce 78
Dilled Cucumbers and Onions 115
Dilled Rye Bread 195
Doan's Dream Bars 265
Double Fudge 106
DRESSINGS
Basic Oil and Vinegar 128
Basil Mayonnaise with Lemon 126
Bleu Cheese Dressing 126
Buttermilk Ranch-Style Salad
    Dressing 122
Herb Salad Dressing 124
Herbed Cream Cheese Salad
    Dressing 127
Herbed Salad Dressing 127

Honey-Mustard Salad Dressing 124
Roquefort Dressing 125
Russian Salad Dressing 123
Vinaigrette for Tomatoes or
    Asparagus 128
Dried Apple Hearts 255
Dried Cinnamon Apple Rings 42
DROP COOKIES
Butterscotch Ice Box Cookies 248
Chocolate Chip Melt-Aways 248
Christmas Cookies 255
Deluxe Pecan-Chocolate Chip
    Cookies 249
Granola Cookies 253
Great Cookies 251
Holiday Cupcake Cookies 258
Little Lemon Tarts 254
Mince Meat Drop Cookies 250
Mother's Fruitcake Cookies 251
Pecan Tarts 254
Pineapple Drop Cookies 249
Soft Molasses Drops 252
Sour Cream Sugar Cookies 256
Sugar Babies 252
Sugar Cookies 250
Williamsburg Ginger Cookies 256
Dutch Apple Pie 238

E

Easiest-Of-All Fruit Punches 102
Easy Candied Sweet Potatoes 174
Easy Frozen Fruit Salad 119
Easy Hot Cross Buns 82
Easy Scampi 137
Easy Swiss-Bacon Squares 92
Easy Thanksgiving Dessert 276
English Date Pudding 88
English Trifle 268

F

Fabulous Lemon Bars 257
Fabulous Pecan Bars 261
Favorite Christmas Salad 112
Favorite Cranberry Salad 120
Favorite Pasta #1 50
Favorite Pasta #2 51
Fettucine and Salmon 130
Figgy Pudding with Brandy Sauce 270
Filled Date Bars 266
Fine Herbes 33
Fine Herbes Butter 35

Index

FISH AND SEAFOOD
  Broiled Salmon with Herbed Lemon
    Butter 134
  Crab Louis 136
  Easy Scampi 137
  Fettucine and Salmon 130
  Herbed Shrimps in Garlic Butter 138
  Linguine with Scallops and Herbs ... 133
  Marinade for Shrimp 131
  Outdoor Grilled and Herbed
    Shrimp 138
  Paella 132
  Sanibel Fish 137
  Seafood Fettucine 131
  Shrimp Creole 135
  Shrimp de Jonghue 135
  Treasure of the Sea 136
  Wild Rice with Shrimp and
    Mushrooms 134
Fluffy Cranberry Salad 118
Fluffy White Frosting 223
Fragrant Herb Bread 69
Fresh Asparagus for a Crowd 178
Fresh Blueberry Pie 236
Fresh Christmas Greens 43
Fresh Herbed Tomato Salad 116
Fresh Herbed Tomato Sauce 89
Fresh Peach Cake 212
Fresh Peaches with Apricot Glaze 164
Fresh Purple Plum Pie 237
Fresh Tomatoes with Herbs 111
Fried Apples 167
Frosted Apricot Salad 119
FROSTINGS
  Caramel Icing 229
  Chocolate Curls 232
  Chocolate-Peanut Butter Frosting 231
  Coffee Cake Glaze 204
  Cream Cheese Frosting 220
  Creamy Maple Frosting 229
  Date Cream Filling 227
  Decorator Icing 230
  Fluffy White Frosting 223
  Honey Glaze 232
  Minute-Boil Fudge Frosting 231
  Peanut Butter Frosting 215
  Old-Fashioned Broiled Frosting 222
  Swiss Chocolate Glaze 232
  Whipped Cream Frosting 230
Frosty Date Muffins 198
Fruit Cobbler 283
Fruit-Flower-Herb Topiary 79
Fruit Salad in Orange Cups 121

Fruit Sauce For Ice Cream 279
Fruit Slices 266
Fruit-Streusel Coffee Cake Topping 206
Fruit Tea 100
Fruit and Spice Christmas Scent 43
FRUITCAKES
  Date Cake 225
  Date-Pecan Fruitcake 222
  Orange Fruit Cake 224
  Superb Apricot Fruitcake 223
FRUITS
  Cinnamon Candied Apples 167
  Company Baked Apples 166
  Fresh Peaches with Apricot Glaze 164
  Fried Apples 167
  Hot Curried Fruit 165
  Hot Fruit Casserole 164
  Layered Fruit Cup 165
  Sherried Peaches 166
  Spiced Oranges 167

G

Georgia Peach Pound Cake 213
Glazed Apple Cake 209
Glazed Cranberry Chicken Breasts 68
Golden Granola Yeast Bread 194
Gourmet Seasoned Salt 32
Graham Cracker Crust 234
Grandma's Mince Meat 294
Granola Cookies 253
Grated Apple Pie 243
Great Cookies 251
Grilled Lamb Chops 157

H

HAM
  Baked Ham with Mandarin Oranges
    and Amaretto 155
  Ham and Cheese Soufflé 154
  Ham and Cheese Stuffed
    Potatoes 171
  Ham-Noodle Casserole 150
  Mother's Ham Patties 151
  Old Fashioned Cider Baked Ham 151
Ham and Cheese Soufflé 155
Ham and Cheese Stuffed Potatoes 171
Ham-Noodle Casserole 150
Hamburger Cheese Bake 160
Herb Butter I 33
Herb Butter II 34
Herb Butter III 34

Herb Rubbed Roast Pork 152
Herb Salad Dressing 124
Herb Vinegars 30
Herbed Cheese Spread 95
Herbed Chevre (Goat Cheese).................. 97
Herbed Cream Cheese Salad
    Dressing 127
Herbed Flour 49
Herbed Mayonnaise 87
Herbed Olive Oil 45
Herbed Olives 57
Herbed Salad Dressing 127
Herbed Shrimps in Garlic Butter 138
Herbed Standing Beef Ribs 159
Herbed Tomato Juice 101
Herbes de Provence 58
Herbes de Provence Toasts 53
Holiday Cupcake Cookies......................... 258
Holiday Ice Cream 277
Holiday Liqueur 295
Holiday Spices for Mini Spice Wreaths 41
Homemade Mayonnaise 87
Honey Glaze 232
Honey-Mustard Salad Dressing 124
Honey Nut Coffee Cake 206
Hot Curried Fruit 165
Hot Fruit Casserole 164
Hot Spinach Salad 123
Hot Stir Fry Oil 48
Hot Water Chocolate Cake...................... 218

I

Ice Cream
    Bailey's Irish Cream Turtle Torte 276
    Easy Thanksgiving Dessert 276
    Fruit Sauce For Ice Cream 279
    Holiday Ice Cream 277
    Ice Cream Crunch Pie 246
    Ice Cream Snowballs 275
    Ice Cream and Toffee Pie 246
    Joan's Vanilla Ice Cream 278
    Marshmallow Sauce For Ice Cream
        Sundaes 280
    N.E.W. Ice Cream 278
    Raspberry Parfaits 277
Ice Cream Crunch Pie 246
Ice Cream Snowballs 275
Ice Cream and Toffee Pie 246
Indiana State Fair Honey Wheat Batter
    Bread 188
Inez's Pear Conserve 290
Italian Bread with Herbed Olive Oil 192

J

Jellies
    Apple-Thyme Jelly 288
    Bluebarb Jam 289
    Christmas Jam 296
    Quick Rhubarb Jam 289
    Rhubarb Marmalade 289
Joan's Best in the West Baked Beans 173
Joan's Vanilla Ice Cream 278
Jody's Pie Crust 234

L

LAMB
    Broiled Lamb Chops with Thyme 156
    Grilled Lamb Chops 157
    Marinade for Leg of Lamb 156
Layered Fruit Cup 165
Lemon Cake 215
Lemon Pie 238
Lemon Chess Pie 241
Lemon-Dill Sauce 52
Linguine with Scallops and Herbs.......... 133
Little Lemon Tarts 254
Louisiana Seasonings 56
Luau Refresher 101

M

Madeira Sauce 142
Maple Butter 83
Maple Cake 208
Maple Walnut Or Pecan Muffins 84
Maple Wheat Bread with Maple
    Butter 83
Margaret's Sausage and Egg Soufflé 152
Marinade for Leg of Lamb 156
Marinade for Shrimp 131
Marinated Antipasto 114
Marinated Green Beans 113
Marshmallow Sauce For Ice Cream
    Sundaes 280
Martha Washington Pie 235
May Wine 105
May Wine Punch 105
Maybe-The-Best Yeast Rolls 189
Mayonnaise
    Basil Mayonnaise with Lemon 126
    Herbed Mayonnaise 87
    Homemade Mayonnaise 87
MEATS
    All-Purpose Marinade 153

Apricot Glaze for Ham or Ham
Loaves 155
Baked Ham with Mandarin Oranges
and Amaretto 155
Baked Steak 160
Barbecue Sauce, Colorado-Style 162
Broiled Lamb Chops with Thyme 156
Grilled Lamb Chops 157
Ham and Cheese Soufflé 154
Ham-Noodle Casserole 150
Hamburger Cheese Bake 160
Herb Rubbed Roast Pork 152
Herbed Standing Beef Ribs 159
Margaret's Sausage and Egg
Soufflé 152
Marinade for Leg of Lamb 156
Mother's Ham Patties 151
Mustard Glaze 154
Old Fashioned Cider Baked Ham 151
Roast Pork with Cinnamon Apple
Brandy 150
Sirloin Tips 158
Spaghetti Bake 153
Taco Burgers 162
Veal Parmesan 161
Vivian's Marinade 159
Mediterranean Salad 116
Mince Meat Drop Cookies 250
Mini Potpourri Wreaths and Mini
Spice Wreaths 41
Minted Iced Tea 100
Minute-Boil Fudge Frosting 231
Mississippi Mud Cake 220
Mix-In-Pan Macaroni and Cheese 169
Mixed Herb Vinegar 30
Mom's Apple Dumplings 280
Mom's Chicken Noodle Casserole 147
Mom's Cream Pie Filling......................... 241
Mom's Easy Baked Custard 286
Mom's Noodles 146
Mom's Pickled Beets............................... 294
Mother's Fruitcake Cookies 251
Mother's Ham Patties 151
Mound Bars 261
Mozzarella Bread on the Outdoor
Grill 191
MUFFINS
Apple Muffins 199
Banana Bran Muffins 200
Cranberry Muffins 198
Frosty Date Muffins............................ 198
Maple Walnut Or Pecan Muffins 84
Poppy Seed Muffins 199

Refrigerator Gingerbread Muffins 197
Squash Muffins 200
Very Best Blueberry Muffins.............. 197
Mustard Glaze 154

N

Nancy Fisher's Zesty Tomato Soup 109
N.E.W. Ice Cream 278
New Little Potatoes with Lemon-Chive
Butter.. 172
Nicoise Salad (Greek Salad) 121
No Bake Cheesecake 226
No-Salt Herb Blend I 31
No-Salt Herb Blend II 31

O

Oils
Herbed Olive Oil 45
Hot Stir Fry Oil 48
Old Fashioned Cider Baked Ham 151
Old Fashioned Oyster Dressing 145
Old-Fashioned Broiled Frosting 222
Old-Fashioned Custard Pie 245
Old Fashioned Homemade Bread 188
Old-Fashioned Peach Cobbler 271
Old-Fashioned Stuffed Peppers 293
Orange Cups 275
Orange Fruit Cake 224
Orange Rum Cake 211
Oriental Chicken with Peaches 145
Outdoor Grilled and Herbed Shrimp 138
Overnight Cauliflower Salad 112

P

Paella 132
Parmesan Potatoes 171
Parsley Butter 35
Party Cheese Ball 93
PASTA
Favorite Pasta #1 50
Favorite Pasta #2 51
Fettucine and Salmon 130
Ham Noodle Casserole 150
Linguine with Scallops and Herbs 133
Mix-In-Pan Macaroni and Cheese 169
Mom's Chicken Noodle Casserole 147
Mom's Noodles 146
Pasta Dough 76
Pasta Primavera 177
Pasta With Fresh Herbs 81

Pasta With Italian Sausages In
Diablo Sauce 78
Quick Pasta Dinner 77
Seafood Fettucine 131
Spaghetti Bake 153
Vegetable-Herb Lasagna 80
Pasta Dough 76
Pasta With Fresh Herbs 81
Pasta With Italian Sausages In Diablo
Sauce 78
Pasta Primavera 177
Pat's Heavenly Apple Salad 120
Peach Conserve 290
Peach Glaze For Ham 86
Peach-Raspberry Pie 236
Peaches and Cream Pie 244
Peanut Butter Frosting 215
Pear and Cranberry Conserve 291
Pecan Tarts 254
Pecan Whiskey Cake 219
Pesto I 48
Pesto II 49
Petite Cherry Cheesecakes 227
Phyllo Cups 75
PIES
Alabama Pecan Pie 240
Anne Byers' Grasshopper Pie 244
Another Old-Fashioned Cream Pie ... 240
Apple Cream Pie
Brown Sugar Pecan Pie 239
Brown Sugar Pumpkin Pie 243
Butterscotch Pie 242
Chocolate Peanut Butter Pie 245
Dutch Apple Pie 238
Fresh Blueberry Pie 236
Fresh Purple Plum Pie 237
Graham Cracker Crust 234
Grated Apple Pie 243
Ice Cream Crunch Pie 246
Ice Cream and Toffee Pie 246
Jody's Pie Crust 234
Lemon Chess Pie 241
Lemon Pie 238
Martha Washington Pie 235
Mom's Cream Pie Filling 241
Old-Fashioned Custard Pie 245
Peach-Raspberry Pie 236
Peaches and Cream Pie 244
Spicy Pumpkin Molasses Pie 239
Pilaf 175
Pineapple Drop Cookies 249
Pineapple Glazed Nut Loaf 181
Pineapple Zucchini Bread 180

Pineapple-Orange Quick Bread 182
Pineapple-Pecan Upside Down Cake 212
Pizza Sauce 157
Pomander Balls #1 40
Pomander Balls #2 40
Poppy Seed Muffins 199
PORK
Baked Ham with Mandarin Oranges
and Amaretto 155
Ham and Cheese Soufflé 154
Ham-Noodle Casserole 150
Herb Rubbed Roast Pork 152
Margaret's Sausage and Egg
Soufflé 152
Mother's Ham Patties 151
Old Fashioned Cider Baked Ham 151
Roast Pork with Cinnamon Apple
Brandy 150
Potato Frills 170
Potato Rolls 196
Potatoes
Easy Candied Sweet Potatoes 174
Ham and Cheese Stuffed Potatoes 171
New Little Potatoes with Lemon-
Chive Butter 172
Parmesan Potatoes 171
Potato Frills 170
Potato Rolls 196
Potatoes with Cheese and Sour
Cream 170
Stuffed Sweet Potatoes 173
Sweet Potato Soufflé 174
Sweet Potatoes with Coconut
Topping 172
Potatoes with Cheese and Sour
Cream 170
Potpourris
Basic Flower and Herb Potpourri 26
Christmas Potpourri 39
Dried Apple Hearts 255
Fruit and Spice Christmas Scent 43
Mini Potpourri Wreaths and Mini
Spice Wreaths 41
Smell of Christmas 42
POULTRY
Best Barbecued Chicken 149
Champagne Sauce 143
Chicken Cashew 144
Chicken Normandy 141
Chicken Wild Rice Casserole 142
Country Style Chicken Kiev 146
Day Later Turkey 149
Madeira Sauce 142

Mom's Chicken Noodle Casserole 147
Mom's Noodles 146
Old Fashioned Oyster Dressing 145
Oriental Chicken with Peaches 145
Raspberry Vinegar Sauced Chicken
    Breasts 148
Scalloped Chicken 140
Sour Cream Baked Chicken
    Breasts 148
Sue Rigg's Lemon-Basil Chicken
    Breasts 147
Thyme-Lime Chicken 143
Pumpkin Bars 264
Pumpkin Bread 180
Pumpkin Cake 216
Pumpkin Pie Spices 55

Q

QUICK BREADS
Angel Biscuits 184
Apple Butter Bread 186
Bread or Muffin Topper 183
Breakfast Bread 185
Date Black Walnut Bread 184
Maple Wheat Bread and Maple
    Butter 83
Pineapple Glazed Nut Loaf 181
Pineapple Zucchini Bread 180
Pineapple-Orange Quick Bread 182
Pumpkin Bread 180
Quick Hot and Crisp Herb Bread 185
Rhubarb Nut Bread 183
Wonderful Orange Bread 182
Zelma's Quick Rolls 195
Quick Hot and Crisp Herb Bread 185
Quick Pasta Dinner 77
Quick Rhubarb Jam 289

R

Raspberry Brownies 257
Raspberry Liqueur 295
Raspberry Parfaits 277
Raspberry Sauce 279
Raspberry Vinegar Sauced Chicken
    Breasts 148
Real Waldorf Salad 122
Red Hot Spiced Peaches 288
Refrigerator Gingerbread Muffins 197
Rhubarb Coffee Cake 203
Rhubarb Crisp 282
Rhubarb Marmalade 289

Rhubarb Nut Bread 183
Rich Biscuit Dough 269
Roast Pork with Cinnamon Apple
    Brandy 150
Roasted Pecans 96
Roasted Peppers 51
Roquefort Dressing 125
Roquefort Spread 95
Russian Salad Dressing 123

S

SALADS
Basic Oil and Vinegar 128
Basil Mayonnaise with Lemon 126
Bleu Cheese Dressing 126
Budapest Salad 117
Buttermilk Ranch-Style Salad
    Dressing 122
Crab Louis 136
Dilled Cucumbers and Onions 115
Easy Frozen Fruit Salad 119
Favorite Christmas Salad 112
Favorite Cranberry Salad 120
Fluffy Cranberry Salad 118
Fresh Herbed Tomato Salad 116
Fresh Tomatoes with Herbs 111
Frosted Apricot Salad 119
Fruit Salad in Orange Cups 121
Herb Salad Dressing 124
Herbed Cream Cheese Salad
    Dressing 127
Herbed Salad Dressing 127
Honey-Mustard Salad Dressing 124
Hot Spinach Salad 123
Marinated Antipasto 114
Marinated Green Beans 113
Mediterranean Salad 116
Nicoise Salad (Greek Salad) 121
Overnight Cauliflower Salad 112
Pat's Heavenly Apple Salad 120
Real Waldorf Salad 122
Roquefort Dressing 125
Russian Salad Dressing 123
Sanibel Salad 115
Special Shrimp Salad 113
Sugared Grapes 117
Tomato, Onion, Mozzarella and
    Basil Salad 111
Treasure of the Sea 136
Vinaigrette for Tomatoes or
    Asparagus 128
Walnut & Roquefort Salad 118

Salmon
 Broiled Salmon with Herbed
  Lemon Butter 134
 Fettucine and Salmon 130
 Salmon-Cheese Ball 94
 Salmon Dip 97
 Smoked Salmon Dip 96
Salmon-Cheese Ball 94
Salmon Dip 97
Salsa 52
Sanibel Fish 137
Sanibel Salad 115
SAUCES
 All-Purpose Marinade 153
 Amaretto-Tarragon Sauce For
  Chicken In Phyllo 73
 Apricot Glaze for Ham or Ham
  Loaves 155
 Barbecue Sauce, Colorado-Style 162
 Blender Hollandaise Sauce 178
 Brandy Sauce 273
 Brandy Sauce for Figgy Pudding 271
 Butter Sauce 281
 Champagne Sauce 143
 Chicago Hot Fudge Sauce 277
 Diablo Sauce 78
 Fresh Herbed Tomato Sauce 89
 Fruit Sauce For Ice Cream 279
 Lemon-Dill Sauce 52
 Madeira Sauce 142
 Marinade for Leg of Lamb 156
 Marshmallow Sauce For Ice Cream
  Sundaes 280
 Mustard Glaze 154
 Peach Glaze For Ham 86
 Pesto I 48
 Pesto II 49
 Pizza Sauce 157
 Raspberry Sauce 279
 Salsa 52
 Vivian's Marinade 159
Scalloped Chicken 140
Seafood Fettucine 131
SEASONINGS
 A Blend of Fine Spices 57
 Bouquet Garnis 32
 Cajun Seasonings 56
 Fine Herbes 33
 Gourmet Seasoned Salt 32
 Louisiana Seasonings 56
 No-Salt Herb Blend I 31
 No-Salt Herb Blend II 31
 Pumpkin Pie Spices 55

Sherried Peaches 166
Shrimp
 Herbed Shrimps in Garlic Butter 138
 Outdoor Grilled and Herbed
  Shrimp 138
 Shrimp Creole 135
 Shrimp de Jonghue 135
 Special Shrimp Salad 113
 Wild Rice with Shrimp and
  Mushrooms 134
Sirloin Tips 158
Smell of Christmas 42
Smoked Salmon Dip 96
Soft Molasses Drops 252
SOUPS
 Beef Vegetable Soup 110
 Canadian Cheese Soup 108
 Chicken Soup 110
 Creamy Chicken Soup 108
 Nancy Fisher's Zesty Tomato Soup ... 109
 Vegetable-Cheese Chowder 109
Sour Cream Baked Chicken Breasts 148
Sour Cream Cinnamon Rolls 192
Sour Cream Sugar Cookies 256
Spaghetti Bake 153
Special Shrimp Salad 113
Spice-Coconut Cake 214
Spiced Apple Cider 104
Spiced Oranges 167
Spiced Sun Tea 99
Spicy Pumpkin Molasses Pie 239
Squash Muffins 200
Stanley Griggs Mushrooms 92
Stir Fry Broccoli, Asparagus or Green
 Beans 177
Stuffed Sweet Potatoes 173
Sue Rigg's Lemon-Basil Chicken in Pita
 Bread 147
Sugar Babies 252
Sugar Cookies 250
Sugared Grapes 117
Superb Apricot Fruitcake 223
Sweet Potato Soufflé 174
Sweet Potatoes with Coconut Topping ... 172
Swiss Chocolate Glaze 232

T

Taco Burgers 162
Taco Dip 97
Tea
 Fruit Tea 100
 Minted Iced Tea 100

Index

Spiced Sun Tea 99
The Best Fresh Herb Butter
   I Know Of! 36
Thyme-Lime Chicken 143
Toasted Herb Roll-Ups 189
Toffee Brownies 263
Toffee Coffee Cake 203
Tomato, Onion, Mozzarella and
   Basil Salad 111
Treasure of the Sea 136
Turtle Brownies 260
Turtle Cookies 259

V

Veal Parmesan 161
Vegetable-Cheese Chowder 109
Vegetable-Herb Lasagna 80
VEGETABLES
   Baked Tomatoes with Fresh Herbs ... 168
   Blender Hollandaise Sauce 178
   Broiled Tomatoes and Cheese 169
   Broiled Tomatoes with Parmesan
      and Basil 168
   Cheesy Cabbage 175
   Company Cauliflower 176
   Easy Candied Sweet Potatoes 174
   Fresh Asparagus for a Crowd 178
   Ham and Cheese Stuffed Potatoes 171
   Joan's Best in the West Baked
      Beans 173
   Mix-In-Pan Macaroni and Cheese 169
   New Little Potatoes with Lemon-
      Chive Butter 172
   Parmesan Potatoes 171
   Pasta Primavera 177
   Pilaf 175
   Potato Frills 170
   Potatoes with Cheese and Sour
      Cream 170
   Stir Fry Broccoli, Asparagus or
      Green Beans 177
   Stuffed Sweet Potatoes 173
   Sweet Potato Soufflé 174
   Sweet Potatoes with Coconut
      Topping 172
   Wild Rice Casserole 176
   Zucchini Provencal 89

Very Best Blueberry Muffins 197
Vinaigrette for Tomatoes or
   Asparagus 128
Vinegars
   Herb Vinegars 30
   Mixed Herb Vinegar 30
Vivian's Marinade 159

W

Walnut & Roquefort Salad 118
Whipped Cream Frosting 230
White Chocolate Cheesecake 286
White Sangria 103
Wild Rice Casserole 176
Wild Rice with Shrimp and
   Mushrooms 134
Williamsburg Ginger Cookies 256
Wonderful Orange Bread 182

Y

YEAST BREADS
   Buttermilk Yeast Rolls 191
   Casserole Bread 187
   Challah 190
   Cinnamon Toast Roll-Ups 187
   Crusty Pumpernickel Bread 193
   Dilled Rye Bread 195
   Easy Hot Cross Buns 82
   Fragrant Herb Bread 69
   Golden Granola Yeast Bread 194
   Indiana State Fair Honey Wheat
      Batter Bread 188
   Italian Bread with Herbed
      Olive Oil 192
   Maybe-The-Best Yeast Rolls 189
   Mozzarella Bread on the Outdoor
      Grill 191
   Old Fashioned Homemade Bread 188
   Potato Rolls 196
   Sour Cream Cinnamon Rolls 192
   Toasted Herb Roll-Ups 189
Yellowstone Park Gingerbread 282

Z

Zelma's Quick Rolls 195
Zucchini Provencal 89

Thyme Cookbooks
Marge Clark
R. 1 - Box 69
West Lebanon, IN 47991

Please send me _____ copies of **It's About Thyme!**   @ $14.95 ea. _____

Indiana residents add applicable tax _____

Plus postage and handling @ $2.00 per book _____

Enclosed is my check ☐   or money order ☐ ....TOTAL _____

Make checks payable to: Marge Clark (address above)

PLEASE PRINT OR TYPE

NAME _____

ADDRESS _____

CITY _____ STATE _____ ZIP _____

Thyme Cookbooks
Marge Clark
R. 1 - Box 69
West Lebanon, IN 47991

Please send me _____ copies of **It's About Thyme!**   @ $14.95 ea. _____

Indiana residents add applicable tax _____

Plus postage and handling @ $2.00 per book _____

Enclosed is my check ☐   or money order ☐ ....TOTAL _____

Make checks payable to: Marge Clark (address above)

PLEASE PRINT OR TYPE

NAME _____

ADDRESS _____

CITY _____ STATE _____ ZIP _____

Thyme Cookbooks
Marge Clark
R. 1 - Box 69
West Lebanon, IN 47991

Please send me _____ copies of **It's About Thyme!**   @ $14.95 ea. _____

Indiana residents add applicable tax _____

Plus postage and handling @ $2.00 per book _____

Enclosed is my check ☐   or money order ☐ ....TOTAL _____

Make checks payable to: Marge Clark (address above)

PLEASE PRINT OR TYPE

NAME _____

ADDRESS _____

CITY _____ STATE _____ ZIP _____